CHRISTIAN
MEDITATION

OTHER WORKS BY JAMES FINLEY:

Merton's Palace of Nowhere

The Contemplative Heart

Thomas Merton's Path to the Palace of Nowhere
  (SoundsTrue Audio)

Christian Meditation (SoundsTrue Audio)

CHRISTIAN MEDITATION

Experiencing the PRESENCE OF GOD

JAMES FINLEY

HarperSanFrancisco

A Division of HarperCollins*Publishers*

Biblical quotes are from the New American Standard Version and the Jerusalem Bible.

CHRISTIAN MEDITATION: *Experiencing the Presence of God.* Copyright © 2004 by James Finley. All rights reserved. Printed in the United States of America. No part of this book may be used or reproduced in any manner whatsoever without written permission except in the case of brief quotations embodied in critical articles and reviews. For information address HarperCollins Publishers, 10 East 53rd Street, New York, NY 10022.

HarperCollins books may be purchased for educational, business, or sales promotional use. For information please write: Special Markets Department, HarperCollins Publishers, 10 East 53rd Street, New York, NY 10022.

HarperCollins Web site: http://www.harpercollins.com

HarperCollins®, 📖 ®, and HarperSanFrancisco™ are trademarks of HarperCollins Publishers.

FIRST HARPERCOLLINS PAPERBACK EDITION PUBLISHED IN 2005.

Library of Congress Cataloging-in-Publication Data
Finley, James.
Christian meditation : experiencing the presence of God / James Finley. — 1st ed.
p. cm.
Includes bibliographical references (p. 287).
ISBN-13: 978–0–06–075064–0
ISBN-10: 0–06–075064–2
1. Meditation—Christianity. I. Title.
BV 4813.F56 2004
248.3'4—dc22 2004047253

05 06 07 08 09 RRD(H) 10 9 8 7 6 5 4 3 2 1

For my daughters, Kelly and Amy

Contents

Acknowledgments

I am grateful to the following people, who, in various ways and to varying degrees helped me in the writing and publication of this book: Maureen Fox, Gustave Reininger, Robert Weathers, Kathleen Deignan, Tami Simon, Matt Licata, Randy Roark, Kim Witherspoon, Alexis Hurley, John Loudon, Frank Cunningham, Msgr. Torgerson, Tom Stella, Keith Egan, Amy Nichols, Lloyd Fredericks, Herb Kaighan, and the members of The Contemplative Way community at Saint Monica Church in Santa Monica, California.

Foreword

Since the time of the Desert Fathers in the third and fourth centuries, Christians have practiced meditation as a way of experiencing and responding to God's presence in their daily lives. Legendary figures such as Meister Eckhart, Saint Teresa of Avila, Saint John of the Cross, and numerous other mystics have left a body of writings that contain trustworthy and encouraging insights into how meditation can help us experience the presence of God in our own lives. This book is intended to serve as a hands-on user's manual for those interiorly drawn to practice meditation in this rich mystical heritage of Christian faith.

The first seven chapters of this book explore the fundamentals of the Christian tradition of meditation. The intention underlying these chapters is not that of stepping back to provide a historical or theological overview. The intention is rather that of exploring, at close range, the Christian tradition's understanding of meditation as a path granting experiential access to God. The shorter chapters that conclude the book consist of a revision of material found in one chapter of my book *The Contemplative Heart*, published by Sorin Books in 2000. These chapters explore the ways in which sitting still, slow deep natural breathing, and other aspects of meditation embody the self-transforming path along which we are awakened to our eternal oneness with God.

Throughout this book I use both the masculine and feminine personal pronouns in referring to God. In the Judeo-Christian tradition God is understood as infinite, and, as such, beyond all finite categories, including the categories of masculine and feminine. At the same time, God is creator of all that is. As such, God is the infinite source, ground, and fulfillment of the feminine and the masculine. But because of the patriarchal culture in which the Judeo-Christian tradition has emerged and in which, for the most part, it has continued to evolve, the Judeo-Christian scriptures and classical texts of theology and spirituality have tended almost exclusively to use the masculine personal pronoun in referring to God. Consistent with current sensibilities in contemporary Christian writings, I have chosen to use inclusive language in referring to God. This seems all the more fitting in a book of contemplative spirituality, which seeks to evoke a graced awareness of oneness with God that recognizes and transcends all finite categories and distinctions.

CHAPTER 1

Divine Destination

The reflections in these pages are intended to serve as a guide in understanding and practicing Christian meditation. In broader terms, these reflections are intended to help those who are being interiorly drawn toward meditation as a grounding place for learning to be a more awake, compassionate, Christlike human being.

In an attempt to be as helpful as I can be to as many people as possible, I have written this book with both the serious beginner and the experienced meditator in mind. For the serious beginner, these reflections will introduce basic ways of understanding what Christian meditation is, along with guidelines on how to practice it. This attention to the particular needs of beginners does not, however, mean that our inquiry will not be, at times, challenging. This is so primarily because meditation itself is challenging in the ways it draws us into a wordless awareness of oneness with God beyond what thoughts can grasp or words can adequately convey. The truth is that we can venture into meditation only in our willingness to be, at times, perplexed. What is more, we must be willing to befriend our perplexity as a way of dying to our futile efforts to grasp the ungraspable depths that meditation invites us to discover.

It is with more experienced meditators in mind that these reflections explore more refined and subtle levels of realized oneness with God. This does not mean, however, that we will be dealing with lofty matters far removed from the concerns of those just beginning their spiritual journey. For, as you have no doubt discovered, the further we travel along the self-transforming path of meditation, the more we realize ourselves to be immersed in beginnings that never end. To be more advanced in meditation means, paradoxically, to discover that the oneness with God we seek was wholly present, without our realizing it, in the humble origins of our spiritual journey. To be more advanced in meditation means to be in the process of realizing that God is wholly present in each step along our way to divine fulfillment. It is to be someone slowly awakening to the divine destination of our journey manifesting itself in the divinity of our own breathing, our own beating heart, our simply being who we are. Or, to paraphrase a line in T. S. Eliot's poem *Four Quartets*, to be more advanced in meditation means to realize that "the end of all our exploring will be to arrive where we started and know the place for the first time."[1]

I am committing myself to being as true as I can to the essential spirit of the Christian contemplative traditions. This essential spirit is the Spirit of God, groaning within us that we might awaken to our eternal oneness with God as revealed to us in Christ (Rom. 8:26). Down through the centuries and into our own day, Christian mystics, monks and nuns living in monasteries, hermits, and countless seekers living in the world have yielded to the transforming power of the Spirit of God within us. It is to these monastic, mystical traditions of Christian faith that we will be turning for guidance and inspiration.

This specifically Christian focus is not, however, intended to suggest that Christians cannot benefit from Yoga, Zen, and other faith traditions. It would, in fact, be tempting as we go through these reflections to note the stunning affinity that sometimes exists between Christian and non-Christian sources of spiritual wisdom. But to do so would take us away from this work's intention of exploring specifically Christian ways of understanding meditation as a way of experiencing oneness with God, one with us in life itself.

This stance of limiting myself to specifically Christian language within a broader context of respect for the contemplative wisdom of non-Christian traditions is something I learned from the contemporary Christian monk Thomas Merton. Near the end of his life, Merton became very committed to Buddhist-Christian dialogue; and in this commitment he went to Asia to have firsthand exposure to Buddhists and the Buddhist tradition. On December 10, 1968, while on that trip, he died. Shortly before his death he wrote a letter back to his own monastic community at the Abbey of Gethsemani in Kentucky. One of the things he said was that in going to Asia he discovered he never had to go there—that everything he was searching for was present in the monastery, was present in his own hermitage, was present in his own Christian tradition. And so it is in this spirit of sensitivity to and respect for the non-Christian contemplative traditions that we will be focusing here on meditation as practiced and understood within the context of the ancient and ongoing contemplative traditions of Christian faith.

In these reflections, I will be sharing with you what I experienced and have come to understand of Christian contemplative spirituality during the five and half years I lived as a monk at the Abbey of Gethsemani, a cloistered Trappist monastery in Kentucky. What may seem surprising is that in my years of living as a monk in the monastery I was not taught how to meditate. In fact, no emphasis was given to practicing any specific method of meditation. This is consistent with the Rule of Saint Benedict, which does not offer instructions in any specific form of meditation. This does not mean that meditation is neglected. To the contrary, Benedict wrote a Rule prescribing a way of life in which the chanting of the psalms in the monastic choir, manual labor, and everything the monk or nun does is to become a meditation. Which is to say, everything becomes a way of entering into a more interior, meditative awareness of oneness with God. It is in this pervasive atmosphere of meditative living that each monk or nun is left free to find his or her way to whatever form of meditation he or she might be interiorly inclined to practice.

It is in this spirit, then, that I express my hope that I might write and you might read these reflections in a meditative manner that will become itself a meditation, which is to say a way of entering into a more interior, meditative awareness of oneness with God.

One way to allow these reflections to become a meditation is to pause and reflect on the simple fact that you and I have most likely never met. As I sit here writing these words, I, of course, cannot see you. But I know something about you that helps me to feel less isolated from you, more connected to you, as I write. I know that you were motivated to read this book on Christian meditation. I do not know with certainty why you are reading this book. But I know that most likely you are reading it in the hope that in doing so you might learn to practice meditation as a way of further deepening your awareness of a response to the presence of God in your daily life. Insofar as this is so, I say, "Me too." It is my intention in sharing these reflections that you find in meditation practice a way of experiencing and responding to God's presence in your life.

As I reflect on this shared intention of our hearts, I come upon a paradoxical fact: It is true that on one level I am alone in this room; I look about me and you are nowhere to be seen. And yet at a more interior level you are here with me as I write. And of course all of this applies to you as well: you look about you and I'm nowhere to be seen. But insofar as you are sincerely reading these sincerely written words, your reading becomes a means of quietly awakening to more meditative modes of awareness in which we are alone together in the shared intention of our hearts.

As the circle of our shared meditative awareness expands we can begin to discern that we are, in some interior sense, one with all who are reading these reflections. As the circle of our meditative awareness expands still further, we can discern the presence of countless men and women, living and dead, who have experienced in their hearts the desire for deeper union with God that we experience in ours. And beyond this we can sense that we are all alone together in God, the awakener of our hearts, the one "in whom we live and move and have our being" (Acts 17:28).

Insofar as we have actually begun to be carried along in this expanding circle of awareness, the divine destination of our lives begins to come into view. In our awareness of being here together in God, we have already begun to meditate. For *meditation is this transformative process of shifting from surface, matter-of-fact levels of consciousness to more interior, meditative levels of awareness of the spiritual dimensions of our lives.*

I will be referring to the more surface, matter-of-fact levels of consciousness as *ego consciousness*. By ego consciousness, I am referring to the consciousness proper—to our self-reflective bodily self in time and space. By ego consciousness, I am referring to the consciousness that manifests itself in saying, "I want, I think, I need, I feel, I remember, I like, I don't like," and so on. Ego consciousness is the day-by-day consciousness in which we tend to get up in the morning, go through our day, and go to bed at night.

Our ego consciousness is a precious gift from God. God wants us to have a healthy ego, because when our ego consciousness is not healthy we suffer and those around us suffer. A great deal of healing has to do with healing the violations and compromises of our ego consciousness. Meditation practice has the potential of playing a powerful and decisive role in this healing process. Through meditation we can learn to be less anxious, less depressed, less addictive—in short, less subject to all the ways in which we as human beings suffer and, in our suffering, contribute to the suffering of others.

But the point is that even if we could manage to become a perfectly healthy ego, there would remain the suffering that arises from experiencing ourselves as nothing more than our ego. For ego consciousness, in and of itself, is not expansive enough to fulfill our hearts. Ego consciousness is not generous enough or gracious enough to bring us all the way home. For God creates our hearts in such a way that only God will do. Scripture says, "God is love" (1 John 4:8). And so we can say that infinite love creates our hearts in such a way that only an infinite union with infinite love will do.

A life hemmed in by the closed horizon of ego consciousness is too impoverished, too one-dimensional to be the subjective ground in which this infinite union with the infinite might be realized. A commitment to daily meditation embodies the paradoxical process of learning to enter more interior, meditative states of consciousness that transcend ego and all that ego can attain. In passing from ego consciousness to meditative states of awareness, we are awakened to that eternal oneness with God that *is* the very reality of ourselves and of everyone and everything around us.

I will be referring to this more interior consciousness as *meditative consciousness.* Sometimes instead of the word *consciousness* I will be using the word *awareness* or the word *experience.* Sometimes I will be using the traditional Christian terms *contemplation, contemplative prayer,* and, in some specific instances, *mystical experience.* But regardless of which of these terms I use, I will always be referring to this interior, rich, mysterious depth of awareness that includes, even as it utterly transcends, the realm of ego consciousness and all that is less than God.

My writing and your reading these reflections on meditation in a manner that becomes itself a meditation is a way of realizing that we are already on the path we are setting out to explore. We start out in ego consciousness, imagining that the union with God we seek is far off. After all, ego consciousness *is* the subjective perception of being a separate self that has to find God, who is perceived as being other than one's self. But then, as ego consciousness yields and gives way to meditative awareness, we begin to recognize the surprising nearness of God, already perfectly present in the intimate recesses of our very being.

Imagine that you are in your car, driving alone on a long journey in a remote area of the country. You are searching for a certain county or small town that your map tells you should be close by, but which you cannot find. Exhausted by your long drive and frustrated that you cannot find your destination, you pull off to the side of the road. You go into a small gas station and ask one of the locals standing there, "Can you tell me how far it is to such and such a place?" The person looks at you, laughs, and says, "You're in it!" You can't believe it. At once pleased and perplexed, you say, "I am?" "Well, yes," the person says, obviously enjoying your obvious surprise. The path to God is like that. God is already here, all about us and within us—the very source, ground, and fulfillment of our being. But, subject to the limitations of ego consciousness, we tend not to experience the divine mystery that is the very reality of who we deep down really are and are called to be as persons created in the image and likeness of God. Subject to the limitations of ego, we do not realize directly the divine reality of reality itself. This is why we meditate: that we might awaken to the already present nature of the oneness with God we seek.

You may feel that you have a long way to go before realizing the degree of habitual meditative awareness of oneness with God exemplified by the great mystics. But the intention of your heart that motivates you to read this book bears witness that a transformative journey, not of your own making, is already under way. Imagine that you go to the ocean, take off your shoes and socks, and wade in ankle-deep. It's true that you are in only ankle-deep, but it's also true that you *are* in the ocean. If you bend down, touch your fingertips to the water, then touch them to your tongue, you taste salt. You feel the wind in your face. You look out at the horizon where the waterline meets the sky. You look down the shoreline. You feel the water about your ankles and, yes, you *are* in the ocean. In order to get in deeper, you simply need to move forward and it will get plenty deep soon enough. Awakening the spiritual path is like this. We have but to remain humbly open to the first stirrings of our journey into God, and our journey, will, in God's good time, get plenty deep, soon enough.

Actually, it's more mysterious than that. Imagine a man and woman who, even in the beginning of their relationship, loved each other very much. Over the course of many years, their love, in the midst of countless ups and downs, continues to grow even deeper.

And yet it's also true that love itself did not get any deeper for all that. For from all eternity love is abysslike. From the very first moment love stirred within them, they were already in water over their heads. It is not that love got deeper, but rather that their awareness of and response to the abysslike nature of love grew deeper. This is how it always is with us spiritually. It isn't as if, in journeying forward, we move into a deeper presence of God, for the presence of God is already infinitely deep. Rather, by moving forward we become ever more deeply aware of the abysslike presence of God in our lives.

To practice meditation as an act of religious faith is to open ourselves to the endlessly reassuring realization that our very being and the very being of everyone and everything around us *is* the generosity of God. For God is creating us in the present moment, loving us into being, such that our very presence in the present moment is the manifested presence of God. We meditate that we might awaken to this unitive mystery, not just in meditation, but in every moment of our lives.

This is how Christ lived. Whether he was seeing a child crawling up into his lap or a leper wanting to be healed; whether he was seeing a prostitute or his own mother; whether he was seeing the joy of a wedding feast or the sorrow of loved ones weeping at the burial of a loved one; whether he was seeing his own disciples or his executioners—he saw God. We meditate that we might learn to see through Christ's eyes the divine mystery of all that surrounds us.

My personal experience of being led along this meditative path has its origins in the years I spent living in the monastery. The sequence of events that led me to the monastery began in my childhood years, in which my father and mother and I and my five younger siblings suffered from the effects of my father's alcoholism and the violence and chaos that were often associated with it.

During the years I was growing up my father seemed to be indifferent toward organized religion. The exception to this was his dislike for the Catholic Church. My mother was a devout Roman Catholic, who relied on her faith to give her the strength to endure the physical, sexual, and emotional abuse that was so much a part of our lives during those years. She taught her six children to do the same. She would take us to Mass on Sundays. She taught us to pray. She would encourage us to turn to God to give us strength. I took all my mother had to say about God to heart. I never doubted her, because I found what she had to say of God to be true.

I found in God a refuge within and beyond myself, and hence beyond the violence and anything it might do to me. It was not that God prevented the moments of explosive rage from happening. Rather it was that, even as the moments of rage continued to occur, I discovered a way of hiding, undetected, in the shadow of God's wing.

When I was in my early teens, I would take the bus alone to Saint Bernard's Church in downtown Akron, Ohio. I would sit alone in the back of the church after Mass and look up into the vaulted ceilings all covered with angels, and I would look at the stained-glass windows with images of Jesus and Mary and the saints. The sacred symbols and rituals of my faith concretized for me this place within and beyond myself. I was somehow, through my faith, hidden in God, where the violence could not destroy me.

I can recall, too, looking at the large cross that hung over the altar. I looked up at the image of Jesus crucified and felt consoled, knowing that Christ was no stranger to suffering and violence. Sitting there, gazing into Christ's eyes as he gazed into mine, I realized that, just as God was not protecting me from the things that were happening to me, God had not protected Jesus from what happened to him. Yet, even so, there was an infinite assurance, an infinite peace—a refuge, a sense of enduring protection—in the midst of it all.

It was at about this same time, when I was in the ninth grade, that an instructor in a religion class at the Catholic high school I was attending told the class about monasteries. I immediately equated monasteries with the refuge within and beyond myself in which I was learning to live my life. I was amazed to discover that there were actually places where I could go to immerse myself in this sense of refuge and to surrender myself to the presence of God concealed in it.

The instructor also told the class about Thomas Merton, who as a young man left a promising career in literature and academia to devote his life to seeking God as a monk in a cloistered monastery. As I began to read Thomas Merton's writings, I sensed that he knew all about the inner refuge in God. A master plan quickly began to take shape within me. I would go through my four years of high school, then go to the monastery. I would become a monk, sit at Merton's feet, and accept his guidance in leading me ever more deeply into the refuge of God within and beyond myself.

In July 1961, just weeks after graduating from high school, I worked up the courage to ask my father if I could go to the monastery to be a monk. He was trimming the hedges out in front of the house at the time. I recall sensing that he might get so enraged at what I was about to ask that he might hurt me with the hedge trimmers. When I nervously told him I wanted to be a monk, he asked me what a monk was. I explained as best I could what I knew about the monastery. He forbade me to leave.

I got up early the next morning while it was still dark. I went into my brothers' and sister's bedrooms as they slept; I sensed it might be the last time I would ever see them. I left a note on my pillow saying that I was leaving home to be a monk. I walked downtown to Saint Bernard's Church and went to 6 o'clock Mass. I kept looking over my shoulder, afraid that my father might come bursting into the church at any moment. After Mass, I went across the street to the Greyhound station, got on a bus to Louisville, Kentucky, and, from there, traveled on to the monastery. When I arrived at the monastery gate I felt as if I had found my way to the gates of paradise.

The five and a half years I lived in the monastery had a profound and lasting effect on me. The early-morning chanting of the psalms in the monastic choir, the monastic liturgy, the study of Scripture, the simple vegetarian diet, the manual labor in the fields, working with the animals—all fit together into a single pattern of paced meditative living.

I went through the monastic formation program, in which Thomas Merton and other senior monks taught a series of classes on Scripture and the mystical, monastic traditions of the church. In these classes and in my own personal spiritual reading I was exposed to the contemplative traditions of Christianity. I learned about the Desert Fathers of the third and fourth centuries, Saint Benedict and Saint Scholastica of the sixth century, Saint Bernard of Clairvaux in the twelfth century, Saint Francis of Assisi and Saint Clare in the thirteenth century, Meister Eckhart in the fourteenth century, Julian of Norwich in the fifteenth century, Saints John of the Cross and Teresa of Ávila in the sixteenth century, Saint Thérèse of

Lisieux in the nineteenth century, and Charles de Foucauld and Mother Teresa of Calcutta in the twentieth century. In short, I was introduced to the depth and richness of the Scriptures and the classical texts of the Christian mystical traditions. Some of this learning took place in listening to and living with Thomas Merton, whom I saw to be a living embodiment of the ancient and ongoing mystical legacy of Christian faith.

The best part of all this for me was that I was living in the midst of the ongoing stream of these ancient contemplative traditions I was learning about. For there I was, a would-be teenage mystic with acne, living in a monastery, wearing monk's robes, bowing and chanting, living in silence, more broken and lost than I realized, and being as sincere as I could be about living a contemplative way of life. I was following a silent path, along which I was being awakened to a sense of oneness with God that utterly transformed my most intimate experience of myself and everyone and everything around me. It was, in fact, the perpetual silence that affected me the most. It is not that I never spoke. I chanted the psalms each day. As a novice, I spoke with Thomas Merton every other week for spiritual direction. There was some limited speaking allowed at work when necessary. But for the most part I lived for five and half years in silence. I gave myself to the silence, found God in it—and for that I am immensely grateful.

I am not saying that all this was healthy, because it clearly was not. I was using my religiosity in the service of psychological defenses against painful memories that I could not bear to let myself feel or to accept. In some ways I went to the monastery as a flight from my own trauma. I was, unwittingly, trying to distance myself from the tragic but very real aspects of my own experience.

It was not until years later, in going through my own psychotherapy and then in becoming a clinical psychologist who works with trauma survivors, that I was able to recognize the regressive nature of my religious quest. It would be years before I would be able to begin turning my spirituality around from being a psychological defense into being a rich resource for the clarity and grace to acknowledge and accept the painful memories of my own childhood.

Learning to turn to spirituality as a way of facing rather than fleeing from daily life is a lifelong process. It is still going on with me. Perhaps I am in part writing this book not only in the hope it might help you in your journey, but also in the hope that it might help me. But the fundamental point remains: God writes straight with crooked lines. Grace uses faltering beginnings to achieve its own unforeseeable ends. At any rate, it is out of the stormy beginnings I have briefly shared with you here that I was first awakened to God in my life and was led to the monastery, where I discovered the path of meditation that I am sharing with you in these pages.

Why I left the monastery is complicated. Certainly this brief narrative is not the place to go into it. I honestly felt when I passed through the monastery gates into the cloister that I had entered a realm of safety in which I no longer had to concern myself about the painful things that had happened to me in my childhood. What I discovered—much to my dismay—was that my own body was a Trojan horse in which I had unwittingly carried into the cloister the very terror I sought to flee from.

I started experiencing flashbacks of the abuse, as well as muscle cramps and dissociative episodes of blanking out. I became depressed. It seemed to me that the destructive power of my father's rage and sexual domination had found its way into a refuge in which I was no longer safe. For reasons that are also complex, I told no one about what I was going through.

My silence further isolated me in my ongoing inability to understand and effectively deal with the flashbacks and other trauma-related symptoms I was experiencing. What I did understand was that I needed to leave the monastery, to go back into the world to face my father and all that I had tried so hard not to face.

The subject matter of this book is not the long process of my inner healing and the role my faith in God and meditation played in that process. Rather, the subject matter is that, after leaving the monastery and returning to the world, I desired as much as ever to continue living the contemplative way of life to which I was introduced in the monastery. The burning question in those days became: "How am I, living out here in the midst of a hectic, complex world, to continue living a contemplative way of life?"

It was certainly true that the demands and pace of my daily life out in the world were no longer conducive to my every act becoming a meditation. But what I discovered was that by learning to meditate day by day, I could learn, day by day, to enter into an ever more habitual meditative awareness of and response to God's presence in my life. In more specifically Christian terms, I realized that daily meditation was a way of following the promptings of the Spirit within me. By way of the silence and poverty of meditation, I might undergo that blessed metamorphosis of mind and heart in which I might realize Christ's life to be my own everlasting life.

And so I resumed the practice of daily meditation that I had begun to explore in the monastery. I did my best to practice daily meditation as a grounding place in learning to live a deeply contemplative way of life in the midst of the world. I resumed reading Thomas Merton and the classical sources of contemplative Christianity. I tried as best I could to internalize and be guided by the spirit and vision of the spiritual path contained in those writings. The journey has continued on for all these years. In this book I am sharing with you what I have learned thus far in my ongoing spiritual journey.

Since the 1960s the term *meditation* has become increasingly popular in Christian circles in referring to what Christianity has historically referred to as *contemplation* or *contemplative prayer*. As we go through these reflections we will be following this current trend by repeatedly using the term *meditation* interchangeably with the more traditional terms *contemplation* and *contemplative prayer*. To avoid any unnecessary confusion in this manner, the following brief review of some traditional terms might prove helpful.

Traditional Christian literature speaks of a graced evolution of consciousness that moves from spiritual reading to discursive meditation to prayer to contemplation. We will be looking at this traditional fourfold development in much greater detail in a later chapter. But for now these four terms can be briefly defined as follows:

Spiritual reading — or, as it is traditionally called, *lectio divina* — consists of the prayerful reading of Scripture of other spiritual writings that inspire and guide us in our search for God. In spiritual reading, the reading itself is an act of faith, a form of prayer uniting us to God. Spiritual reading naturally leads to *discursive meditation*. The term *meditation* is used in traditional Christian literature to refer to discursive meditation, in which we prayerfully reflect on what we have read. When we are engaged in discursive meditation, we are prayerfully thinking about the things of God and filling our imagination with images that inspire and guide us in our spiritual journey. Reading and discursive meditation awaken our desire for God, which we express in *prayer*. When engaged in prayer, we express our feelings, desires, and deepest yearnings to be one with God.

Spiritual reading, discursive meditation, and prayer prepare our hearts for *contemplation*. Contemplation is a state of realized oneness with God. When engaged in contemplation, we rest in God resting in us. We are at home in God at home in us.

Our role in contemplation is essentially receptive, in that when we are engaged in contemplation we receive a gift of divine awareness. Contemplation, in its essentially receptive aspect, is sometimes referred to as *mystical experience* or *mystical prayer*. The word *mystical*, as used in the classical Christian texts, does not refer to having visions, hearing God's voice, or experiencing any other similar, extraordinary events. Although these kinds of experiences can and do occur, they do not necessarily arise from God, and even when they do, they can become hindrances if we cling to them. The Christian mystics use the terms *contemplation* and *mystical union with God* to refer not to visions and other similar experiences, but rather to a life-transforming realization of oneness with God. In this mystical realization of oneness with God we are liberated from our tendencies to derive our security and identity from anything less than God. In specifically Christian terms, we enter the mind of Christ, who realized oneness with God to be the reality of himself and of everyone and everything around him.

While essentially passive or mystical in nature, contemplation is also active, insofar as we must freely choose to open ourselves in a willingness to be wholly transformed in contemplative oneness with God. Contemplation might come flooding in as an overwhelming realization of oneness with God. Contemplation might gently and quietly begin to illumine the most intimate of moments. But then we are left to say yes or no to the contemplative experience to which we have been awakened. In this sense, contemplation is an act of freedom, in which we say yes to God's eternal yes to us in having created us in his image and likeness, as persons called to share in God's life to the point of realizing a graced identification with God's own infinite actuality.

Contemplation, or contemplative prayer, evolves within these dynamics of active receptivity to a oneness with God, which, in our powerlessness to attain it, grants itself to us as the very reality and fulfillment of our lives. It is with regard to the active aspect of contemplation or contemplative prayer that the Christian tradition suggests methods or guidelines for freely opening ourselves to and actively sustaining states of receptive openness to God. In the traditional Christian sources we will be exploring here, these methods include ways of detaching ourselves from our customary reliance on thoughts, memories, and other aspects of ego consciousness that tend to block the subtle, wholly spiritual contemplative states of realized oneness with God.

Since the 1960s there has been a growing popularity of Yoga and Zen and other forms of Buddhist meditation—the critical point being that when these non-Christian traditions use the term *meditation*, they are not referring to discursive meditation using thoughts and images. Rather, these traditions use the term *meditation* in a manner that parallels both the active and passive aspects of Christian contemplation. That is, in the practice of Yoga or Zen meditation, one actively seeks to let go of one's customary reliance on and identification with thought, memories, and other ego-based forms of experience in order to open oneself to a direct experience of oneness with the sacred mystery that wholly permeates all of reality. The methods of Yoga and Zen—and, for that matter, the methods of the Jewish mystical tradition of the Kabbalah and the Muslim mystical tradition of the Sufis—all resonate with the Christian mystical tradition. All share various spiritual practices that, when engaged in with heartfelt devotion and commitment, can evoke or invite a profound, life-transforming realization of oneness with the divine.

The trend in some Christian circles today to use the term *meditation* interchangeably with the term *contemplation* makes sense as long as there is a basic understanding of the distinctions that have been briefly summarized here. With these distinctions in mind, we can read the term *meditation* and understand it in the context in which it is used. When the term *meditation* appears in classical Christian sources, it most likely means discursive meditation—that is, a form of prayerful reflection, using thoughts and images. When the term appears in non-Christian literature or in some contemporary Christian writings, including this book, it most likely means what the traditional Christian literature means by contemplation or contemplative prayer. As used in this latter sense, Christian meditation includes both the act of inviting and opening ourselves to a graced realization of oneness with God and the mystical fulfillment received in this active seeking.

I hope those of you who are just now beginning to explore meditation have been fairly comfortable with the pace and tone of this first chapter. For it is at this same pace and in this same tone that we will continue our attempt to lay bare the fundamentals of understanding and practicing Christian meditation. I encourage you not to be discouraged at those points that are particularly difficult to understand. Be confident that matters not yet clear will become clear as your own meditation practice matures and deepens. The eighteenth-century Christian artist, poet, and mystic William Blake wrote: "If the doors of perception were cleansed, every thing would appear to man as it is, infinite."[2] In the beginning we might be able to recognize and appreciate the poetic beauty of Blake's statement even as the truth it proclaims remains obscure, beyond what we have yet to experience. But as our perceptions become cleansed in our ongoing fidelity to meditation, we begin to see through meditative eyes the infinity of all that we see. And suddenly Blake's words become clear in the intimate sense in which we realize Blake is putting into words what we ourselves have come to experience. The whole path is like this. So be patient with yourself. For it is in this very patience with yourself that you will continue to be transformed in the lifelong learning process of becoming one seasoned in the meditative awareness of the divinity of daily living.

I hope, too, that those of you who are more seasoned and experienced in meditation have found this opening chapter to be helpful as well, for the pace and tone begun in this chapter will continue to be the context in which I will present the more subtle and refined aspects of realized union with God. As you know by your own experience, this is how it tends to work in real life: the truly profound is found in the truly simple. The acclaimed jazz musician John Coltrane was known to practice scales throughout his musical career. When asked why he, as an accomplished musician, did this, he said he did it to become a saint. In this book we will, in effect, be practicing scales so as to become saints. For us to become saints in this context is to become a man or woman who never ceases to be amazed by the generosity of God that ceaselessly flows through all that is most simple and immediate in life itself. It means allowing the generosity of God to flow through us into others.

When I am leading silent meditation retreats, a room of eighty to a hundred or so men and women gather for sessions of group meditation. When the meditation sessions begin, each person present starts meditating right where he or she is in his or her own longer-than-life journey into God. But as the communal silence begins to settle on the group, each person there is gathered into the one communal mystery in which we all journey into God together. It is like that here. I, in writing these reflections, and each of you, in reading them, are right where each of us is in this particular moment of our spiritual journey. And yet we are all journeying on together toward an ever deeper realization of the ever present divine destination of our lives. Regardless of where you might be on this journey, I hope you find in these pages encouragement and guidance in surrendering to God in the silent simplicity of meditation. I hope you find here insights into how meditation might be for you a grounding place in your own spiritual journey of learning to be a truly awake, compassionate, Christlike human being.

CHAPTER 2

Learning to Meditate

The very fact that you sincerely desire to practice meditation means you are being blessed in a most extraordinary way. You are being led into the waters of meditative awareness, in which hermits, monks and nuns living in monasteries, and countless devout women and men living in the world have found a deep and abiding experience of oneness with God. In order to join all these kindred spirits, you must courageously step into the stream of meditative experience that they entered, and in which their lives were transformed. You must entrust yourself to God, who is this river's origin, its steady, strong current, and the ocean of endless fulfillment to which it leads.

When I entered the monastery I was not taught any specific method of meditation. That this was the case is not surprising if meditation is understood in the broadest possible sense—as including all the ways in which we might enter into more interior, meditative states of realized oneness with God. Monastic life was the method of meditation, in this broad sense, that was being taught. The daily silence and the chanting of the psalms in the monastic choir, the manual labor, the study of Scripture and spirituality—all were aspects of a single self-transforming process of learning to live in a habitual state of meditative oneness with God.

Each monk would then be open to all the ways in which the meditative practice of the monastic life was to be internalized and followed on his unique, interior journey to God.

When I would go in for my one-on-one spiritual-direction sessions with Thomas Merton, we would frequently talk about my prayer and meditation practices. I would ask questions about where I felt stuck, about things I did not understand. He would answer in ways I found to be very helpful and clarifying, but he never told me how I should meditate.

The point is that there is no such thing as Christian meditation, formally and officially designated as such, if by that we mean some specific way to meditate. As we shall see later on in this book as we get into the writings of the Christian mystics, the methods the mystics suggest for meditation vary from one mystic to the next. But when this diversity of methods is carefully examined one finds the methods themselves to be strikingly similar. This is so because each method embodies a specifically Christian way of understanding and entering into acts and attitudes inherently endowed with the capacity to awaken more interior, meditative states of awareness.

The same holds true of the guidelines for meditation that I am about to introduce in this chapter. The guidelines consist of acts or attitudes inherently endowed with the power to awaken more interior, meditative states of awareness. This is why the basic guidelines suggested here can be found in one form or another in all the mystical traditions of the world's great religions. In a more specific sense, the guidelines for meditation that I am about to share here are specifically germane to the

Christian tradition in that they are found, in one form or another, in the classical texts of contemplative Christianity. And in a still more specific sense, the guidelines I am proposing here are personal. They embody the universal and specifically Christian ways in which I have been drawn into more interior, meditative ways of experiencing God's presence in my life. I hope you find these guidelines helpful as a way to begin meditating. As you settle into your own practice, you will, with God's grace, settle into the method of meditation that is most natural and effective for you. It is in learning to grow in your own evolving meditation practice that your meditation will continue to embody your own unforeseeable journey into God.

The guidelines for meditation practice that I suggest are, with respect to the body, to sit still, to sit straight, to close your eyes or lower them toward the ground, to breathe slowly and naturally, and to place your hands in a natural or meaningful position in your lap. With respect to the mind, the guideline is to be present, open, and awake, neither clinging to nor rejecting anything. And with respect to attitude, the guideline is to maintain nonjudgmental compassion toward yourself as you experience yourself clinging to and rejecting everything, and nonjudgmental compassion toward others in their powerlessness, one with yours.

The first guideline for meditation is to sit still. When you sit still, do so in a natural and relaxed manner. Take a few moments to settle into a felt sense of simply sitting there. Then sit still with all your heart. Allow your bodily stillness to embody your heart's desire to realize your eternal oneness with God. Be simply present in a "Here I am, Lord" (I Sam. 3:4) stance of openness to God. Allow your bodily stillness to embody a child-like faith in God present all about you and within you as you sit.

The second suggested guideline for meditation is to sit

straight. Sitting straight fosters a state of relaxed alertness. We are accustomed to associating relaxation with sleepiness, and alertness with being tense. But meditation is a way of learning to be deeply awake and deeply relaxed at once. It is this stance of being deeply relaxed and deeply awake at once that invites and embodies entrance into more interior, meditative states of realized oneness with God.

The third suggested guideline for meditation is to close your eyes or lower them toward the ground. You may find it is most natural to close your eyes while you meditate. If closing your eyes promotes sleepiness and an excess of images, you may find it most natural and helpful to meditate with your eyes left slightly open, lowered at a forty-five-degree angle toward the ground. This visual dimension of meditation merges with sitting still and straight as a way of entering into more interior, meditative states of awareness. Closing or lowering our eyes embodies a "Lord, that I might see" stance in which we seek to see, through meditative eyes, the mystery of God eternally loving us into the present moment for himself alone.

Sitting still and straight, with your eyes closed or lowered toward the ground, breath in and out slowly, in a natural, relaxed manner. Settle into your breathing. Listen to each life-sustaining breath. Allow your breathing to embody a childlike openness to God giving herself to you, whole and complete, in and as your very breath.

Sitting still and straight, with your eyes closed or lowered toward the ground, breathing slowly and naturally, place your hands in a comfortable or meaningful position in your lap. By a meaningful position I mean, for example, with your open hands palms upward on your thighs, expressive of an interior stance of receptive openness to God. Or you may find yourself sitting still and straight with your hands joined in prayer. Or you may be inclined to simply rest one hand gently in the other in your lap.

If you did nothing but simply sit each day, silent and still, attentive to your breathing, with your eyes closed or lowered toward the ground, you would be doing yourself a huge favor. You would already be starting the long journey home into God, who lies hidden deep within your bodily being.

But there remains the question of what to do in meditation with what we tend to think of as our minds. That is, there remains the question of what to do with the thoughts, feelings, and sensations that we experience in meditation. The guideline for meditation with respect to the mind is to be present, open, and awake, neither clinging to nor rejecting anything. This guideline applies to all the thoughts that arise in the mind. As each thought arises, simply be present, open, and awake to the thought as it arises. As the thought endures, simply be present, open, and awake to the thought as it endures. And as the thought passes away, simply remain present, open, and awake to the thought as it passes away.

In order to understand the intuitive logic of the guideline with respect to thought, pause for a moment to recall those moments in your daily life in which you are spontaneously awakened to a more interior, meditative awareness of the moment in which you find yourself. Recall, for example, those moments in which you have spontaneously given yourself over to the beauty of a sunset, or a child at play, or a compelling work of art. In such moments, you are deeply awake. And yet you are not thinking! Or, if you are thinking, your thoughts do not constitute the living essence of the moment. For in gazing at the sunset or the face of a friend you are deeply awake in an interior, meditative manner that transcends all the thoughts that may be passing through your mind at the moment. In such moments you spontaneously enter into a meditative awareness that qualitatively transcends thought. In meditation we freely choose to enter into this meditative, nonthinking mode of awareness. And we do so by neither clinging to nor rejecting the thoughts that may be flowing through our mind. In meditation the goal is to neither think our thoughts nor try not to have any thoughts. Rather, the goal is to sit still and straight, meditatively aware of each thought as it arises, endures, and passes away.

The stance of gazing deeply into each thought as it arises, endures, and passes away pertains to all thoughts, whether they are pleasant or unpleasant, superficial or profound. This stance applies as well to all thought about God. For, as the author of the anonymously written Christian classic *The Cloud of Unknowing* reminds us, when we meditate we are not seeking to have thoughts of God. Rather we are seeking to know God "in his naked existence,"[1] infinitely beyond our most profound thoughts about him.

The stance of remaining present, open, and awake is to be maintained as well with respect to all bodily sensations that arise in meditation. These may include a slight pain between the shoulders. This sensation may then give way to being aware of the coolness or warmth in the room, or perhaps of the weight of our hands resting in our lap. As we sit, we are to remain present, open, and awake to each bodily sensation as it arises, endures, and passes away.

So, too, we are to remain present, open, and awake to all that our senses perceive in our surroundings: the sound of a car driving by, the refrigerator motor turning on or off, the room suddenly filling with light as the sun breaks through the clouds. With respect to all these passing phenomena, we are to remain present, open, and awake to them as they arise, endure, and pass away.

The stance of remaining present, open, and awake is to be maintained as well with respect to the feelings that flow through us as we meditate. This applies to all feelings, whatever they may be: sad feelings, peaceful feelings, angry feelings, sexual feelings, confusing feelings, and many other kinds of feelings. With respect to them all, the guideline remains: be present, open, and awake to each feeling as it arises, endures, and passes away.

This stance toward feelings pertains as well to all the spiritual consolations and feelings of God's presence that may arise in meditation. The sixteenth-century Spanish mystic Saint John of the Cross reminds us that, as wonderful and consoling as feelings of God's presence might be, they are not God. All consolations and spiritual gifts, he reminds us, are finite and as such are infinitely less than God, who is infinite. We are not to reject any consolations that may come along. But neither are we to cling to whatever consolations or other spiritual gifts we may experience. For God made our hearts in such a way that only God will do. Or we might say infinite love made our hearts in such a way that only an infinite union with infinite love will do. Since all consoling feelings of God's presence are finite and infinitely less than God, we are not to cling to whatever consolations we may be fortunate enough to experience as we meditate. We are rather to remain simply present, open, and awake to all consolations and spiritual experiences as they arise, endure, and pass away. By the way, if our meditation is devoid of any sense of God's presence, we are to remind ourselves that the absence of spiritual consolations, though perhaps difficult, is but the absence of what is infinitely less than the infinite union with God that alone fulfills our heart. It is with this sense of equanimity in the face of consolation and aridity that we are to remain present, open, and awake to God wholly present in, yet wholly transcending, both consolation and aridity.

The title of the Christian classic *Abandonment to Divine Providence*, by Jean-Pierre de Caussade, provides a way of putting words to the deep awareness of oneness with God that can occur in meditation.[2] When Christian writings speak of abandonment to divine providence, they usually do so in the context of trusting in the big picture of God's providential hand at work in guiding us through the course of our lives. But when the Christian mystics offer guidance in contemplation and meditation, they are clearly opening up a more refined understanding of what abandonment to divine providence means. For meditation practice recalibrates abandonment to divine providence to an ever more refined and subtle awareness of God at work in the hidden recesses of the concrete immediacy of each passing moment.

The Gospels tell us of how Jesus abandoned himself to the Father's will in the big picture of his own unfolding life. But Jesus gave witness to a more finely tuned awareness of God's providential presence revealed to us in the way Jesus saw the flowers of the field or the birds of the air or a small child climbing up into his lap. In meditation we imitate Christ by abandoning ourselves to the providential flow of such simple and concrete things as the sound of children who happen to be playing outside the window. Sitting still and straight, we remain present, open, and awake to the providential flow of the sound of the clock chiming, just now, on the mantel. We abandon ourselves to the utterly trustworthy providential flow of the room in which we sit as it darkens at sunset. We sit abandoned to the providential flow of our own breathing, to the thought passing, just now, through our mind. We sit surrendered to the divinity flowing through the never-quite-this-way-before, never-quite-this-way-again immediacy of the moment just as it is.

As you sit given over to this simple intention of being present, open, and awake, neither clinging to nor rejecting anything, you are likely to experience just how inept we humans beings are at doing such a simple thing as being simply present in the present moment. To enter into meditation entails a willingness to recognize and accept just how restless our restless mind tends to be. Then, in this stance of humble acceptance, we are to simply reinstate the meditative stance of being present, open, and awake each time we realize we have drifted off yet again into the clinging and rejecting ways of our wandering mind.

I would like to mention here two methods that can help to stabilize meditative awareness. The first is to use your awareness of your breathing as an anchoring place in present-moment attentiveness. Each time you realize you have once again drifted off into sleepiness, daydreaming, or clinging to this or that sensation, thought, or feeling, simply renew your awareness of your breathing as a way of regrounding yourself in meditative awareness of the present moment.

The silent, interior repetition of a word or phrase is another traditional method of sustaining present-moment attentiveness. You may choose a single word such as God, mercy, or Jesus. Or you may use a phrase taken from Scripture or from a prayer or hymn that is particularly meaningful to you. Each time you realize you have once again drifted away from being present, open, and awake in the present moment, simply reinstate the sustained attentiveness of practice by silently saying your word or phrase within yourself.

A practice I have found particularly helpful is to pair up breath awareness with the phrase "I love you." Each time you realize you have drifted off into this or that thought, silently say, "I love you" as you exhale, allowing your exhalation to be an expression of your whole being as an act of love to God. Then, as you inhale, silently take in and surrender to God's life-giving "I love you."

Even with the help of your breath awareness, the use of a word or phrase, and your most sincere efforts, you are likely to experience just how inept we human beings can be at such a simple, fundamental thing as being simply present in the present moment. Truth is, meditation has a way of laying bare our poverty. We start out with the sincere intention to be present, open, and awake, only to discover that the very simplicity of the intention reveals the wayward complexity of our mind and heart. This is why the prevailing attitude of meditation is to have *nonjudgmental compassion for yourself as you discover yourself clinging to and rejecting everything.*

Our faith in Christ reveals that God is infinite compassion—that love that recognizes and goes forth to identify with the preciousness of all that is lost and broken within ourselves and everyone around us. Our meditation fosters and embodies a Christlike compassion in which we realize our own mind and heart to be the one lost sheep that we must lovingly gather up and bring back to the fold of present-moment attentiveness.

As we learn to see ourselves through the eyes of Christlike compassion, we learn to see others through the eyes of Christlike compassion as well. In learning to be compassionate toward ourselves as precious in our frailty, we learn to be compassionate toward others as precious in their frailty. In this way we begin to sense how meditation renders our heart ever more sensitive and responsive to ourselves and others. This is one of the refrains that run throughout the lives and teachings of the Christian mystics—that only love and all that is given in love is real. Love is at once the means and end of the journey into God, who is love itself. And since love impels us to act lovingly, we can begin to see as well the radical and intimate connection between a nonviolent, Christlike response to our own suffering and our response to the suffering of those we encounter in walking out our own front door or in watching the evening news on television.

As each meditation period comes to an end, you might fold your hands in prayer and bow in gratitude. The meditation went the way it went. It was more than enough, and you can bow to God in gratitude for it. You might then ask God for help in learning how not to break the thread of meditative awareness as you go through your day. Then rise from your meditation and go about your day, knowing that tomorrow, with God's grace, you will sit in meditation again. And so with each day of your life as you find in meditation the grounding place of your whole life, open to the divine mystery your daily life embodies.

Let each session of meditation become the hearth at which you and God sit together, sharing inexpressible things. Discover for yourself how true it is that meditation grants entrance to more interior, meditative states of awareness. Enter into meditative awareness. Learn to live in this awareness in which you are laid bare to God, who is eternally laid bare to you in the sheer immediacy of what simply is as it simply is.

Do not be in a hurry. Know that no matter how hard you push, you cannot push yourself beyond where you are, just as you are, in the present moment. Nor do you need to. For it is in the unplumbed depths of your being just the way you are in the present moment that your eternal union with God lies hidden. Remember that meditation is a way of slowing down so as to descend into the depths of yourself in the present moment, where God lies waiting to grant you a deep experience of your eternal oneness with God. But don't confuse this slowing down with continuing to postpone the inner journey that leads to an unforeseeable rendezvous with God. Don't delay in letting today be the day you renew your efforts to seek God in meditation by simply opening yourself to God in a spirit of whole-hearted sincerity and simple, childlike faith.

As you develop the habit of meditation, you will become more skilled in learning to enter more directly into a quiet state of meditative openness to God. Little by little you will experience yourself becoming more familiar with the inner landscape of your newly awakened heart. As your newly awakened heart is allowed to repeatedly rest in meditative awareness, it slowly discovers its center of gravity in the hidden depths of God.

By meditating day by day, the meditative awareness fostered and sustained in meditation will flash forth with ever greater frequency in all sorts of unexpected ways as you go through your day. You might, for example, be standing at the sink doing dishes. As you look up, your heart is quickened in the recognition of God in the gentle breeze that barely stirs a leaf on a branch of the tree just outside your kitchen window. You interiorly smile back at God, grateful that you are no longer surprised by these little surprises.

Lovers delight in surprising one another with little signs of love. They consider themselves most fortunate in being in a loving relationship in which they are not surprised by these surprises. They know this is what love is like—always delighting in catching one another off guard with unexpected manifestations of love. Since "God is love" (1 John 4:8), God's ways are the ways in which love awakens you again and again to the infinite love that is the reality of all that is real. As you ripen and mature on the spiritual path that meditation embodies, you will consider yourself blessed and most fortunate in no longer being surprised by all the ways in which you never cease to be delighted by God. Your heart becomes accustomed to God, peeking out at you from the inner recesses of the task at hand, from the sideways glance of the stranger in the street, or from the way sunlight suddenly fills the room on a cloudy day.

Learning not to be surprised by the ways in which you are perpetually surprised, you will learn to rest in an abiding sense of confidence in God. Learning to abide in this confidence, you learn to see God in learning to see the God-given Godly nature of yourself, others, and everything around you. Learning to abide in this meditative awareness of oneness with God, you will be impelled to pass on to others the divine generosity of God that has been and continues to be so graciously passed on to you.

There are some practical considerations that tend to come up as one begins to commit oneself to daily meditation. One such practical consideration is the value of meditating every day, or nearly every day. If your schedule permits and you are inclined to do so, meditating twice a day may be even better. The reason for this suggestion is that meditation practice is a habit that grows and develops over time. It takes a while to get acclimated to the often subtle transformations that occur as one moves into more interior, meditative states of awareness. Added to this is the simple fact that the more firmly established the habit of daily meditation becomes, the more likely it is that meditative awareness will become your habitual awareness in your day-by-day life. As habitual meditative awareness grows and deepens, you will grow in your ability to rest in God, present in whatever you are doing at the moment.

Another practical matter that often comes up as people begin to meditate is how long each session of meditation should last. As you go along you will naturally fall into a pattern of meditation, including a tendency for each period of meditation to last a certain length of time. But a time frame that seems best for many people is twenty to thirty minutes. This is short enough to be practical with respect to our busy schedules, while at the same time being long enough to allow us to begin to settle into the meditative state. If twenty or thirty minutes seems too long for you, especially at first, then cut the time back to something you feel you can manage. Our compassion in pacing ourselves as we go along is an important aspect of learning to give ourselves, in our own unique way, to God, who eternally gives herself to us.

As you sort out the practical details of time, you may find that it is best to use a timer as a way of freeing you from the need to do any clock watching as you meditate. Of course, your situation may be such that there is no need to stop meditating at a certain time—in which case you can simply sit in meditation and trust the felt sense of your meditation coming to a close.

You will also have to decide where you are going to practice meditation. You can, of course, meditate anywhere. The goal, in fact, is to habituate meditative awareness throughout your whole day, so that you would quite naturally take opportunities to meditate here and there, wherever you might find yourself. But in the beginning and for the duration of the journey, many people find it helpful to have a grounding place, a place to which they go each day to meditate. In time, the mind and heart grow accustomed to what goes on there. In time, the very act of walking toward the place of meditation opens up our hearts to the meditative state of receptive openness to God.

The place you choose for your meditation will most likely be a place in your own home—a corner in your living room, bedroom, or some other room—that seems a fitting place to commit yourself to your daily practice. You may want to set up some kind of altar in this place, on which you can place various items expressive of your tradition of Christian faith and what is personally meaningful to you. If you are in the Protestant tradition of Christian faith, the items you choose to have at your place of meditation might include a plain wooden cross, a picture of Christ, and a copy of the Scriptures and other devotional works that are especially meaningful to you. If you are in the Episcopal, Roman, or Eastern Rite Catholic tradition, the items you choose might also include a crucifix, or possibly pictures or icons of Christ, Mary, and a saint to whom you have a personal devotion. Following your personal inclination, your place of meditation might also include a candle, some incense, perhaps a houseplant, or perhaps a few small stones brought in from outdoors. Along with the Scriptures, your place of meditation might include one or more spiritual books and perhaps a journal. The point is that your place of meditation practice will tend to have a certain quiet order about it, expressive of sincerity and faith. Just seeing the place set aside for meditation will suggest to you that something important happens there.

There is also the practical question of how to begin each session of meditation. You might simply sit, settle in for a moment, and begin to meditate. Or you might begin by standing before a picture of Christ, a cross, or some other sacred image. Folding your hands in prayer, you can take a moment to renew your awareness of God, in whose presence you are about to meditate. You might bow as an act of reverence to God. Then you might light a candle or a stick of incense. You might then spend some time slowly reading a few verses from Scripture. Then you might begin with a simple, sincere, heartfelt prayer, asking God for guidance in your meditation as a way of opening yourself to God, who is author, sustainer, and fulfillment of your heart's desire for God.

The sacred images with which you choose to adorn your place of meditation and the prayers you say are, in some, essential sense, unimportant. This is so because the self-transforming journey into God is a radical wonder that transcends the minutiae of arranging spiritual bric-a-brac on little altars, bowing to pictures, and the like. The entire matter of meditation is a self-consuming fire. It is a river of grace that carries us to the sea. It is way of becoming utterly transparent to the divine light that our very being manifests. It is our way of yielding to a God-given awakening to God, giving himself to us, whole and complete in and as who we simply are. And so whether you put a cross on a table or bow to a picture or light a candle is hardly the point.

And yet is it not so that lovers say and do the simplest, most tender, and seemingly foolish things to express and embody the depths of their love for one another? Is it not so that parents get down on the floor and do the silliest of things simply to revel in the sound of their child's laughter? Do not parents do this again and again so that their hearts might be grazed again and again by the mystery of loving their child into being? And so it is that such a simple act as lighting a candle or bowing in silence before an image of Christ can embody the mystery of yielding ourselves to ever deeper realizations of oneness with God. And in this sense, simply bowing in childlike sincerity hits the mark. Simply gazing at a plain wooden cross embodies the essential point of realized oneness with God, who is the reality of all that is real.

This is what a commitment to seeking God in meditation does for us—or, I should say, does *to* us. It opens up a new center of gravity in the depths of our being. When we are sincerely open to this new center of gravity within ourselves, the simplest of acts embodies that which cannot be explained. Such a simple thing as bowing can embody the mystery that cannot be achieved or attained. Simply lighting a candle in a mindful, meditative manner can cast a light deep into the darkness that blinds us to the divinity of our lives.

My maternal grandmother had five children. The youngest, a boy named James, died in her arms at age nine. I was named after him. For some time after his death my grandmother was too broken by the loss and pain of his death to pray or go to church. When she did start attending church again, she did so by way of a little ritual. She would walk alone to the church, light a candle, and sit in the empty church and pray. She would then walk home. I do not know how often she did this, or for how many months or years it went on. It was an odd thing in a way, certainly not the kind of thing that can be accounted for or made sense of in practical or logical terms. But in a deeper, more interior sense her acts of simple faith made perfect sense. For walking to the church, lighting a candle, and sitting in silence embodied her broken heart on a healing journey.

It is such deep and simple faith that renders our meditation real, fruitful, and true. The issue here is not grief and sadness. Rather, the issue is the depth of intimately realized oneness with God that is, from time to time, obscurely disclosed to us in moments of grief and joy, and in every human experience in between. You have your story. I have mine. But running through all our stories is the way in which we are each, from time to time, awakened in the midst of sorrow and joy to the mysterious ways in which God sustains us in our powerlessness to sustain ourselves. Meditation rings true when we bring to it nothing less or other than our own heart, broken and made whole in ways we cannot even begin to grasp or explain. It is in this attitude of bringing to our meditation nothing less or other than our lives up till now that we begin to find in meditation nothing less than God, giving herself, whole and complete, in the life we are living.

A musical score does not become music until the musician begins to play. So, too, guidelines for meditation, such as the ones being presented in this book, remain but words on the printed page until you begin to meditate. I encourage you, then, to allow these guidelines for meditation to inspire you to begin meditating. That is, if you have not already done so, consciously make a decision to enter into a more intimate relationship with God. Then ground your fidelity to this decision in some form of daily meditation and prayer.

The beloved says from the other side of the door, "Open the door and come in, so we can experience just how one we might become." You stand outside the door, reading one more book about how to open the door. You note in your journal one more thought about what it might be like to walk through the door. And all the while the longings of your heart remain unconsummated. And so let today be the day you open the door of your heart to God, whose heart, from all eternity, is open to you. This is the Good News of Christian faith—that God has left the door unlocked and even slightly ajar. God is waiting for you to open it and come walking through to experience that oneness with God that is the fullness of life itself. It is in the midst of this poetic imagery of passing through the door into God that we find ourselves in the living essence of Christian faith. And it is here, too, that we find ourselves in the midst of the living essence of Christian meditation as a way of intimately realizing the eternal oneness with God that Christ came to proclaim.

Realizing the awesome and mysterious nature of the self-transforming journey your commitment to daily meditation embodies, you might more readily allow yourself to be open and responsive to all the discoveries that lie along the way. These discoveries will include pleasant surprises, joyful moments, and deep consolations. The self-transforming journey will also entail arduous struggles, hardships, and difficulties. There is nothing less at stake than your very life. There is nothing less at stake than dying to your most cherished illusions, so as to awaken to that blessed oneness with God that is the source, foundation, and fulfillment of your very life.

If you have already begun this interior journey of opening yourself to God in meditation, you know that these words of encouragement, aimed at those just beginning to meditate, apply to you as well. I know they apply to me. For there is in me that which has long since passed through the open door into God. There is that in me that, in the very act of writing this sentence, is passing through the open door into God. And there is that in me that loiters just outside the door, still reluctant, confused, and afraid to enter. This reluctant, not yet awakened part of me can always use a little pep talk, a little encouragement and support.

I am assuming you have your own version of this same ongoing conversion process going on in your own life. There is that in you that long since passed through the open door into God. There is that in you that is perpetually passing through the door in the reading of this very sentence. And there is that in you that still hesitates, in fear and confusion, to enter through the open door into God. This confused and still frightened part of you needs all the encouragement it can get in beginning, yet one more time, to pass through the open door into God.

Take courage, fellow traveler, as you perpetually renew your efforts to begin again and again the journey that was already well under way before the creation of the universe. Listen to what your own heart tells you to be true. Do not be afraid to consider that the most bold and far-reaching statements of the mystics apply to you. For the yearnings for God that stir within you are but faint and distant echoes of God's infinite yearnings for you. To listen to the yearnings for God that stir within you is to listen to God, the living source and fulfillment of these yearnings. Learn to trust and befriend these yearnings for God, as faint and subtle and hidden as they might be. Learn to yield to these yearnings as the reverberations of God, drawing you along the ancient and ongoing path marked by the Christian mystics down through the ages.

Take to heart whatever you find in these guidelines that might be helpful. As for what does not seem right or helpful, let it pass over your shoulder, as something that is possibly meant for somebody else. Simply be sincere and open in your willingness to let God lead you into the silent simplicity of meditation. For it is in that silent simplicity that you will be transformed in ways you cannot and do not need to comprehend or imagine.

CHAPTER 3

Meditative Experience

You do not have to meditate very long to begin experiencing more interior, meditative states of awareness. There is something about simply sitting still, quietly attentive to your breathing, that tends to evoke less agitated, less thought-driven modes of meditative awareness. When this shift toward more interior, meditative states of awareness embodies a sincere desire for God, a new capacity to realize oneness with God begins to emerge. Resting in this awareness offers the least resistance to God. As resistance to the divine diminishes, you learn to follow God, who alone knows, and is, the dark and luminous path that leads into the depths of God.

To express the matter in specifically Christian terms, meditative experience offers the least resistance to the Spirit of God within us, who, with unutterable groaning, yearns that we might awaken to that eternal oneness with God that Christ reveals and proclaims. As our resistance to God's quiet persistence diminishes, our experience of ourselves as other than Christ dissolves into a meditatively realized oneness with Christ. Little by little, or all at once, we come to that point of blessedness and freedom in which we can say, along with Saint Paul, "For me to live is Christ" (Phil. 1:21). That is, for me to live is for me to be that oneness with God that Christ embodies and proclaims.

Sensing, then, the centrality of the question, we ask: What is the nature of the meditative experience that meditation practice evokes and sustains? And how can we draw upon our understanding of meditative experience to enhance our efforts in meditation and the contemplative way of life that a commitment to daily meditation embodies?

As a way to begin, I invite you to pause and ponder those moments in which meditative experience unexpectedly manifests itself in the midst of your day-by-day living. I have in mind one of those moments in which you are going along, caught up in the concerns of the day, when something wonderful happens. Suddenly, your awareness of whatever it is you are aware of at the moment occasions a subtle expansiveness of awareness, a subtle quickening within your heart.

Suddenly, your awareness of *this* awakens you to *that which transcends this*. By "this" I mean whatever it is you might happen to be aware of at the moment when the awakening occurs. What catches your eye might be *this* friend's unexpected act of kindness. Or perhaps the unexpected expansion of awareness occurs as you are looking down into the upturned face of *this* child, perhaps your own child or grandchild, tugging at your pant leg, asking for a glass of water. Or the moment of awakening may be occasioned by your looking up to see *this* lone bird circling in a cloudless sky. Or the precipitating event might be *this* wind that is just now picking up, signaling an upcoming storm.

It is nothing special, really. Your friend does many kind things. Your child or grandchild often asks for a glass of water. You have often looked up to see a bird circling in a cloudless sky. You have noticed many times how the wind picks up before a storm and what it feels like against your face, how it stirs the trees. In your customary day-by-day experience of these day-by-day things, nothing special is going on. It is just that in these moments of which I speak your customary, day-by-day experience of these things instantaneously yields to an intimate awareness of that which transcends all these things. In some wondrous manner your customary way of experiencing the friend's act of kindness or the child's open-faced presence yields and gives way to an interior, meditative experience of something vast and ungraspable.

The moments of spontaneous meditative awareness that we are now exploring can, at times, break in on us with great psychological intensity. The humanistic psychologist Abraham Maslow referred to these monumental moments of awakening as *peak experiences*. In my one-on-one talks with men and women who have attended silent meditation retreats with me over the years, and in my own life as well, I know how true it is that just one such experience can change your whole life. Sometimes, when still quite young, we can be granted a spiritual awakening that we spend the rest of our life learning to understand and be faithful to.

At present, however, I am referring primarily to the much more frequent, subtle, and often barely noticed moments of meditative awakening that occur in the course of daily living. What is it these moments awaken us to? We are not inclined to say. For that which is glimpsed in these moments is intuitively recognized as transcending anything we might say concerning it. The momentary flash of awareness leaves us momentarily speechless. We do not know what to make of it. It is just that for a fleeting moment we are awakened to the sheer miracle of simply being alive.

Continue pondering your own moments of spontaneous experience and you will see what happens next. No sooner does the moment of awakening occur than it passes away as mysteriously as it came. As it does so, we return to our own customary way of experiencing things. At least this is what tends to happen to many people. And this is what has happened to us many times: we are graced with moments of spontaneous meditative experience of God's presence in the midst of our daily living, only to go on as if no awakening had been granted.

Fortunately for us, we, at some point, experienced a shift within ourselves. The moments of awakening continued to pass as mysteriously as they came. In their passing we returned to our customary way of experiencing things. But not quite. For the coming and going of our moments of awakening began to graze our hearts with longing. This is what makes us seekers of the inner way—this longing, in which we find ourselves going about with a certain holy discontent, a holy restlessness, a kind of homesickness. Consciously, and unconsciously, we go about asking: Why do I spend so many of my waking hours trapped on the outer circumference of the inner richness of the life I am living? How can I learn to live in more daily abiding awareness of the transcendent depths so fleetingly glimpsed?

Perhaps by trial and error, with no one to guide us, we find our own way to respond to the unconsummated longings of our awakened heart. We, in effect, discover our own personal ways to meditate. By meditation I mean, in this context, *any act habitually entered into with our whole heart as a way of awakening and sustaining a more interior meditative awareness of the present moment.* The meditation practice we might find ourselves gravitating toward could be baking bread, tending the roses, or taking long, slow walks to no place in particular. Or we might find ourselves being interiorly drawn to painting or to reading or writing poetry or listening to certain kinds of music. Our meditation practice may be that of being alone, truly alone, without any addictive props or escapes. Or our practice may be that of being with that person in whose presence we awakened to what is most real and vital in our life. Or we might find ourselves slowly reading the psalms or stopping on the way home from work to slowly walk through a cemetery or to sit in the back of an empty and silent church. We cannot explain it, but when we give ourselves over to these simple acts, we are taken to a deeper place. We become once again more grounded and settled in a meditative awareness of the depth of the life we are living.

We discover we cannot make our moments of spontaneous meditative awakening occur. But even so, we unwittingly find our way to the strategy that underlies all methods of meditation. The strategy is that of freely choosing to make ourselves as open and receptive as possible to the graced event of awakening to that meditative sense of oneness with God one with us in life itself.

This is the strategy that underlies the guidelines for meditation introduced in the previous chapter. We sit, attentive to our bodily stillness, until little by little, or all at once, our awareness of *this* moment of bodily stillness once again awakens us to that which transcends this stillness. We sit, quietly attentive and receptive to our breathing, until, by God's grace, our awareness of *this* breath awakens to the presence of God that wholly transcends this breath. We sit in this moment of attentive silence until, by God's grace, our awareness of this moment of silence awakens us to the eternal silence of God. Little by little, or all at once, the unconsummated longings of our awakened heart find a hallowed clearing in which we learn to quietly rest with a sense of trusting expectancy.

The transformative power of meditation is often not easy to recognize at first. Meditation is a habit that grows slowly, over time. But as we cultivate the habit of meditation, a more habitual meditative awareness slowly becomes our way of experiencing our day-by-day lives. It is in this manner that daily meditation becomes a way of learning to live in a more daily abiding awareness of the depths so fleetingly glimpsed. So it is through our fidelity to daily meditation that we might learn to be the contemplative man or woman we know we, deep down, really are and are called to be. Which is to say, we might learn to be someone who upon entering a room is immediately awakened to the mystery that transcends walking into a room, transcends whatever might be happening at the moment.

It may seem as if I am exaggerating by attributing such immensity to the simple, unassuming moments I am reflecting on here. But it seems to me that the opposite is true. It seems to me that we are trying to put words to that which it is impossible to exaggerate. For no matter how far-flung our words might become, no matter how expansive the imagery, our words pale in significance to that which transcends all that words can say.

In the moment we look down into the child's upturned face, how are we to find the words that would begin to convey that which we fleetingly glimpse in that little face? How can we ever speak of it in a manner that does justice to it? We cannot. Our hearts break when we try. Seeing how this is so helps us to understand that meditation practice goes far beyond what can be properly understood in terms of methods and techniques. For when we sit still in meditation, we sit still with all our heart. As we do so, our eyes are opened to the hallowed light in which we live out our lives.

As we sit in meditation, silent and still, and as childlike as we can be, we realize ourselves to be immersed in the mystery to which we are awakened. This is what I want to reflect on next. I want to go back and pick up where we left off in our reflections on moments of spontaneous meditative experience, so as to better understand ways in which we, in these moments, realize ourselves to be one with the mystery to which we are awakened.

In reflecting on our moments of spontaneous meditative experience, we saw them to be moments in which we are awakened to that which transcends whatever we are aware of at the moment. The person, thing, or event is experienced as a door that suddenly flies open to a previously unrecognized mystery. But look closely and you will see that to stop at this point would be to leave unexplored one of the most stunning aspects of these moments. For in our moments of spontaneous meditative experience, our awareness of *this* awakens us to that which transcends this, *manifesting itself in and as this.*

To see how this is so, consider a moment of spontaneous meditative awareness in which a woman sees her beloved. She holds her beloved. And in doing so she is awakened to a love that transcends the concrete immediacy of the beloved. By this I mean that the love to which she is awakened transcends whether or not his hair is combed, or even whether or not he even has any hair. The love she experiences transcends whether or not he is wearing matching socks. Every detail about him is transcended by the love to which his presence awakens her. But look and see how true it is that the love to which she is awakened is *not* experienced as being dualistically *other than* who she, at this moment, experiences him to be. She is not in this moment awakened to an ethereal realm of love above and beyond what he or she can reach. Rather, she is awakened to the mystery of love manifesting itself *in and as* who he simply is! The love to which she is awakened is found in drawing closer to him, as she settles into who he simply is, as she settles into who they simply are together.

This is why it rings true for this man and woman to call their moments of sexual union "making love." Their "loving making" makes love present *in and as* their very lovemaking. Seen in this way, their making love is meditation practice. That is to say their making love is a way for them to make themselves as open and vulnerable as they can be to the more interior, meditative awareness of the love in which they are one.

This *in-and-as* aspect pertains to stones and stars and the smell of burning leaves. It holds true with respect to the loaf of bread we are slicing, the berries we are rinsing off in the sink, or the dust we're sweeping into the dustpan. Suddenly, without warning, we can find ourselves in the midst of such simple things, being fleetingly awakened to that which transcends all that we see manifesting itself in and as all that we see.

Look for yourself and see if it is not so: that to which you are awakened in the moment the friend gives the unexpected gift is not experienced as being dualistically other than the friend's loving act. Similarly, the mystery to which you are awakened in looking down into a child's upturned face is not dualistically other than that very child. The mystery to which you are awakened by a bird's flight or the blowing of the wind is not other than the bird's flight itself or the very wind that now sends you off closing windows as the rain begins pouring down all about the house. In each instance, it is just so: the mystery to which you are awakened awakens you to itself in and as the concrete immediacy of what just is.

We now have our finger on Christ's pulse. For Christ was always calling out to those around him to join him in seeing the Godly nature of everyone and everything he saw. We now have our finger on the pulse of the mystics. It is out of this meditatively realized oneness with God in life itself that Saint Francis called the sun his brother and the moon his sister.

It is this in-and-as awareness that Saint John of the Cross speaks of—the transformative process in which, at the beginning of our spiritual journey, the beauty of created things distracts us from our search for God. We sense that we have to be careful so as not to love a person, place, or thing too much lest it hold us back from loving God, who is infinitely beyond all that God creates. Then, as we mature in our spiritual path, we look about the world to discover that, as Saint John of the Cross observes, the beloved has passed this way in haste. That is, in our moments of meditative awakening we intuitively recognize traces of the divine in ourselves, others, and everything around us. As our meditative journey ripens and matures still further, we look out at the mountains and are amazed to discover ourselves silently crying out, "My beloved is the mountains." We discover that we can spend a day alone in the mountains—sensing, in doing so, that we are spending the day in God, wholly present in and as the mountains.

It is with respect to this *in-and-as* aspect of meditative experience that we have our finger on our own pulse as we lose our footing in our perceived otherness from God in the midst of things. To see how this is so, we have but to go back to the moment of gazing at the setting sun. As you give yourself over to the beauty of the sunset, you do not turn into the sun. Nor does the sun turn into you. You and the sun do not become each other. And yet in the moment of meditative awareness you are not other than the sun. In giving yourself over to the beauty of the setting sun you cannot find the place at which that beauty ends and our own begins. Nor are you inclined to try to do so. The moment is such that you and the beauty of the sunset are experienced as being simply and unexplainably one.

The Catholic writer Romano Guardini makes this same point about our relationship with God.[1] Beginning with a basic principle of logic, Guardini observes that A cannot be B at the same time and in the same respect that it is A. This pen with which I am writing these words cannot, at the same time and in the same respect, be this piece of paper on which these words are being written. Similarly, in the Christian tradition an emphasis is made on honoring the revealed truth of creation, in which a distinction remains between an infinite creator and ourselves as God's finite creation. In this stance God is known as the transcendent source of ourselves as finite creatures of God's love. In this stance we sing, "Praise God from whom all blessings flow. Praise God all creatures here below." But then we are given to realize that although we are not God, neither are we other than God. The paradoxical truth, Guardini suggests, lies at the heart of all religious experience. It is this paradoxical truth that lies at the heart of our moments of spontaneous experience. In fact, meditative experience is the experiential intimacy of faith. Our faith proclaims that God, who is infinitely beyond us, is infinitely one with us—as Saint Augustine phrased it, "closer to us than we are to ourselves." In moments of spontaneous experience we fleetingly realize this closer-than-close presence of God, as intimately and unexplainably as we know the palms of our own hands.

I am referring in this book to God present *in* ourselves and everything around us to preserve the distinction between God and creation. I am referring to God present *as* ourselves and everything around us to give witness to the sense of oneness with God germane to all religious experience, and to meditative experience in particular. In a similar manner, I am referring in these reflections to the God-given nature of our lives to give witness to the Judeo-Christian revelation of God as creator. I am referring to the

God-given godly nature of our lives to give witness to the truth proclaimed by Meister Eckhart and other Christian mystics that God holds nothing back, in being so generous as to make our own deepest reality nothing less than all that God is.

Awareness of the *in-and-as* aspect of meditative experience can help us to understand the nature of meditation practice, in which we seek to open ourselves to ever deeper levels of discovering God already present in life itself. We can begin to appreciate how, as we sit in meditation, we serendipitously lose our footing in our perceived otherness from God in the midst of what just is. We sit in meditation, attentive to our breathing, so that we might be intimately awakened to God giving herself to us whole and complete in and as our breathing. We sit in meditation, neither clinging to nor rejecting the thoughts that flow through our mind, that we might awaken God giving herself to us whole and complete in and as the gift of thought. We sit, gazing deeply into the feelings that arise, endure, and pass away within us, that we might awaken to God given whole and complete in and as the gift of our sadness and happiness and all the emotions we experience. Awakened to this divinity of the life we are living, we can end our meditation practice with a prayer of gratitude. We can bow to the cross or to the image of Jesus, who, through the power of the spirit within us, reveals to us the absolute oneness of all that God is and all that we really are and are called to be. We can then go eat lunch, knowing that as we do so God is given, whole and complete, in and as our ordinary experience of simply eating lunch.

We can now take our reflections on moments of spontaneous meditative experience one final and important step further by focusing on how moments of spontaneous meditative experience instantaneously leap clear of each aspect of ego consciousness. By this I mean that in moments of spontaneous experience we leap clear of the intellect, the memory, and the will. We leap clear of feelings and bodily sensations. In a moment of spontaneous meditative experience the I that says, "I think, I remember, I want, I feel, I experience this or that bodily sensation" is instantaneously transcended. By learning to understand and appreciate how this is so, we can better understand and appreciate the self-transforming power of meditation practice. For in meditation we seek to cultivate more interior, meditative ways of experiencing oneness with God transcending the ego and all that the ego can attain.

We can begin by reflecting on how moments of spontaneous experience leap clear of thought. To see how this is so, I invite you to once again situate yourself in a moment of giving yourself over to the beauty of the setting sun. As you stand there, all kinds of thoughts might be passing through your mind. Perhaps some of these thoughts are about this particular sunset or about sunsets in general. But the meditative awareness that constitutes the living essence of the moment is neither dependent on nor reducible to any of these thoughts. In fact, as you gaze at the sunset, you can sense how even the most sublime thought about this sunset falls short of what you, in this moment, intimately experience this sunset to be. You sense that dwelling on your thoughts about sunsets would compromise your nonthinking awareness of the ultimately unthinkable beauty of the setting sun.

Free of thought, in all its modes, you are, in this moment, momentarily free of all questions and answers, all problems and solutions, all that is agreed on or disagreed on. For a fleeting instant there is nothing to prove, nor is there anything being experienced that could even be proved. There is nothing to solve, nor is there anything about what you are experiencing that needs solving, or even could be solved. In the twinkling of an eye you are fleetingly immersed in a nonthinking awareness of the unthinkable depths of what just is.

Reflecting on this aspect of meditative experience can help us to understand the practice of meditation as a way of learning how to wean ourselves off our customary dependency on thought. The strategy at work here is that of quietly establishing ourselves in an interior stance of neither clinging to nor rejecting whatever thoughts might arise in our mind as we meditate. As we meditate, we do not try to have no thoughts. Nor do we think the thoughts that come into our mind. Rather, we simply sit, in sustained meditative awareness of each thought as it arises, endures, and passes away. By assuming this interior stance, we freely choose to offer the least resistance to a graced liberation from the tyranny of thought. As we do so, we open ourselves to the mystery of knowing God in ways that utterly transcend what thought can grasp or contain.

This does not mean that we reject thought as we meditate. Rather, it means that we refrain from our customary tendency to think. As we meditate, we simply gaze with meditative eyes into the flow of thoughts that arise, endure, and pass away within us. As we do so, we are awakened to God manifested, whole and complete, in and as the God-given godly nature of thought. As the meditation practice comes to a close and we return to our day-by-day lives, we do so liberated from ideological living based on thoughts about God, ourselves, others, or anything else. At the same time we learn to live in a new appreciation of the gift of thinking with a clear, simple, and open mind.

As you continue reflecting on what actually happens in moments of spontaneous experience, you will see that as you leap clear of thought, you simultaneously leap clear of your own will. You can see how this is so by observing how impossi-

ble it is to have a repeat performance of a moment of spontaneous meditative experience. Just because you are graced this
evening with a deep experience of the setting sun is no assurance that tomorrow's sunset will usher in another moment of
intimately realized grandeur. You can go into a church, attend
a retreat, sit and pray, and be blown away by a moment of realized oneness with God. You return to the same spot at some
later date, bracing yourself for a repeat performance of wonder
and grace, only to be left empty-handed, barren of any sense of
meditative awakening. It is in this way, then, that we are given
to realize that we, in our moments of spontaneous meditative
awareness, leap clear of our own will. For in these moments we
are immersed in an awareness that we, by the sheer brute force
of our will, are powerless to produce or make such moments
happen whenever we please.

We can also recognize how we leap clear of our own will in
those moments of meditative awakening, which take us completely by surprise, without our consciously willing them to
happen in any way. Perhaps you are walking along at sunset,
completely preoccupied with many things. Pausing to experience the beauty of the setting sun might be the furthest thing
from your mind. Then, without warning, a single glance at the
setting sun occasions an unforeseen, unchosen moment of
awakening. As lovers, poets, artists, those who meditate, and all
spiritually awake people know, it is so good that life is like this.
Without our even seeking to be awakened we are, from time to
time, awakened. Without even baiting our hook and throwing
it into the water, a huge fish jumps right into the boat.

Moments of spontaneous meditative experience leap clear
of the will even in those instances in which they are granted to
us in the midst of our desiring and hoping that a moment of

renewed awakening might occur. Perhaps your rendezvous with the beauty of the setting sun has been carefully thought out and prearranged. Perhaps you intentionally came to this spot with the intention of being as open and receptive as possible to a moment of meditative communion with the beauty of the setting sun. But even here the awakening that is granted leaps clear of the will. For as the moment of graced awareness begins to occur, its inner richness and depths transcend anything that could be explained or accounted for purely in terms of your efforts to evoke it.

Lovers often plan their moments of intimacy. For they are not fools. They have learned by experience how unwise it is simply to wait passively for each moment of renewed oneness to serendipitously appear. And so they stack the deck in their favor. They go to great efforts to arrange moments conducive to renewed awakenings of their love. But when the premeditated moment of renewed oneness catches fire, it burns with a light that qualitatively transcends anything that could be accounted for by their efforts to bring it about. Note, too, how they watch over their moments of reawakened intimacy. The intimacy can drain away if diversions and distractions from it are not recognized and let go of so as to sustain the flow of their intimacy. Their will is active at this point in the paradoxical sense of freely willing to remain open and receptive to an experience of love beyond what their will can produce or attain. And as the moment passes, they must will as well to be faithful to what they were privileged to experience in each other in the moment they looked into each other's eyes and recognized that which makes life worth living. Even here, in their day-by-day fidelity to each other, they are freely willing to honor what lies beyond their will to produce or attain. It is this way with poets and artists and with every venue of self-transformation. The will is always at hand in the free decision to honor and sustain that which transcends what the will can attain.

Understanding how moments of spontaneous awareness transcend the will helps us to understand our meditation practice. We cannot, by the sheer brute force of our will, make moments of meditative awareness of God's presence occur. For it is our situation as human beings that we are powerless to produce by our efforts that union with God that alone fulfills our hearts. But what we can do is freely will to make ourselves as vulnerable and receptive as possible to the influx of grace. And so we sit in meditation, being as open and receptive as we can be to God, the awakener of hearts. As seekers of a more habitual meditative experience of God's presence, we do not simply go about our business, leaving our moments of meditative awakening to chance. We stack the deck in our favor. We tend to show up for sunsets. We see to it that we do not miss that quiet moment alone in the morning on the back porch with a cup of coffee before the hectic pace of the day begins. We are quick to slow down, if just for a moment, as those little things that happen during the day unexpectedly flash forth that certain something we cannot define or describe. And we practice meditation. Day by day, we set aside time to sit still and straight—a "Here I am, Lord" stance of receptive openness to an experience of God that transcends the power of the will to attain. And in those moments the desire for realized oneness with God catches fire; it burns with light that transcends what can be accounted for by our efforts to evoke it.

We might at first imagine that when we meditate we are stacking the deck in favor of a heightened possibility of some kind of extraordinary experience of God's presence. Such an attitude often leads to disappointment. It is helpful to pause and consider that lovers do not live in a perpetual ecstasy of love.

Rather, their moments of ecstatic union open their eyes to the true nature of all their ordinary moments with one another. Artists do not live in a perpetual avalanche of creativity. Rather, their moments of extraordinary creative energy open their eyes to the true nature of all the ordinary moments of patient toil and effort that their fidelity to their art requires. Similarly, as we meditate we are not attempting to will our way toward extraordinary experiences of God. Rather, our moments of extraordinary experience of God's presence open our eyes to the endlessly holy nature of our ordinary experience of ordinary daily living. Seen in this way, our meditation practice embodies our desire to stabilize ourselves in a quiet confidence in God, present, whole, and complete, in and as our ordinary experience of our ordinary day-by-day lives.

Even during periods of spiritual desolation and hardship, we can discern how meditative experience transcends our will. For even as our desire for God remains painfully unconsummated, we, in some ever so subtle manner, can discern something of God's presence flowing in the hidden recesses of our powerlessness. Even as our desire to experience God's presence remains unfulfilled, we are secretly fulfilled in ways we can neither grasp nor explain. Some of the deepest and most profound aspects the meditative path to God occur in the midst of this "dark night" experience, in which the grace we seek is granted in the very depths of our ongoing powerlessness to attain it.

As we leap clear of our own conceptualizing mind and our will, we simultaneously leap clear of our memory. In our ego consciousness we are guided by memory. We navigate our way around by remembering our past experiences, which serve as the basis for interpreting what we are currently experiencing. If someone holds up an apple and asks us what it is, we, by virtue of our memory, say it is an apple. If someone holds up a pear and asks what it is, we, by virtue of our memory, say it is a pear. We could not survive without the functional power of memory. To have a family member or loved one with Alzheimer's disease or some other form of dementia is to experience firsthand how precious memory is and how tragic the loss of memory can be.

And yet if we are always going about wholly identified with our remembering and remembered self, we tend to remain exiled from who we are in the virginal newness of the present moment. This is what makes our moments of spontaneous experience so freeing. In a flash we are set free from the tyranny of memory. We are set free of the illusion of going about imagining we are nothing more than the ongoing momentum of who we used to be. We gaze at this sunset in this never-quite-this-way-before, never-quite-this-way-again present moment in which our lives unfold. God did not speak to Moses from the burning bush, revealing himself as "I Am Who I Used to Be. Come with me." Rather, God reveals himself as "I Am Who I Am. Come be with me." In meditative experience we taste firsthand the eternal newness of the present moment. And in the newness of the present moment we taste something of the eternal newness of God. We glimpse, however obscurely, that God is the infinity of the perpetually unfolding newness of the present moment in which our lives unfold.

It is true that our memory is active in moments of spontaneous meditative experience. As we stand in a moment of quiet awe before the setting sun, no one has to tell us what we are looking at. For we remember what sunsets are by virtue of our past experiences of sunsets. And yet the meditative awareness that awakens within us in this moment transcends memory. For our experience of the setting sun is clearly not simply a matter of recognizing what the sunset is by virtue of remembering previous sunsets. In this moment, our remembering and remembered self falls into the background. Immersed in the newness of the present moment, we are given to realize that nothing that has happened to us in the past, nor anything we have done in the past, has the power to name who we are. In this moment we realize ourselves to be one with the virginal newness of the present moment, which is always just now appearing, fresh and free of all that used to be.

Understanding the ways in which our moments of spontaneous experience transcend memory helps us to understand the strategy at work in meditation practice. Each thought that arises in meditation is a remembered thought, one that we neither cling to nor reject. So, too, with all the images that arise in our minds as we sit in meditation. Each is a remembered image that we neither cling to nor reject. As we sit in meditation, neither clinging to nor rejecting our remembered thoughts and images, we learn to wean ourselves off our tendency to identify with our remembered and remembering self. Sitting this way, we learn to be free at last from the tyranny of the past. And in this dying away of all that used to be, there arises the eternal child, ever present and radiant with a newness that never dies.

Moments of spontaneous meditative awareness are also moments in which we leap clear of feelings and bodily sensations. Reflecting on a moment of gazing at the setting sun, we can readily recognize that there is nothing antiseptic about this moment in which we are bathed in the sensuous richness of the colors and hues that are before us.

Nor is the moment void of feelings that may come welling up within us, adding to the richness of the moment. The moment is one of vulnerability to all that is flowing through our body. The greater the degree of unguarded bodily openness, the broader and richer the meditative experience that comes rolling through. If we have been shut down or constricted just prior to this moment, the awakening eases the tightness. Our body recognizes just what it is to do, as evidenced by how we instinctively relax into all that is welling up and passing through us in this graced and expansive moment.

This bodily relaxation and surrender is a primitive and profound form of faith. It is an act of trust in God and in God's world as a trustworthy and safe place to be. In spite of all the scary things that can and do happen, we can let down our guard. We can open the gate of our heart to discover not a threatening force to overtake us, but a love that wills to have its way with us and set us free.

Look, too, and you will see that it is not simply the tendency to reject painful or disturbing feelings and bodily sensations that can hinder the flow of a moment of spontaneous meditative experience. For equally detrimental is any attempt to cling to consoling or otherwise pleasant feelings and bodily sensations that we might experience.

Any attempt to grab hold of the consoling aspects of a moment of meditative experience so as to "have" this moment on our own terms only constricts the flow of the moment. In attempting to cling to the consoling aspects of the moment, we pull back into the constricted ego space of wanting to possess, rather than simply be blessed by, pleasant and consoling experiences. Any attempt to use the sensuous delight of the moment to soothe ourselves at the end of a hard day dissipates the mysterious sense of being consoled in a willingness to cease grasping at consolations. So it is that our moments of spontaneous meditative experience flow unobstructed and free to the extent that we neither cling to nor reject the feelings and bodily sensations the moment brings our way.

Truth is, there is no way of knowing in advance just what feelings and bodily sensations might come welling up out of the unguarded openness of a spontaneous meditative experience. Sometimes the feeling aspect of the moment is barely discernible. The moment consists of a calm, lucid awareness. Sometimes the moment occasions a sense of deep joy that prompts us to yield to joy completely in sensing how joy filled life can be. Sometimes moments of awakening can evoke an unexpected encounter with our untended-to and wounded heart. The joy we may feel in a moment of awakening may bring to the surface a sense of deep sadness in realizing how rarely we feel truly joyful. The feelings of tenderness a moment of awakening might evoke might evoke as well a sense of how little tenderness there is in our life. To be open, truly open, to that moment of spontaneous awareness is to be open and accepting of ourselves as we really are.

Understanding the bodily, feeling dimensions of our moments of spontaneous experience can help us to understand the strategy at work in meditation with respect to our feelings and bodily sensations. As we sit in meditation, we sit silent and still, neither clinging to nor rejecting the stream of bodily sensations the moment brings—the ticking of the clock on the mantel, the crow cawing in the tree just outside the window, the coolness or warmth of the air. We sit, open to all these bodily sensations, that we might awaken to the way our body bodies forth the love that is just now loving us into being. Sitting thus, we recognize something of God in our awareness of the clock's ticking, the crow's incessant cawing, the breeze that stirs the curtains, the way the room slowly, unrelentingly becomes dark as day comes to a close. It is not that our experience of seeing, hearing, smelling, tasting, and touching is suspended. Rather, we sense something of God, the creative source of our seeing, in the intimate texture of our experience of seeing and in all that we see. We sense something of God, the creative source of our hearing, in the intimate texture of our experience of hearing and in all that we hear. And so with each of the five bodily senses and each aspect of the world around us that we experience through our senses.

So, too, with all the feelings that flow through us as we meditate. Neither clinging to pleasant feelings nor rejecting painful feelings, we remain open and free with respect to all of our feelings. In this way we make ourselves as vulnerable and receptive as possible to a renewed and deepened experience of the way our bodily being bodies forth the love that utters our feelings into being. As our practice deepens, we learn to discern something of God, the creative source of our feelings, present in the intimate texture of our feelings and in all the people and events and circumstances we have feelings about.

As we go through these reflections we will be touching on these matters again and again, viewing them first from one angle and then another. In fact, this whole book is nothing but a series of meditative glances into the ways in which meditative experience lays bare the living essence of Christian faith in every aspect of our day-by-day lives. But as a way to distill what has been shared in this chapter into a succinct summary, I invite you to consider the following:

Meditative experience thinks nothing. It gazes deeply into the nature of thought. Meditative experience wills nothing. It gazes deeply into the nature of willing, and of all desire. Meditative awareness believes nothing. It gazes deeply into the nature of belief. Meditative awareness remembers nothing. It gazes deeply into the nature of memory. Meditative experience feels nothing. It gazes deeply into the nature of feelings. And meditation experience sees, hears, tastes, smells, and touches nothing. It gazes deeply into the nature of the bodily senses. Gazing deeply into each aspect of ego consciousness, meditative experience transcends ego consciousness. Transcending ego, meditative experience realizes God to be in no way reducible to the ego, nor reducible to anything other than ego and all that ego consciousness is conscious of.

As I write this chapter I am listening to a Gospel hymn, "Down to the River to Pray." The refrain of the hymn is: "As I went down in the river to pray, studying about that good old way, and who shall wear the robe and crown. Good Lord, show me the way." The good old way is the way of those who follow Christ, who began his public ministry by entering the River Jordan to be baptized. The event occasioned a spiritual awakening. As Christ came up out of the water, God's voice was heard: "Behold my beloved son in whom I am well pleased" (Mark 1:11). Perhaps because of hearing this hymn playing away as I write, I feel moved to conclude this chapter by recasting its central message in a parable about entering a river.

The parable provides a way of sharing how my journey through Yoga, Taoist, and Buddhist meditation practices has brought me back full circle to an enriched understanding and appreciation of the mystical heritage of my own Christian tradition. I hope that those of you in the Christian tradition whose spiritual odyssey has been expanded and enriched in opening yourself to other religious traditions will relate to this parable. I hope you might find in it truths that relate to the experience of coming back full circle to be consoled and reassured by following the universal path of spiritual self-transformation in the mystical legacy of your own Christian faith.

The first and most basic thing that happens when you enter a river is that you get completely wet. It does not matter whether you have entered the river after a great deal of deliberation or you have fallen in accidentally off the end of a pier. Either way, you get completely wet. It does not matter whether you are entering the river for the first time or whether you have entered it countless times before. You get completely wet either way. No matter how many times you enter the river, the river never says you are running out of turns, allowing you to get only slightly damp. No matter how many times you go down into the river, you are as completely wet as the first time you entered it.

It also does not matter whether you enter the river alone in the middle of the night, so as to have the river all to yourself, or whether you enter in broad daylight along with thousands of other people. You get completely wet either way.

Nor does it matter whether you enter the river for only a brief moment or linger there for a long time. You get completely wet either way. Even in the briefest of forays into the river, you get completely wet.

It doesn't matter whether you have lived on the banks of the river all your life or whether you had to travel a great distance to arrive at its shores. You get completely wet either way. There is no bonus package of extra wetness granted to those who travel a great distance to get to the river. Everyone, whether coming from near or far, gets completely wet.

It doesn't matter whether you are a man or a woman, or whether you are old or young. It doesn't matter whether you are a great saint or a scoundrel. It doesn't matter what you believe. It does not matter whether you have accumulated great wealth or are as poor as poor can be. When you enter the river, you get completely wet.

We might call this the graciousness of the river. She accepts all who come to her. Jesus taught that we are completely drenched through and through with God's love. In the parable of the prodigal son, in his miracles of healing, in his love for everyone he encountered, his message rang out to one and all: you are drenched through and through with a divine benevolence that gives itself to you whole and complete in and as your very life. The fact that you do not see this unitive mystery is the source of all sorrow. Your incremental degrees of awareness of this mystery are incremental stages of realizing what is from all eternity the brimming-over fullness of your true and everlasting life.

This is just what moments of spontaneous meditative experience disclose to us. In a fleeting flash we realize there is nothing missing anywhere. Our very life is manifesting the fullness of life itself. The reality of everything around us is manifesting the fullness of reality itself. Moments of spontaneous meditative experience give witness to the anarchy of the ineffable. For these moments come to whom they come; they are granted to whom they are granted. Anyone, at any time, might find himself or herself falling into the river, becoming completely drenched in a graced and childlike clarity.

What must be dealt with, of course, is the way in which the clarity granted in moments of meditative awakenings tends to dissipate. It is in this awareness of how unaware we tend to be of the mystery to which we have been made aware that we experience the desire to be a river enterer. That is, anyone at any time might be interiorly drawn to enter the river intentionally as a conscious act—a choice to be awakened. Any one of us at any time might be interiorly drawn to become a river enterer, choosing to enter the river, day by day, until we remain, even in the scorching sun, drenched through and through with sustained, clear-eyed awareness of the divinity of our lives. Any of us might be drawn to seek this habitual awareness and to give witness to this clarity by the honest, vulnerable, and loving way in which we seek to live our life. That is, any of us might be drawn to commit ourself to daily meditation, in which the meditative experience of oneness with God might become the habitual way in which we experience and respond to God's presence in our daily life.

Now, if you are going to be a river enterer, it is wise to seek out the wise counsel of a seasoned river enterer. For there are drop-offs and undertows and other hazards to be aware of. It is best not to drown if you can at all help it. But even if you do drown, it is not that you did not get completely wet. It is just that you were not careful. This is what spiritual teachers are for: to help us not drown in the deep waters in which we, in entering the river, find ourselves. Be patient, be compassionate, be humble, be careful, the teacher tells us, so that we can get acclimated to living a life beyond our powers to grasp, control, or sustain.

Now imagine that you are a river enterer. Imagine, too, that you have learned to be a river enterer in the religious tradition that traces its roots back to Jesus. Jesus is the great river enterer, who calls others down into the river that they might discover that they are created in God's image and likeness, that they are God's children, in whom God is well pleased.

But there is something missing, something that is not right. Seeking to sort out just what the difficulty is, you study the history of your river-entering community. You discover that at first it was very simple. At first, men and women simply entered the river. Soon a path began to form leading down to the water's edge. Word got out, and a growing number of people began showing up to use the path.

One day someone observed that river entering is so important it seemed only fitting there should be a ceremony celebrating the admission of new members into the river-entering community. Someone else suggested it might also be nice to have a ceremony to reconcile wayward river enterers back into the community. And before long there arose rituals with hymns and candles as people gathered at the river.

Then one day someone observed that river entering is so special that there should be some kind of little tent over the path that goes down into the river. Others agreed. And a festive, brightly colored tent was built over the path. Then someone observed that river entering is so special that a tent was hardly a suitable way to honor all the ways that river entering enriched their lives. Others agreed. And so there was the first fund drive to raise money to build a large and beautiful building over the tent that covered the path that went into the river. And everyone agreed that it was an inspiring and uplifting building indeed.

Then someone wrote a book titled *The Meaning of River Entering*. Someone read the book, did not agree with its premise, and so wrote another book refuting the teachings of the first book. Someone read both books, disagreed with both, and wrote a third. Soon there was a proliferation of books on the meaning of river entering. A second fund drive was required to build a library adjoining the building over the tent that was over the path going down into the river. And everyone agreed what a fine library it was.

Then someone suggested that a school be build to promote the study of riverology and the granting of degrees to learned riverologists. Another fund drive raised the moneys to build a fine school, a seminary of sorts, next to the library, next to the building that was over the tent that was over the path that went down into the river.

Then someone observed that it was getting so crowded, it might be best if everyone did not enter the river. It might be better if only certain members of the community entered the river, and then distributed river water to the others. And who would be better suited to do so than the riverologists who held degrees in river entering? The decision was made to create a new ritual to celebrate authority invested in the riverologists to distribute river water to the community.

Somewhere along the way, the riverologists tended not to enter the river nearly as much as they used to. At some point they began to pipe river water into the building. And there were rumors that the water was actually shipped in from undisclosed sources. This is the situation that has developed in the river-entering community in which you find yourself. It seems that most everyone is content to sip bottled river water, read books on river entering, attend river-entering ceremonies, and agree and disagree with each other about the meaning of river entering.

Disheartened, you walk alone one day down by the river, trying to grasp just how everyone got into this predicament. As you are walking along, you slip and fall into the water. In doing so, you discover that the river is so gracious as to accept you completely in your solitary mishap. All alone, unplanned— with no building, no teaching, no ceremony—you get completely wet.

You come out of the river and start walking down the shore, and you are surprised to come upon a group of people who have built a large building over a tent that is over a path that goes down into the river. You are inclined at first to tell them they can't do what they are doing. You are tempted to tell them they are not even really getting wet. They only think they are getting wet. You are tempted at first to tell them that if they want to really get wet they are going to have to travel with you to join the river-entering community from which you came. Or perhaps some riverologists from your community could come to show them the correct and truly effective way to get wet.

But then, in recalling the personal journey that has brought you to this place, you decide instead to ask if they would mind if you used their path that goes down into the river. In doing so, you get completely wet. Relieved and grateful, you venture farther down shore to discover other buildings where river enterers gather. You use their path that goes down into the river and, in doing so, discover how completely wet you get, regardless of the color of the tent that is over the path, the architecture of the building, the teachings in all the books about the meaning of river entering. For what you discover is that although the teachings regarding the meaning of river entering vary greatly, one thing remains clear: each time you enter the river you get completely wet. Everyone who enters the river gets completely wet. And in each community you discern the presence of seasoned river enterers, men and women who even in the scorching sun remain drenched in the graciousness of the river.

In venturing on still farther down the shore you eventually come to the point at which the river empties into the sea. As you wade out into the water, there is only water as far as you can see. Silenced by the vastness of it all, you realize that you and the river have come to rest in the vast depths toward which all reality and all of life ceaselessly flows.

Taking all this in, you are surprised to discover yourself being interiorly drawn back to the river-entering community from which your journey first began. As you arrive back at your origins, you enter the large building and head straight for the path that goes down into the river. You are touched by the sincerity and devotion that went into setting up the festive little tent that covers the path. You are touched, too, by the depth of religious feeling and commitment that went into each detail of the building. You see all these things not as diversions from river entering, but as sincere efforts of men and women attempting to honor and reverence a grace and mystery they hold dear. You realize that perhaps you were a tad too judgmental. Perhaps, had you humbly done more river entering yourself, you would have realized that more river entering was going on than you had realized.

As you stand at the water's edge, the spirit of God blows over the water. You enter the river, and in doing so you become completely wet. Coming up out of the water, you hear the words that Christ heard as he came up out of the water, now spoken directly to you: "Behold my beloved child in whom I am well pleased."

As those standing about see how completely drenched you are as you come up out of the water, they are moved to enter the river as well. In doing so they, too, become completely wet. You, together with them, rediscover the origins of your own tradition of river entering. Together you seek to give witness to the good news that we are, from all eternity, completely wet. We are all drenched, through and through, with that oneness with God that Jesus, the one who calls us down into the river, proclaimed to be the very fullness of life itself.

CHAPTER 4

A Ladder to Heaven

As you commit yourself to seeking God in daily meditation, you will inevitably experience many graces and challenges along the way. The challenges might not appear at first. Sometimes there is a honeymoon period in which meditation seems to be nothing but a way of resting in God's arms. Sometimes no honeymoon is granted: right from the start there are issues to be faced and dealt with.

If you are going to be a fair-weather meditator, meditating only occasionally in moments that seem conducive to it, you are likely to avoid many of the challenges a commitment to daily meditation can bring. But then again you will also miss out on the full potential of self-transformation and spiritual fulfillment that meditation provides. It is in committing yourself to daily meditation that you stand to benefit the most from the ways in which meditation can revolutionize your life.

Just meditate long enough and you will inevitably begin to encounter your own unique version of the challenges that tend to be woven into the very fabric of meditation itself. You might, for example, discover yourself spending the time you had intended to set aside for meditation doing any number of other important or not so important things. As you meditate you will inevitably have to deal, at times, with distracting thoughts, invasive memories, and disturbing emotions. There will be times of sleepiness, boredom, confusion, discouragement, and other hardships as well. As you settle more deeply into the substance of the matter, you will discover that your own poor wounded ego is simply not up to the transformative process of dying to its most cherished illusions about itself. You will discover, firsthand, your ineptness in yielding yourself over to the joy of that sweet death to all that is less than God. You will discover yourself to be, at times, baffled and dazzled by utterly unmanageable realizations of oneness with God.

At first, and for quite some time, it may seem as if the task is that of working through all the challenges you encounter along the way so that you can move on to a state of realized oneness with God that lies beyond them. There is some truth to this perspective. Look closer, however, and you will find that the challenging aspects of meditation are themselves among the greatest graces that meditation brings. For it is in working through the challenging aspects of meditation that you *are* learning to die to your illusions about yourself. It is in learning to die to your illusions about yourself that you *are* dying that sweet death to all that is less than God.

One of the graces inherent in the challenging aspects of meditation is the humbling realization that we need to build foundations within ourselves capable of sustaining a life devoted to seeking God in meditation and prayer. It is strange how we as human beings can get ahead of ourselves. We can break through into dimensions of reality we do not have the maturity to sustain. A man and woman, for example, can experience profound feelings of passion and oceanic union only to discover they lack the maturity to sustain the love to which they have been awakened. Similarly, an artist may discover he or she lacks the maturity to effectively sustain and contain the giftedness that has awakened within him or her. The path that lies ahead in both love and creativity is often paved with the hard work of learning to be a down-to-earth human being, transparently open to ever more expansive levels of self-transformation.

The same point applies to the domain of religious experience. It is true that we can experience moments of realized oneness with God that are beyond anything we have ever known before. Extraordinary experiences of God's presence can be the catalyst that sets us on the path of meditation. But it is also true that moments that occasion a precipitous vertical ascent to God tend to be followed by a descent back into one's customary unawareness of God's presence. Likewise, any attempt to use force in meditation, as if to pole-vault into heaven in a single bound, can result in injuries. Any enthusiastic "mystical union or bust" approach to meditation is likely not to have any staying power. It often proves to be the case that the path of meditation is paved with the hard work of building within ourselves all that goes into being an awake, compassionate, Christlike human being. For it is in building the foundations of psychological and spiritual maturity that we are able to grow in an ever more expansive and habitual meditative awareness of oneness with God, one with us in life itself.

In our efforts to gain some clarity in these practical matters we will be turning in this chapter to a classical text titled *The Ladder of Monks*.[1] This simple and profound masterpiece of Christian spirituality was written by the monk Guigo in the latter half of the twelfth century. In recognition of his holiness, he is sometimes referred to in manuscripts as Guigo the Angelic. He is more commonly referred to as Guigo II because he was the second prior named Guigo at the Carthusian monastery of La Grande Chartreuse near Grenoble, France.

Guigo wrote his *Ladder of Monks* in the medieval literary genre called the monastic letter. That is, while written as a letter to his friend and fellow monk Gervaise, his text is obviously a carefully crafted exposition of the spiritual life, written not just for Gervaise but also for all who might benefit from reading it. Down through the centuries monks and nuns living in monasteries, as well as countless devout seekers living in the world, have been among his grateful readers. We will now join their ranks as we begin to prayerfully explore Guigo's insights into the spiritual path on which we find ourselves.

By reading Guigo's letter in this personal manner we can begin to appreciate how the mystical traditions of Christian faith render the passing centuries irrelevant in the face of the timeless mystery that unites Guigo's heart with our own. It is true that reading a work written centuries ago requires a certain translation into the language of our own day. But as we get into the inner recesses of Guigo's letter we begin to appreciate that it is as current and fresh as anything that might show up in today's mail. It is in this spirit, then, that I invite you to consider that the graced desire for a more interior, meditative union with God that stirred in Guigo's heart now stirs in your heart as well. If it were not so, you would not be interiorly drawn to the silent simplicity of meditation. It is in this spirit, then, that I encourage you to follow along with me as I turn to Guigo's letter for inspiration and guidance in building the psychological and spiritual foundations supportive of a lifelong commitment to seeking God in meditation.

Early on in his letter, Guigo shares with Gervaise, and with us, the experience that awakened him to the understanding of the spiritual life presented in his letter. He writes:

One day when I was busy with my hands I began to think about our spiritual work, and all at once four stages in spiritual exercise came into my mind: reading, meditation, prayer, and contemplation. These make a ladder for monks by which they ascend from earth to heaven. It has a few rungs, yet its length is immense and wonderful, for its lower end rests on earth, but its top pierces the clouds and touches heavenly secrets.[2]

Before we move on to reflect on Guigo's insights into each of the rungs of the ladder to heaven, it is worth pausing over the introductory paragraph cited above. For his disclosure concerning the context and content of the intuitive vision that inspires his letter gives witness to several aspects of the ground on which the ladder to heaven is to be firmly placed.

One aspect of the solid ground that supports the four-runged ladder to heaven is the way in which fidelity to spiritual practices increases the frequency, depth, and impact of moments of spiritual awakening that occur spontaneously throughout the day. Here is Guigo, perhaps washing out a pot or fixing a broken gate, as he ponders the nature of the spiritual path. "All at once" he is graced with an intuitive vision, a sudden gift of awareness. What is worth noting is that Guigo's sudden gift of awareness did not come to him while he was at prayer or absorbed in deep meditation. Rather, the flash of awareness came to him while he was doing the chores. But it seems safe to say that his fidelity to reading, meditation, prayer, and contemplation contributed to his having the sudden gift of awareness that he shares with us in his letter. It seems safe to say, as well, that it is his fidelity to prayer and meditation that allowed him to recognize and appreciate the insights into the spiritual path granted to him in his vision.

In my work with therapy patients I am struck by how often it happens that some of the most life-changing insights that occur in therapy do not occur in the therapy sessions themselves. Rather, the patients will come in to a session, sharing how as they were waking up in the morning or sitting in their car at rush hour or fixing dinner, they all at once realized something they never quite realized before. But what seems clear is that if their spiritual sensitivities had not been awakened by being in therapy, the insight might not have occurred. Or if the moment of insight had occurred, they might not have recognized it and been moved to ponder its significance to their life. Artists and writers will often say something similar. They will share how often it happens that the flashes of insight and inspiration that set things off in a whole new direction occur while they are standing in the shower or pouring a cup of coffee. And they share as well that there is something about fidelity to the creative process that tends to enhance the frequency, clarity, and impact of the flashes of intuitive awareness they experience

Guigo helps us to understand that the life of prayer and meditation is like this as well. The transformative events that occur in a life devoted to seeking God in meditation often do not occur during the times of meditation and prayer. Rather, the flashes of awareness come in the midst of the most unassuming moments of one's day-by-day life. But the point is that if we are not practicing meditation, these breakthroughs tend not to occur as often. Nor does the graced aura of awareness and gratitude these moments leave in their wake endure as long.

Nor are we able to find within ourselves a stabilized field of meditative awareness in which the graces granted in these moments might grow and develop into a habitual meditative awareness of God's presence in our day-by-day lives.

But it is not just fidelity to prayer and meditation that heightens the likelihood of our experiencing God's presence in the midst of our daily responsibilities. For what is also true is that the ladder to heaven will fall over if it is not firmly established on being responsible to ourselves and others in carrying out the chores and duties of everyday life. When I was going through the novitiate training at the monastery, there was little emphasis on reaching lofty states of mystical union with God. There was, however, an emphasis on not slamming doors, not leaving crumbs all over the table after meals, and not coming late to vespers. There was a daily emphasis on learning to be a decent citizen of the earth, one who could be relied on to tend to what needed tending to.

When I was in the monastery I would feel a sense of awe in the presence of some of the holy old monks who had lived there for fifty years or more. Thomas Merton once said they went around like transparent children. I would watch these old monks closely to see what they could teach me about becoming one with God. What came through to me was their sense of quiet dedication to daily responsibilities. They had somehow vanished into the ordinariness of the daily round of work and prayer, and in doing so they stood forth as present in some uncanny, childlike, and wondrous way.

Reading, meditation, prayer, and contemplation—the elements that make up Guigo's four-runged ladder to heaven—are to be firmly planted on learning to do what our daily responsibilities require of us. For by our being right where the daily round of our responsibilities would have us be, God will not have to go looking around trying to find us to grant us whatever the grace of the moment might bring.

There is a third and final aspect of the ground on which the ladder to heaven is to be solidly placed—namely, a down-to-earth, loving concern for one's own happiness and the happiness of others. This aspect of the solid ground of the interior life is found in the fact that Guigo's vision does not send him off into mystical realms devoid of the need to think about his own suffering and the suffering of others. To the contrary, his vision focuses his attention on "our spiritual work." In going to such great care in crafting his letter, he gives witness that this work entails a willingness to be sensitive and responsive to the plight of the human heart in its longing to realize true happiness and spiritual fulfillment. The writing of his letter is a labor of love. It is a way of passing on to others what has been passed on to him regarding how we are to come to God, in whom true spiritual fulfillment and happiness lie hidden.

The lesson we are invited to ponder is that meditation embodies a desire for God that brings us back full circle to a more clear-minded, Christlike compassion for others and ourselves. The more deeply we enter into meditation, the more we prayerfully ponder sound spiritual teaching, the more we are brought to a surprising realization that the whole journey, from start to finish, is inseparably bound up with how we talk to the woman next door. It is bound up with how we talk to ourself about ourself when we wake up in the morning and go through our day. The ladder to heaven will topple over if it is not firmly established on a sincere love and concern for ourselves and those around us. We simply never know just how far a single act of loving consideration will travel, or the ripple effects it might have on those we have never met. Just look at Guigo's letter. He wrote it centuries ago in his monastic cell in France, and here we are, centuries later, being touched and enriched by the compassionate concern that it contains.

Guigo says that anyone who inquires carefully into the properties and functions of each of the four rungs of the ladder to heaven "will consider whatever trouble and care he may spend on this little and easy, in comparison to the help and consolation he gains."[3] Taking Guigo at his word, let us now carefully ponder each rung of the ladder that symbolizes a foundational stage of spiritual development needed to sustain a life of meditation and prayer.

READING

The first rung of the ladder to heaven is *reading*. By reading, Guigo means a "careful reading of scripture, concentrating all one's powers on it."[4] He likens reading to the act of eating, saying that when we read God's word we take in spiritual nourishment. To clarify what he means by reading, he invites us to read with him these words of Jesus: "Blessed are the pure of heart, for they shall see God." Using this verse to demonstrate what he means by reading, Guigo writes:

I hear the words read: "Blessed are the pure of heart, for they shall see God." This is a short text of Scripture, but it is of great sweetness, like a grape that is put in the mouth filled with many senses to feed the soul. When the soul has carefully examined it, it says to itself, there may be something good here. I shall return to my heart and try to understand and find this purity, for this is indeed a precious and desirable thing. Those who have it are called blessed. It has for its reward the vision of God, which is eternal life. And it is praised in so many places in sacred Scripture. So wishing to have a fuller understanding of this, the soul begins to bite and chew upon this grape as though putting it in a wine press to ask what this precious purity may be and how it might be had.[5]

Being open and receptive to the words that flow right from Christ's heart into our own, then savoring the sweetness and depth of the words that are heard, is, for Guigo, the first rung of the ladder to heaven. This is a safe and reassuring way to begin; here is where all Christian life begins — in this sincere stance of receptive openness to Christ and his teachings.

If we look closely at the experience Guigo refers to as reading, we begin to realize that he is describing an experience that we ourselves have had. For each of us is no doubt familiar, at least to some degree, with the experience of being suddenly and interiorly touched by the beauty or depth of a passage of Scripture or some other spiritual work. It is just that we rarely read in the slow, attentive manner that invites these moments. And when these moments do occur, they tend to be so fleeting and subtle that we often do not realize the inner richness and full potential of what is happening.

Imagine you are reading the Scriptures in the manner Guigo describes. As you slowly and prayerfully read each verse, you come upon these words of Jesus: "Blessed are the pure of heart, for they shall see God." This is not the first time you have read this verse. You have read it, or heard it read, perhaps many times. But you now sense in these words new levels of beauty or meaning not quite seen before. The words suddenly become deeply personal, evoking a personal response. You say to yourself, "There may be something good here. I shall return to my heart and try to understand this purity of which Jesus speaks."

The transformative power of reading, as described by Guigo, holds true in a unique sense in the reading of Scripture. For to read the Scriptures as an act of faith means that the words of the living God are on your lips. The power of God's words works as leaven in the heart, awakening us to a personal experience of the presence of God that Scripture reveals. Read in this way, the Scriptures are one long love letter from God. Each verse tells the story of the love that perpetually calls us to itself.

There is no method here, no technique. For Guigo is encouraging us to read in a manner that is too sincere, heartfelt, and childlike to be reduced to any strategies of the ego whatsoever. The reading of which Guigo speaks is none other than our awakened heart actively seeking, coming upon, and surrendering to the first intimations of the love that has awakened it.

When I was in the monastery, the reverence given to Scripture was manifested in a simple devotional practice of kneeling on the floor of the library or wherever one might be, as one began to read the Scriptures. You might want to incorporate this devotional practice into your own reading of Scripture. Or you might be naturally inclined to begin your reading by bowing to the Scriptures or kissing the Scriptures or lighting a candle. Explore whatever might help you to open yourself to the Scriptures as the living word of the living God speaking personally to you and to the community of believers.

Note that in reading, as Guigo describes it, there are both Christ's words and the thoughts that come into Guigo's mind as he reads. But notice that these thoughts remain as yet unthought. That is, while engaged in the aspect of reading that Guigo invites us to explore, we are, as yet, not thinking about the thoughts that arise in our mind as we read. That will come later, in meditation, which forms the second rung of the ladder. This first rung of the ladder is that of reading the Scriptures as a way of seeking God. Then, in the midst of a quiet, sincere seeking, there is the graced event of coming upon words that embody that which we seek. As we read, we come upon something of God's presence in that which we are reading. And in coming upon that which we seek, we descend into the depths of our awakened heart, from which there emerge thoughts, images, and connotations that simply flow out, without being seized or grasped hold of in any way.

I first experienced what Guigo refers to as reading when I was in the monastery. When I first entered the monastery, the psalms were chanted in the monastic choir in Latin. Before I learned Latin well enough to conceptually grasp what I was chanting, the rhythmic cadences of the chant opened up a kind of interior listening or attentiveness. A sense of God's presence would come pouring into this sustained openness, granting a certain understanding not dependent on, nor reducible to, thought. When I learned Latin well enough to follow what I was chanting, and later when the office was chanted in English, the intuitive, visceral recognition of God's presence in the words continued to hold sway over conceptual understanding.

Spiritual reading is not limited to the reading of Scripture. As this chapter is attempting to demonstrate, reading Guigo and other works of spiritual wisdom can embody our search for God. As we search for God in the writings of the mystics, we can experience in their words something of the experience of God the mystics are writing about. I first experienced reading the mystics in this way in the monastery, when I started reading the sixteenth-century Spanish mystic Saint John of the Cross. I could tell that much of what I was reading was going right over my head. But I experienced that, however much was passing over me, something essential in his words was passing right into me, penetrating my chest and stomach. As I read his words, he seemed to be personally inviting me not to be afraid to abandon myself to the mystery he spoke of. I would read his words about that mysterious night that "transforms the lover into the beloved." As I read, I sensed within myself a desire to enter into that night, to experience the transformation into God that secretly unfolds within it.

As you continue on in your own spiritual journey you will no doubt come across those spiritual books, written by authors both ancient and contemporary, that you will learn to cherish. These are the books we never really finish. For each time we open them and read a few passages, we once again recognize something of ourselves and the path along which we are being led. By the way, Guigo's letter has been, for me, one such source of renewed and deepened spiritual awareness. I was first introduced to it in the monastery by Thomas Merton, and over the years have found it to contain the richness of insight that I am attempting to pass on to you here.

To commit ourselves to seeking God in the practice of meditation as described in the second chapter of this book assumes that we are learning to read the Scriptures and other spiritual writings, both ancient and contemporary, in the manner Guigo describes. That is, it assumes that we are committed to the ongoing process of quietly and unhurriedly reading, as a way of seeking and coming upon intimations of God's presence manifested to us in the midst of our reading.

The mode of consciousness embodied in reading as described by Guigo extends beyond the narrow sense of simply reading the Scriptures and other spiritual works. For Guigo is describing a mode of consciousness germane to an important phase of psychological-spiritual development in which we learn to seek, recognize, and rest in God as we remain present in whatever it is we are doing at the moment.

Artists, poets, those who serve the poor, and those committed to healing suffering in themselves and others learn to cultivate the stance of receptive openness we are here referring to as reading. The reward for serving the poor, for example, is found not outside the experience of serving the poor, but rather within the experience itself. In the very act of learning to read the faces of the poor, one is granted glimpses of God's presence in the world.

Lovers advance in love as they learn to cultivate within themselves the receptive openness that Guigo refers to as reading. Imagine a woman opening a letter from a man with whom she has recently risked disclosing her deep feelings of love. It is with a sense of excitement that she begins to read, seeking to find in his words some indication that he feels for her something of what she feels for him. As she begins to find such disclosures of love, she revels and rests in each self-disclosure. She reads his words over and over again. For in doing so, the words descend ever deeper into the hidden recesses of her heart.

Staying with romantic love as our example, we take in a yet richer appreciation of the foundational nature of reading as a stage of psychological-spiritual development. Imagine a man and woman who are in a deep and loving relationship. She is sharing something with him that she really wants him to hear and take to heart. If he is distracted by his own inner agenda, there will be no room in him to take in what she is sharing. He will be unable to be fully present and receptive to her self-disclosures unless he is willing to set aside whatever thoughts and concerns may be preoccupying him at the moment. He sets his foot on the first rung of the ladder to heaven experienced in human intimacy in his willingness to let go of his preoccupations with his own thoughts so as to really listen to all the beloved has to say. It is in his willingness to leave behind his preoccupations with his own thoughts that he begins to enter the open field of meditative awareness. It is in this interior, open field that she is waiting for him to be with her in her moment of self-disclosure.

Once he shows up for their rendezvous in receptive openness, he can remain there only by watching over his heart so as not to drift away from his receptive openness to her heart. Love asks of him not to go dashing off but to linger in the arena of receptive openness in which love grows and deepens. There is, it seems, nothing more painful than opening our heart to someone who is not there. Unless, of course, it is opening our heart to someone who is there, only to have that person disappear, leaving us alone in the midst of our self-disclosure. And so as she lays bare her heart, he must let love teach him to set aside all of his preoccupations and concerns. He must then let love teach him to sustain his meditative openness to all the beloved has to share. For sustained intimacy rides the waves of deep, uninterrupted openness to all that love has to offer. As she learns to listen to him in this same way, they learn from each other how to read the stuff the heart is made of.

To commit yourself to seeking God by practicing meditation in the Christian tradition assumes that you are learning how to read. In a specifically Christian sense this means you are grounding your meditation practice in receptive openness to the Scriptures and other sources of sound spiritual reading. In a broad sense, this means you are grounding your meditation practice in an ongoing process of learning to discover and rest in God's presence recognized in receptive openness to whatever you might be engaged in at the moment.

Daily meditation practice goes best as we learn to stand firmly on the first rung of the ladder to heaven. By this I mean learning to be attentive to God's voice reverberating in a poem, a novel, the refrains of a song, a report on the evening news, or a conversation overheard in the waiting room at the doctor's office. In learning to stand firmly on the first rung of the ladder to heaven, we learn to be receptive and open to God, uttering us into existence as we wash out a pot, or fix a broken gate, or slip off our shoes at the end of the day.

DISCURSIVE MEDITATION

The second rung of the ladder to heaven is *meditation*. In reading Christ's words "Blessed are the pure of the heart, for they shall see God," Guigo says, we take in nourishment. We put food into our mouth and begin to savor its richness. Then, in meditation, we begin to chew the food, as we begin to prayerfully reflect upon what is being read. Jesus said, "Seek and you shall find." Guigo, echoing Christ, advises us to seek in reading and we will find in meditation.

Guigo demonstrates what he means by meditation by sharing with us a reverie of other Scripture passages that come into his mind as he reads Christ's words "Blessed are the pure of heart, for they shall see God." He then meditates—which, in this context, means he prayerfully reflects on each verse that comes into mind to see what light it might shed on the purity of heart he seeks to realize.

Recall for a moment that in practicing meditation, we do not think. That is, we do not reflect on the thoughts that come into our mind as we meditate. Meditation practice is a way of entering into meditative awareness of oneness with God in which we pass beyond our customary reliance on thought.

Guigo, however, is here using the term *meditation* in a very specific sense as referring to what is traditionally referred to in Christian literature as *discursive meditation*. Discursive meditation is a process of prayerful introspection in which we move from point to point, carefully thinking through the thoughts, memories, images, and connotations that come into our mind as we sit in the receptive openness of our reading.

Guigo at this point is helpful in reminding us that in following the path of Christian meditation we are not trying to pass over or banish thinking. Rather, we are trying to build strong foundations in clear-minded thinking. The clearer and more penetrating our thinking becomes, the more readily our awareness begins to move outward and inward into more meditative modes. A single thought can, at any moment, catch fire, becoming an insight, an intuitive vision that can transform our life.

We ascend to the second rung of the ladder to heaven as we learn to ponder the thoughts that flow into our mind out of our childlike vulnerability to God. Discursive meditation—we might call it *meditative thinking*—is as intimate and personal as reading. This is so simply because the unguarded openness of reading tends to give rise to equally unguarded and unforeseeable insights into ourselves and the life we are living. While leading silent meditation retreats I have asked a hundred or so people to listen to Christ's words "Fear not." Then after a period a silence I invite all who care to do so to share the thoughts, images, and memories the verse brings to mind. As I listen to all that is shared, it becomes quickly apparent how intimate and personal discursive meditation tends to be. For inevitably there are not one or two but many different connotations, each personally meaningful to the one who shared it.

So it happens that reading a single verse of Scripture sometimes becomes a leaping-off place into the ways in which the truth revealed in that verse has been or is active in our life today. For example, you might read in Scripture the reassuring words that "if our heart condemns us, God is greater than our hearts" (1 John 3:20). As you ground yourself in a receptive stance of reading these words, savoring their sweetness, a host of insights and connections might come to mind.

You might, for example, begin to reflect on the suffering that has come into your own life and the lives of others as a result of your own past hurtful behavior. You might reflect on how you are at times still tempted to allow that self-condemning voice to pummel you for the ten thousandth time for your past, or perhaps ongoing, infractions. Then you reground yourself in prayerfully reflecting on what Scripture reveals: that God is infinitely greater than both your infractions and your self-condemnations. In this way you are consoled and reassured. So it is that as we deeply read and meditate upon each verse of Scripture, Scripture becomes personalized and internalized, to the point where it becomes an ongoing, coauthored work you and God are continually working on together.

The transformational process of moving from the first to the second rung of the ladder to heaven is a delicate one. Prayerful discernment is called for in learning not to leave the first rung of the ladder too soon. The process of allowing the heart to open and rest in its God-given openness to God takes time. There is no need to rush into thinking. In fact, an essential characteristic of reading is its potential to liberate us from the illusion of the need to rush at all.

T. S. Eliot advises us to "[w]ait without thought, for you are not ready for thought."[6] Here, we might say that to think too soon is to think the wrong thing. Or, more precisely, to think too soon is to remain trapped in the one-dimensional nature of conceptual formulations and answers. We must first steady ourselves on the first rung of the ladder in learning how to establish ourselves in receptive openness to the depths our reading discloses to us. It is only then that we can ascend to the second rung of the ladder, without ever leaving the first rung, as we learn to stabilize ourselves in quietly thinking through all the thoughts, memories, images, and connotations that come welling up out of the depths, flowing into our open and receptive mind.

A small child falls many times as part of what goes into learning to walk. This is why parents who have a child who is learning to walk are careful to do all they can to protect their child from getting hurt. This is what we must do as well, by padding our efforts with lots of patience, compassion, a sense of humor, and confidence in God's providential care. This willingness to fall many times as we keep ourselves safe in the process is what builds character and prepares us for what lies ahead.

It takes time to mature in the process of learning not to get hooked by fear-based, possessive, and otherwise controlling modes of thinking. It takes time to become someone who thinks deeply about the ultimately simple and unthinkable things that really matter. It takes time to become so immersed in the unthinkable depths of oneness with God that our thinking flows from and manifests those depths. And it takes time to learn to ascend to the second rung of the ladder to heaven without ever leaving the first. By this I mean it takes time to think thoughts that embody, express, and give witness to an abiding openness to what thought cannot grasp. It takes time for thought to blossom into wisdom that liberates us from the tyranny of thought as having the final say in what it means to know all that we know.

There are moments between lovers that help us understand the psychological-spiritual stage of development embodied in all forms of discursive meditation. In singling out romantic love to demonstrate the more broadly based understanding of discursive meditation, I encourage you to keep in mind that a number of other examples could be used as well. Committing oneself to solitude, or to the service of the poor, or to following one's consciousness in painful complex situations, or to the protection of the environment, or to attempting to be a teacher or someone committed to healing others—all require some degree of clear-minded, heartfelt thinking about what matters most and how to be faithful to it.

Imagine the two lovers mentioned earlier, in the moment in which she is sharing some deep matter of her heart. We saw how true it is that if he does not first establish himself in a stance of receptive openness to her, he will not be able to take in what she has to say. Her heart will remain unmet in the moment that she risks her self-disclosure. But now we go on to consider that if he never says anything, he might leave her heart unmet as well. I say "might" because there is a silence that is itself a deep response to what has just been shared. Sometimes we are grateful that the one to whom we have just laid bare our soul says nothing. Sometimes silence is a way of honoring that which only a respectful, even reverential silence can honor. But there is as well the silence that betrays the fact that what we have just disclosed cannot be responded to because the person was not attentive enough to really hear and take in what we revealed.

Truth is, the woman in her moment of self-disclosure will be met insofar as he allows her words to flow from her heart into his. Her heart is met when he keeps guard over his heart, keeping at bay anything that would not leave the clearing between them open and free. Up to this point, they are standing on the first rung of the ladder to heaven, that of receptive openness to the depths.

Then, there is the moment her heart is met in hearing him respond back to her in a way that leaves the root meaning of her self-disclosure intact. That is, her heart is met in hearing him say back to her, intact and unaltered, the intimate texture of that which she disclosed. And her heart is met in hearing her self-disclosure enriched by the ways in which in her words come back, intact and unaltered, yet woven with his insights and observations into what has been so deeply heard. As she listens to what he has heard in all that she shared, she is able to see and understand herself in new and more insightful ways. This is the art form of discursive meditation—taking a word into the depths of our sustained receptive openness, then allowing the word to resurface, intact and enriched by our own reflections upon it.

Thinking is the second rung of the ladder to heaven. Not the thinking that springs from that ceaseless round of commenting on our own and everyone else's existence. The thinking germane to discursive meditation is rather a deep, heartfelt thinking that comes welling up out of the depths of meditative openness. Such thinking does not disturb the stillness of meditative openness. To the contrary, such thinking allows the light that plays in the silent depths to be refracted and mirrored in thought. When you share such thoughts with others, the light that plays in the depths is expressed in words. Such are the words of Scripture. In a broader sense, such are the words of mystics and poets. Such are the words that come from your own lips in those moments when your words come from the depths of your heartfelt ponderings. Such are the words your heart impels you to speak in your efforts to free yourself and others from suffering. Such are the words of Guigo's letter. Such words do not convey information. Rather, such words draw us, once again, down into the luminous depths of receptive stillness in which we learn from God how to recognize God's presence in our lives.

PRAYER

Prayer is, for Guigo, the third rung of the ladder to heaven. When Guigo writes of prayer, he does so in terms of the heightened desire for union with God that reading and meditation evoke within us. It is this way in human love as well. Lovers never tire of sharing again and again the story of how they first met, the first time they sensed that something special was happening, the way each felt inside the first time they kissed. Listening to each other in this way, they yield to a reverie of thoughts and images that come welling up out of all that they share. In yielding to this reverie, renewed and deepened desires to be one awakens within them. In a similar fashion, in our reading and discursive meditation we and God tell the story of how we first met. The telling of the story embodies a reverie of thought and images that awaken and reawaken feelings and desires to be one with God. Prayer for Guigo is the living substance of our heartfelt feelings and desires for greater union with God.

Prayer embodies the emotional energy that carries the journey forward. This emotional energy includes the entire range of human emotions that flow out of, and merge into, a single desire for ever greater oneness with God. Guigo says that meditation without prayer is sterile. By this he means that meditation without prayer lacks the energy and momentum of the longings characteristic of a heart impelled toward a union not yet realized.

Guigo says that the desire for God that prayer embodies tends to take on certain demanding qualities. Lovers know all about the demanding qualities the longings of love can have.

This is particularly so in those moments when the couple are unable to fulfill the desire for union that their heart demands. This demand is not that of stomping one's foot, like a child in a tantrum over not being able to have what it wants (though lovers have been known to do this). Rather, the demand arises from longings so profound that one does not know how one can continue to go on unless the longings are fulfilled. As we stabilize on the third rung of the ladder to heaven, we stabilize in pleading and demanding that love finish off that which it began. Saint John of the Cross, the great poetic master of these longings, prays to God, saying:

> Why, since you wounded
> this heart, don't you heal it?
> And, why, since you stole it from
> me,
> do you leave it so,
> and fail to carry off what you have
> stolen?[7]

The longings that form the visceral energy of prayer are not necessarily felt and expressed in concrete and tangible ways that are easy to recognize. Sometimes—often, in fact—the longings of prayer are diffused and muted longings that one barely feels at all. What we notice is that we tend to be entirely too indifferent and uncommitted to the spiritual path. But in looking more closely, we can discern a sense of discontent with our apparent lack of zeal. The discontent belies a subtle desire hidden beneath the surface of an ongoing apparent lack of desire. There is a tender sadness in the shrug of the shoulders, the pretending, even to ourselves, that we do not feel a desire that is, in fact, there. We pretend we do not care about what we, at some deep level that is hard to access, actually care about very much. There is, it seems, a deal that the heart makes with itself not to admit that it harbors a desire so deep it could not go on without that desire being fulfilled. To commit ourselves to seeking God in meditation is to recognize that this deal is a con game played on us by the powers of darkness.

Crock-Pots were in vogue for a while. In the morning you put in your meat and potatoes or whatever it is you are going to have for dinner that night. You turn on your Crock-Pot, and all day long the pot sustains a steady low-level heat that thoroughly cooks the food. The prayer of longing is, for many people, a Crock-Pot version of barely perceptible longing that, over time, achieves its transformative effects.

Whenever someone on the spiritual path shares with me their concerns about their lack of desire for and commitment to their path, I often sense the tender sadness in all that they share. The tenderness lies in the sincerity in which they obviously do care. For if they did not care, their perceived lack of caring would be of no concern to them. And the sadness lies in their inability to see how God loves them so in the midst of their real and imagined lack of commitment to God.

CONTEMPLATION

The fourth and highest rung of the ladder to heaven is contemplation, in which we are awakened to a nondual experience of oneness with God. But to see how the longed-for event of contemplative oneness with God tends to occur, we must go back to our awakened heart's demands for more intimate union with God. That is, we must continue to stabilize ourselves on the third rung of the ladder, where we are being consumed by a desire for union with God that we are powerless to fulfill. The situation is precarious—but in a most mysterious and wondrous manner. For in our felt sense of powerlessness our guards are down; we are left open and defenseless and unwittingly poised on the brink of unexpectedly realizing the union with God that we long for but are powerless to attain.

In attempting to help us discern the mysterious ways in which the union we long for is perhaps much closer than we realize, Guigo focuses on weeping. As prayer, and the longings that prayer embodies and expresses, continue to deepen, we begin to shed tears. We might, at times, begin to experience ourselves feeling tearful or actually crying. Most often, however, the tears of which Guigo speaks are hidden, interior tears of unconsummated longings. Whatever our unique experience of these tears might be, Guigo says our tears are the "generous draught which He gives you to drink. Let these tears be your bread day and night." He asks, "Can it be that the heralds of and witnesses of this consolation and joy [of contemplation] are sighs and tears? If it is so, then the word consolation is being used in a completely new sense, the reverse of its ordinary connotation."[8]

We typically think of being consoled by anything that might help us to feel better. But what if we are suffering because we have become smitten by a love that preempts all other loves? Then it would be sad to be consoled by anything other than the fulfillment of this one love alone. It is consoling to see how utterly unconsoled and inconsolable we are with anything less or other than the consummation of that love for which we now live and, in yearning for, we now die.

Can it be, we say, that I could actually love this much? Can it be that my poor heart, with all its ragged edges, could be ravaged by infinite love to the point that only an infinite union with infinite love can console me? To the extent that we are amazed to discover that such may indeed be the case, we are consoled in realizing how unconsoled and inconsolable we have become with anything less or other than the love that has awakened us. We are consoled and reassured in knowing how unconsolable we will remain so long as we have yet to experience that infinite union with the infinite love on which our heart is now so unexplainably fixed as its sole fulfillment. In being unconsoled and inconsolable in this way, we begin to know God in a new, more intimate sense. For we begin to know within ourselves a faint shadow or echo of God's utterly unbearable and unmanageable love for us.

It is in the very midst of these unbound and boundaryless longings that the contemplative experience of oneness with God occurs. Guigo writes:

> So the soul by such burning words inflames its own desire, makes known its state . . . But the Lord, whose eyes are upon the just and whose ears catch not only the words, but the very meaning of their prayers, does not wait until the longing soul has said all it has to say, but breaks in upon the middle of its prayer, runs to meet it in all haste . . . and He restores the weary soul, He slakes its thirst, He feeds its hunger, He makes the soul forget all earthly things: by making it die to itself He gives it new life in a wonderful way, and by making it drunk He brings it back to its true senses.[9]

Reaching the third rung of prayer, we discover we are powerless to ascend any higher. For we have come to the summit of the ego's powers. That is, we have reached the uppermost limit of what the ego, guided by grace, can attain. The summit is that of unbearable yearnings for an infinite union with the infinite that we, by our finite powers, are powerless to attain. It is on this third rung of prayer's unconsummated longings that God unexpectedly does what God most loves to do. God bends down and unexpectedly places the fourth rung of the ladder firmly beneath our feet. Perplexed and bewildered, we gaze directly into God's eyes eternally gazing into ours. Everything is suddenly homecoming and communion. Everything is a love that comes rolling through, leaving in its wake nothing but love alone.

As Guigo brings his letter to a close, he notes how moments of contemplatively realized oneness with God tend, like all moments, to pass away. As they pass, we are left once again with our ordinary experience of our day-by-day self. He writes:

> [S]ince, however, the eye of the human heart has not the power to bear for long the shining of the true light, let the soul descend gently and in due order to one or the other of the three degrees by which it made its descent.[10]

As the moment of contemplative oneness with God dissipates, we return to our customary way of experiencing ourselves. Yet we do so with a new appreciation of the previously unrecognized presence of God hidden in the midst of every aspect of our daily life. There is something subtle and profound about how Guigo brings his letter to a close. For he suggests that as the moment of realized oneness with God passes, we are left with a new understanding of how God is always uniting us to himself in our *ordinary* experience of our ordinary day-by-day lives. As Guigo puts it, God "goes, it is true. For this visitation ends, and with it the sweetness of contemplation; but yet He stays, for He directs us, He gives us grace. He joins us to Himself."[11]

The moment of contemplatively realized oneness with God vanishes as mysteriously as it came. What are we to do next? Taking Guigo as our guide, we can do our best to descend gently back onto the solid ground on which the ladder to heaven is firmly placed. That is, we can descend gently back into renewed willingness to return to the lifelong process of learning to be mindfully present to the graced nature of our daily round of duties and activities. We can descend gently back into a renewed willingness to engage in the lifelong process of learning to be truly generous and loving to ourselves and those around us. We can learn to descend gently back to the first rung of the ladder, consisting of our receptive openness to the divinity of the life we are living. We can gently descend back to the second rung of the ladder, consisting of the lifelong process of learning to think through the deep and simple things of God disclosed to us in our receptive openness. We can learn to descend back to the third rung of the ladder, consisting of prayers, expressive of our feelings and desires for loving union with God. We can, in short, learn to live our ordinary life, knowing and trusting that in the midst of it all God ceaselessly joins us to herself.

We can turn, one last time, to a moment of human intimacy to see what it reveals of this mysterious return to a newly discovered holiness of ordinary experience. Imagine a man or woman in the moments after making love, or some other manner of being mutually caught up in a sense of oceanic oneness. Lying in one another's arms, lingering in the aura of the oneness they have just experienced, she says, "Look how one we have become. I never knew that such oneness was even possible." He agrees, and feels with her how true her words are.

Then, without knowing just where the words are coming from, she asks, "I wonder just how one we will become? What I mean is, I wonder how far we will go into this oneness before we get to the point beyond which no greater degree of oneness is possible?" As soon as the question leaves her lips, they know together that which they cannot and do not need to explain. They know that no matter how one they become, they will never arrive at a degree of oneness beyond which no greater degree of oneness is possible, for no such point exists. And in this moment they taste together something of the already perfectly present mystery that never ends. They know that this endless oneness is the very oneness to which they are awakened and in which they are living out their lives. This never-ending oneness is the very oneness in which they learn to be content and grateful as they go through their days and nights, facing and experiencing together all that their days and nights might bring.

Guigo reminds us that moments of contemplative oneness with God come and go. But in their passing, we are given to realize that God goes nowhere. We come to realize there is no real way to live other than in a willingness to love and be loved by a love that breaks our heart open ten thousand times a minute. Breaking our heart open, this love makes our heart whole in awakening us to the mysterious ways in which it invincibly and eternally unites us to itself in every detail of our day-by-day lives.

The arising and passing away of moments of contemplative oneness with God awakens us to the baffling realization that we have scaled the ladder to heaven without ever leaving the ground. We come to see and appreciate that daily life is all there is. It is just that daily life never ends. For each moment of it is nothing less or other than all that God is, given to us, wholly and completely, in and as all that each moment simply is.

CHAPTER 5

A Monastery Without Walls

I was only eighteen years old when I entered the monastery. I was unaware of so many things. But I was keenly aware of the silence that pervaded my new life. The silence was particularly striking in that the monastery I entered belongs to the Cistercian Order, also known as Trappists. Trappist monasteries are known for their silence. When I was there it was still the custom for us to use a monastic sign language so that we could communicate with each other without "breaking silence." Even then we were not supposed to make unnecessary, conversational sign language. We ate together in a large refectory in silence. We worked together side by side in silence. Day in, day out, seven days a week, there was the pervasive silence of living together without speaking to each other. The ideal was that of being alone with God in community.

Seeking God in perpetual silence had a profound effect on me. It seemed to me I was dreaming all day long. It was a waking dream, in which everything I saw and touched had turned into God. It seemed that when we were chanting in the monastic choir, God was chanting with a deep reverence that had neither beginning nor end. When it rained, it seemed that God was falling from the sky into all the green woods and brown plowed furrows of herself. There was a lot in this dream, I am sure, that was a disassociate way of attempting to escape from my past. But even so, there was something given to me there that was graced, real, and true. And that something (there is no name for it) utterly transformed my life. In the day-in, day-out silence, the edges of what I thought was reality gave way. I fell through the center of myself into an interior landscape of oneness with God. I was very happy.

And then I became very sad when I discovered that the nightmare I had fled from—my years of child abuse—began to intrude itself into the dream of realized oneness with God. Once the pain of the trauma had found its way into my awareness, it would not stop flooding in. The pain kept flowing in to the point that it drove me out of the Garden of Eden, and I eventually left the monastery. William Blake says it in a poem:

> Oh rose, thou art sick!
> The invisible worm
> That flies in the night . . .
> Has found out thy bed
> Of crimson joy:
> And his dark secret love
> Does thy life destroy.[1]

It has been thirty-some years since I left the monastery, but I keenly remember my sense of culture shock in being suddenly thrown back into the everyday world in which the vast majority of us human beings live out our lives: traffic, billboards, televisions and radios, a hectic pace in which everyone seemed to be talking all the time and to be in some tremendous rush to get somewhere. More interiorly, I felt like a refugee who had been cast out of the interior landscape of oneness with God in which I had lived in the monastery.

I went kind of crazy for a while. I got drunk a lot, dropped out of the church, got depressed, and, to make myself feel better, got married to someone as wounded as I was. But then I began to practice daily meditation. It started with yoga, and then deepened with Zen meditation. From there my practice slowly swung back around into the Christian mystical vision embodied in the simple practice that I have described in the second chapter of this book. As I allowed myself to enter the silent simplicity of meditation, I once again discovered that secret passageway into the interior landscape of oneness with God that I first learned to enter in the monastery. The unbroken continuity between monastic life and meditation practice led me to realize that meditation is a monastery without walls.

It is out of this personal journey that I am writing this book to assure you that you do not have to be a monk or nun living in a monastery to live a meditative way of life. It may seem as if meditative living would be easier in the silence of the monastery. And in a way it would be. After all, the walls of the monastery mark off a place of prayerful silence intended to create optimal conditions for meditative living. But deeper down, the optimal conditions for *you* to live a more meditative way of life are the conditions of your own life. You might be a college student or senior citizen. You might be a single adult or someone married with children in a house with big mortgage payments and a leaky roof you cannot afford to fix. Whatever the specifics of your life might be, the truth is that God, who is love, is within you and all about you, loving you into the present moment. And when the indwelling spirit begins to awaken you to the divine love that is your life, what real choice do you have but to slow down, to calm yourself, so that this love might have its way with you?

If you are inclined to do so, you could pause right in the midst of reading this page, close the book, and open yourself to a childlike receptive openness to God. You could sit for a moment of meditative oneness with God, sustaining you, breath by breath, in this and every moment of your life. Or it might be most natural for you to simply continue reading, not so much to gather information as to allow the words to invite you into an ever more refined awareness of that oneness with God that words cannot express. It is always like this. At any given moment you can choose to grow where you are planted. You can yield to the subtle inclination that tugs at your heart to open yourself to the presence of God that is always there.

It does not matter whether you are reading this book or standing in line at the grocery store or sitting in your car waiting at a red light or wiping off the kitchen counter before going to bed. You can always choose to open yourself, in the midst of a thousand graces and setbacks, to the oneness with God that is the reality of all that is real. To learn to see that this choice is always there, and to learn to make this choice over and over until it becomes the habitual way you live your life, is to live in a monastery without walls.

I will at this point summon Saint Benedict from the mists of the past to serve as our tour guide through the monastery without walls. Saint Benedict lived in the sixth century in Nursia, a region of central Italy, where he wrote his Rule for monks. His sister, Saint Scholastica, who founded communities of women based on her brother's Rule, joined him in forging the beginnings of the great Benedictine monastic tradition that continues to this day.

LEARNING TO BE SILENT

If we summon Saint Benedict to help us, he will surely come to our aid. We have only to read his Rule in a sincere and prayerful manner to discover how he speaks to our heart of the timeless truths of meditative living. Silence is the first of these timeless truths. When Saint Benedict greets us at the gate of the monastery without walls, he leads us into a lifetime of learning to be silent. In the chapter of his Rule devoted to the practice of silence, Saint Benedict says, "[O]n account of the importance of silence, let permission to speak seldom be granted even to perfect disciples."[2] He is saying, in effect: no matter how eloquent or holy a monk you might be, be silent. And he says the same thing to us as we sit in meditation. When I was living as a monk in a monastery that followed the Rule of Saint Benedict, I experienced directly the transforming power of the practice of silence. After I left the monastery I discovered in meditation a way to reenter the silence that had so transformed my life in the monastery.

I realize that life out here in the world, where the vast majority of us live our lives, is considerably more noisy, and requires a lot more talking, than the life lived by monks and nuns in their cloisters. I realize, too, that the hectic pace in which many of us live our lives makes it difficult to slow things down enough to relax into the subtle silence that opens out into God. But the great thing about meditation is that it directly embodies the essence of silence. The moment you begin to silently sit in meditation, you *are* silent. It may be true that this silence is, at first, only the silence that begins when you stop speaking. But you can choose to turn toward this initial taste of silence. You can choose to savor silence, to open yourself to it, so as to enter more deeply into its hidden depths.

Each day you come to your meditation. You might have there an icon or picture of Christ or a plain wooden cross. You might stand for a moment in silence, with the palms of your hands joined in prayer. In silence you might bow to God, or to Christ, or to the self-transforming path on which you find yourself. Sitting still and straight, you sit in silence. Becoming aware of your breathing, you allow your breathing to open the way to a yet deeper, more interior silence. Settling into silence, you give yourself to the silence as the silence gives itself to you. This giving of yourself to silence as silence gives itself to you happens of itself as you simply become open and receptive to the silence in which you sit.

There are no doctrines to which you must submit to gain access to silence. In fact, as long as the mental noise of ascribing to or refusing to ascribe to doctrines continues, you are not yet silent. There is nothing you have to figure out before silence will allow you to enter into all that lies hidden in it. In fact, as long as the mental noise of imagining anything needs to be figured out, or even can be figured out, you are not yet silent. All that is needed is for you to simply become silent, in a willingness to become more silent still.

Entering into silence is comparable to entering a warm home on a chilly day. As soon as you step through the door, the warmth surrounds you and immediately makes itself felt. But if you are chilled to the bone, it takes a while for the warmth to sink in. The same is true of silence. The moment you sit in meditation and become silent, the silence surrounds you and immediately makes itself felt. But if the chatter of your wandering mind and the frayed edges of a hectic day have a real grip on you, it takes a while for the silence to sink in.

Sitting in silence, breathing in silence, opening yourself to silence, you become, little by little, more and more silent. So much of what meditation has to offer lies hidden in our willingness to allow the last echoes of egocentric noise to dissolve in silence. The silence of a single session of meditation can open up more mystery and depth of oneness with God than a lifetime of speaking could even begin to explain.

As you quietly learn the ways of silence, you begin to discover for yourself that there are no handles in silence to hold on to. Silence has no shape, no boundaries, no horizon. There are no toeholds in silence to stop your descent into depths you cannot comprehend. It is in learning to rest in silence that you are led by the indwelling spirit into the eternal silence of God.

In reading the creation narrative in the Book of Genesis, we discover that God never said, "Let there be silence." Silence is, then, uncreated. Being uncreated, silence has no beginning. And in having no beginning, silence never ends. God eternally dwells in the uncreated mystery of the very silence that underlies and pervades our lives. Surely, then, silence is a trustworthy place to be. When you die you will enter into this silence forever. Entering the monastery without walls is to get a head start in learning to live in the silence that soon enough will be your eternal and endlessly trustworthy home. We might say that in practicing meditation we are practicing what it will be like to be dead. Which is to say, we are practicing what it will be like to be, at last, eternally, fully alive with the very silence of God.

It is out of God's eternal silence that God eternally speaks the world and everything in it into being. If only we could become truly silent and attentive, we could hear God uttering us and all of creation into being. The difficulty is that we do not hear so well. The din of our egocentric noise drowns out the silent voice that is uttering us and all things into being. But Christ has come as lord and master of our true self, inviting us, teaching us to listen. As Saint Benedict welcomes us into the monastery without walls, we can look up to see, inscribed over the gate as we enter, the opening words of his Rule: "Listen, my child, to the precepts of the master, and incline the ear of your heart."[3]

Saint Benedict's master plan, inherent in the invitation to be silent, now becomes clearer. We become silent that we might learn to listen to Christ calling us to love. It is the love revealed to us in Christ that breaks our heart open and teaches us to listen. Our learning to love as Christ has loved us breaks down the barriers that close us off from ourselves, God, and others. Meditation is an act of love. It is a way of becoming silent so that the egocentric noise of our mind can fall into the background. Sitting still and straight, grounded in silence, we become a listening presence.

It sounds beautiful on paper. But as you know if you have been meditating very long at all, actual fidelity to this simple, transforming path can be quite demanding. There is something about sitting every day in meditation that opens up a whole new way of life, filled with unforeseeable challenges and blessings. Truth is, a sincere commitment to the simplicity and poverty of daily meditation opens up meditative states of awareness that call for serious adjustments in our customary way of experiencing ourselves and the world around us.

PREPARING OURSELVES FOR A MEDITATIVE WAY OF LIFE

Reflecting on what Saint Benedict has to say about admitting new members into the community can help us understand and prepare ourselves for what we are getting ourselves into as we learn to meditate day by day. He writes:

> To him that newly comes to change his life, let not an easy entrance be granted. For the apostle says to try the spirits that they be from God. If, therefore, he that comes perseveres in knocking, and after four or five days, is seen to endure patiently the wrongs done to him and the difficulty made about his coming in, and to persist in his petition, let entrance be granted him. And let him be in the guesthouse for a few days. Afterwards, let him go to the Novitiate, where he is to meditate and study, to take his meals and to sleep. Let a Senior who is skilled in gaining souls be appointed over him, to watch over him with utmost care, and to see whether he is truly seeking God, and is fervent in the work of God.[4]

This passage expresses the essence of the entire matter. Someone has to come to the monastery to change his or her life. The tone and content of the entire Rule leaves no doubt that the change the newcomer seeks is that which gravitates toward the fullness of life that Christ came to reveal and proclaim. The same is true of us in our commitment to seeking God in meditation. We meditate that we might change our lives by becoming the clear-minded, Christlike human beings we really are and are called to be. We would do well, then, to linger with this passage as our way of lingering at the gate of the monastery without walls. In this way we can get our bearings. We can begin to grow in our understanding and appreciation of all that learning to live in the monastery without walls entails.

It is in coming up against our own difficulties and moments of uncertainty in meditation that we can appreciate the wisdom of Saint Benedict in suggesting that a senior monk or nun "skilled in gaining souls" watch over the entire process of passing through the gate into all that lies within. I was most fortunate in that Thomas Merton, who was, by anyone's standards, quite skilled at "gaining souls," was the senior member of the community assigned to watch over my transition into the community. He had, in a sense, already gained my soul even before I arrived, in that it was through reading his books that I experienced him to be my spiritual teacher. I went to the monastery in the hope that I might sit at his feet in the classical sense of allowing him to lead me to God.

As you sit at the gates of meditation, it might not seem to you at first that you have a wizened old monk or nun to help you. And perhaps you do not, if by that is meant having an experienced person in the ways of meditation to whom you go to guide and support you in your efforts. If such is the case, it might be worth trying to find a spiritual director who is experienced to some degree in meditation. Or, if such a person is not available, a friend, a fellow meditator with whom you can take turns sharing each other's journey might be helpful. But the fact is that most people who follow the interior path spend most of their journey without such a person. This lack of supportive insight from a concerned and experienced meditator is for many people part of the solitary nature of their inner journey. It is in this solitude that one learns to trust in God's guidance, which comes in meditation practice, prayer, Scripture and other spiritual reading, and the events and circumstances of one's daily life.

But I am also telling you that if you risk the silence of meditation, the wizened old monk or nun will appear. The wisdom source will be there in your willingness to be who you simply are when you are not trying so hard to be something else. So much of the monastic-meditative path to God is found in the willingness to rest in the silence in which we listen to ourselves in this unforced, unhurried manner. In this patient, heartfelt attentiveness, our awakened heart is laid bare. And it is in the laying bare of ourselves as we really are, in silence, that we unexpectedly make our way through the gate into God. Truer still, we are surprised to discover God passing through the gate to meet us, delighted that we have finally begun to see and accept who God knows and accepts us to be from before we were born.

The way in which you experience meditation and the universal meditative states of awareness it evokes is as personal and unique to you as anything you could mention. Perhaps your troubles will be few. Perhaps you will, right from the start, encounter all sorts of questions and concerns. What matters most is to remain as honest and vulnerable with yourself in God's presence as you can be, taking the journey as it comes, one step at a time. Know that some degree of doubt and uncertainty is a normal and, in some ways, important part of your transformation.

You might be tempted to use the Scripture quotes as a kind of Cliffs Notes, hoping to come up with rote answers that might put the nagging questions and self-doubt to rest. But even a right answer, said by rote, is not the response that indicates a readiness to continue coming through the gate. In fact, the questions and concerns that arise within you as you begin to settle into your practice of meditation are in themselves the embodiment of the wizened old monk or nun who is there to test the spirits, asking, "What are you looking for? What do you want?"

It says in the Gospels that Mary, the mother of Jesus, pondered in her heart just who this Jesus was she had given birth to. To ponder is to silently sit with what we cannot comprehend. Meditation embodies the silent pondering of what we cannot comprehend. As we sit in meditation, attentive to our bodily stillness, we cannot comprehend all that our bodily stillness really is. As we sit, silent and still, attentive to our breathing, we cannot comprehend all that a single, life-giving breath really is. Sitting in the incomprehensibility of ourselves and everything around us, we incomprehensibly find our way through the gate into all that lies within.

Saint Benedict knows, better than we, the struggles that lie ahead. It is out of this understanding that he says, "[L]et not an easy entrance be granted" to all who seek to enter. This seemingly less than cordial treatment is actually an act of love on Saint Benedict's part. It is as if he is saying, Look, I owe it to you to give you a small taste of what you are in for. The difficulty you are experiencing in arriving at the gate is but a preview of coming attractions. What lies just inside the gate is not a lifetime of getting what you want when you want it. It is, rather, a lifetime of learning how to wait, with respectful, quiet persistence, in the midst of ongoing delays and difficulties, interspersed with unexpected and sometimes unmanageable graces and blessing.

Saint Benedict knows, too, that all difficulties, at all stages of the journey, are themselves the very stuff the journey is made of. Patience with one's slow beginnings and false starts is itself a good beginning in learning to realize that, in the end, everything is right on schedule. Learning to be patient with yourself in your slow and inept efforts has within it the potential of an experiential knowledge of God's infinite patience with us as we spend our lives fumbling around at the entrance into the depths of the life we are living. It is our growing trust in the loving patience of God that sustains and supports us as we make our way into a meditative way of life.

Your first steps along this path may not be slow at all. The first step may occasion a lightning bolt that catapults you into realms of realized oneness with God that makes your ordinary ego self reel. If this be the case, be patient with that, too! The same compassionate, grounded presence in your own life, as it really is, pertains to ecstasy as much as it does to an apparently endless array of unmet expectations.

Saint Benedict knows that you will have to discover for yourself that life in the monastery without walls is simply your life just as it is. You live your life as best you can. You try to love God, yourself, and others as Christ loved God and all of us. You go each day to meditation, where you seek to cultivate a habitual meditative awareness of God. As each session of meditation comes to an end, you stand and go about your day, trying as best you can not to break the thread of meditative awareness of the divinity of the life you are living. Living this way, you come to a habitual meditative realization that there are no walls between you and God, no distance, no separation. Looking out through meditative eyes, you see there is no distance, no separation, from others or from the earth that sustains us all.

FIVE MISTAKES

I will now share with you five mistakes I made in my assumptions about what my life in the monastery would be like. Since leaving the monastery, I have continued to make these same mistakes concerning my understanding of the nature of meditation. In my talks with many people on meditation retreats over the years, I have come to realize that I am not alone in making these mistakes. These mistakes are, it seems, the universal mistakes the ego, in its estrangement from meditative experience, makes about itself and God.

The genius of the monastic-meditative path, as mapped out by Saint Benedict, is that it leads us directly into the silent attentiveness in which we can catch ourselves in the act of making these mistakes. Seeing and accepting ourselves as invincibly loved by God in the midst of making these mistakes proves to be the surprising way we are awakened to our eternal oneness with God.

Thoughts

The first mistake I made when entering the monastery was assuming I could leave my wandering mind outside the gates. During my four years of high school, in which I read books by Thomas Merton and looked at pictures of monks in monasteries, I had fantasies of myself walking through silent cloisters and sitting in secluded places with a quiet and grounded mind. When I entered the monastery I became silent. In the silence I tried to listen to Christ whispering in my heart. But my wandering mind often seemed to drown out God's still, small voice. I told my wandering mind to calm down, to stop the ceaseless chatter. Sometimes my mind would calm down. There were times of profound silence. But often—very often, in fact—my own chattering mind continued chattering on and on.

It was in this way that I discovered my error in imagining I could extinguish the thoughts that kept intruding themselves into the silence in which I was attempting to listen to God. But it was in the very process of discovering that I simply could not get rid of my thoughts that I discovered I could learn to humbly listen to my thoughts. I could listen in silence to my own mind as my only way of ever learning how to listen to God. For if I continued to see my own mind as something to get rid of or to cancel out, I would continue feeling that my own mind was an albatross around my neck. I would continue trying to get rid of myself, and in so doing I would continue to estrange myself from God, the creator and sustainer of the miracle of my thinking mind.

This became a cornerstone of both how I lived my life in the silence of the cloister and how I learned to meditate. I learned to be present, open, and awake, neither clinging to nor rejecting my own thinking mind. To cling to my thinking mind was to continually think about the thoughts that arose, endured, and passed within me. Living in this way, my subjective awareness tended to never break free of the gravitational pull of thought and all that thought can attain. To reject thought was to reject God manifesting and giving herself in and as each thought arising, enduring, and passing away within me. What I could learn to do was to become silent and attentive to the stream of thoughts arising, enduring, and passing away within me, while at the same time refraining from thinking about the thoughts that kept flowing through my mind. What I could do was to learn to let go of my perception of myself as being the thinker of my thoughts. I could learn, instead, to become the silent observer of the thoughts that arose, endured, and passed away within me.

This is the meditative stance toward your thoughts that I am suggesting you explore in your own meditation practice. Sit silent and still, and simply refrain from your customary tendency to abandon your thinking mind by slipping off into daydreaming or sleepiness. Sit silent and still, and simply refrain from your customary tendency to invade your thinking mind with your thoughts, opinions, and reactions. Simply let go of your perception of yourself as the thinker of your thoughts. Instead of sitting there thinking your thoughts, learn, instead, to simply sit, silently attentive to the thoughts that arise, endure, and pass away within you. This quiet, nonobtrusive, nonabandoning mind *is* meditative mind. Meditative mind excels in the light touch of being quietly attentive to each thought without slipping into the tendency to think about those thoughts.

The meditative state that begins to emerge as we learn to cease invading and abandoning our thinking mind may seem quite strange at first. This is understandable in that most of us are not accustomed to freely weaning ourselves off our tendency to think. The experience can be frightening as well. For as we pass beyond the frontiers of thought, we momentarily lose the control we think we have over the life we think we are living. Our ego self might understandably try to pull back into its own realm, where it can think through what is happening. And yet, if the conditions are right, the moment of passing beyond the frontiers of thought can bring with it a wave of the peace that surpasses understanding. Resting in this peace, even for a moment, can occasion a taste of paradise.

As we patiently learn to listen to the thoughts that arise, endure, and pass away within us, we come to a deep experiential knowledge of ourselves as we really are. We learn to befriend our own wandering mind, neither abandoning it through daydreaming or sleepiness, nor invading it with more thoughts about the thoughts that are already there. By quietly persevering in sustained nonthinking meditative attentiveness, we come to a new groundedness within ourselves. The meditative mind that neither thinks nor is reducible to any thought grows stronger, calmer, and more stable. In time we learn to listen with God's ears to our wandering mind while at the same time passing beyond all that our wandering mind can comprehend.

Memories

The second mistake I made as I entered the monastery was imagining I could leave my memories outside the gate. But, of course, I quickly discovered that my remembering self and all its memories had come through the gate with me. I would be chanting vespers in the monastic choir. As we all bowed over at the end of a psalm, chanting, "Glory be to the Father and to the Son and to the Holy Spirit," rock and roll songs that were popular on the radio at the time I entered kept echoing through my mind. As I walked about the silence of the monastery there were memories of my mother and sister and four brothers that made me feel homesick, because I felt I might never see them again. Eventually, my memories of things that happened in the monastery were added to the ones I had from home. All these memories kept intruding themselves into the silence in which I was attempting to listen to Christ, silently whispering within my heart.

Then I came to realize that if I was always living out of my memories, I would remain estranged from the virginal newness of the present moment. But if I tried to rid myself of my memories, I would be doing violence to myself and to God, the author and sustainer of the miracle of memory. I discovered that what I could do was to learn the delicate touch of being present, open, and awake, neither clinging to nor rejecting the memories that arose, endured, and passed away within me.

You can try this delicate touch of neither clinging to nor rejecting the memories that arise, endure, and pass away within you as you sit in meditation. The delicacy lies in remaining attentive *in the present moment* to the memories of the past without slipping out of the present moment into the past. As each memory arises, endures, and passes away within you, simply let it do so. Do not abandon the memory by slipping into daydreamy indifference toward it. Do not reject the memory, regardless of how unpleasant it might be. Do not cling to the memory, regardless of how pleasant it might be. In this way you will learn, little by little, to remain meditatively present to each memory that arises in the present moment without slipping out of the present moment into the past.

As we learn to stabilize ourselves in this delicate meditative attitude toward our own memory, we learn to listen with God's ears to the miracle of memory. We learn to reverence the telling and retelling of our own unfolding story, which is being perpetually revised and renewed with each passing moment.

As we learn to stabilize ourselves in present-moment meditative awareness of our memories, we realize in the most intimate fashion that we cannot make the past be other than it is. We cannot make ourselves into someone other than who we remember ourselves to be. Even to respond to someone calling our name is an act of our remembering our self, recognizing itself in this name we know to be our own. And yet neither are we simply who we used to be and nothing more. For the present moment, and who we are in it, is perpetually new. And who God eternally knows us to be in this perpetually new present moment is infinitely more than anything we remember ourselves to be.

As we settle into meditative freedom in the midst of our memories, we are awakened to the great and liberating truth that nothing we have done in the past, nor anything that has been done to us in the past, has the power to name who we are. Freed from the tyranny of memory, we are free to live in the virginal newness of the one unending present moment in which our lives unfold. Freed from sequential time with respect to the past, we are simultaneously freed from sequential time with respect to the future. Looking into all that lies ahead, we ask, What is the joy that death does not have the power to destroy and how might I discover it? In meditative awareness we find this joy in awakening to the timeless joy of God that ceaselessly plays itself out in the fleetingness of our day-by-day life.

Intentions

A third mistake I made when entering the monastery was assuming that in passing through the gates I could leave behind my own wayward will by submitting myself to God's will in all things. But, again, I was mistaken. Saint Paul disclosed, "I am not practicing what I would like to do, but I am doing the very thing I hate" (Rom. 8:15–16). In the silence of my daily life in the monastery I watched myself doing just that. I watched at close range how I could not live up to my own ideals of being the perfect monk. Nor could I stop doing the things that made my hopes of being the perfect monk impossible to achieve. At the same time I could feel within myself the desire to be one with God, and I could feel, too, how powerless my finite will was to attain this oneness with God.

I began to discover that the only way for me to resolve my inability to will myself into my desired state of perfection was to accept God's free choice to love me unwaveringly in the midst of all my imperfections. I was to continue on in my efforts to be the best monk I could possibly be. But in doing so, I discovered the deepest perfection was to be found laying myself bare to God, invincibly loving me in the very midst of my powerlessness to live up to my own ideals.

It was then that I discovered meditation to be a way this paradoxical transformation of my will could sink into the innermost recesses of my being. Sitting in meditation, I would enter into the simple, wholehearted intention to remain present, open, and awake, neither clinging to nor rejecting anything. At first I was dismayed to discover how powerless I was to actually sustain this stance of simple presence. Every few minutes, sometimes every few seconds, I discovered myself clinging to pleasant or consoling thoughts and feelings. The very next moment I discovered myself rejecting unpleasant and disturbing thoughts and feelings. Then I discovered that these difficulties were opportunities for me to breathe God's compassionate love into my ongoing and seemingly endless frailty. Each instance of clinging and rejecting provided renewed opportunities to open myself to the utterly disarming experience of being cut clean through by God, invincibly loving me in the midst of all my wayward ways.

This is the approach I am inviting you to explore in your meditation. If you do so, you will experience for yourself just how powerless your will is. Instead of being discouraged by this, see it as an opportunity to grow in experiential knowledge of God, sustaining you in being invincibly loved in the midst of your frailties.

Meditation practice is not humiliating. But it is humbling to see again and again how our will is so weak that we cannot sustain our simple intention to be present in the present moment just as it is. Surely if our efforts to reach God are left up to us, we are in serious trouble. But as we repeatedly experience and accept the impotence of our will, we learn to trust in God's will, sustaining us in being, breath by breath, just as we are. As we learn to trust in God in the midst of our ineptness, we are amazed to discover how we pass, like water through a sieve, into the arms of God.

Feelings

A fourth mistake I made when entering the monastery was assuming I could leave my feelings outside the gates. I knew at some level that I would continue to have pleasant and unpleasant feelings after entering the monastery. But it never occurred to me that my feelings would matter. I just assumed that once I got inside the monastery my feelings would all be devout, sincere feelings of my love for God. Again, I was mistaken. I did have feelings of love for God, sometimes very strong ones. I often had quite pleasant, normal feelings as well, about all sorts of things. Often, I was simply peaceful, without awareness of any feelings, pleasant or unpleasant. But sometimes—often, in fact—the felt sense of God's presence would vanish completely. And while I had to deal with this loss of a felt sense of God's presence, I was bombarded by feelings of sadness, loneliness, confusion, and a host of other emotional burdens. The silence in which I lived provided little diversion from all these disturbing feelings. I could not find the off switch for these feelings, which often seemed to drown out the serene and tranquil self I so wanted to be.

I discovered that I could learn to be present, open, and awake, neither clinging to nor rejecting the feelings that flowed through me. I could learn to grow in self-knowledge by learning to know on intimate terms my own feeling self. I discovered that meditation was a way in which I could enter into a nonintrusive, nonabandoning attentiveness to each feeling as it arose, endured, and passed away within me.

This is the approach I am suggesting you can try as well. As you sit in meditation, you can practice learning to be quietly attentive to each feeling that arises, endures, and passes away within you. You can practice learning not to abandon your feelings by trying to block them out or ignoring them. You can practice learning not to invade your feelings by rushing in and trying to hold on to consoling, peaceful, or otherwise pleasant feelings. You can learn not to reject the painful feelings you might experience. In this way you can learn to become grounded in a meditative awareness of your feeling self and all the feelings that pass through you in each passing moment. Open to all feelings, neither clinging to nor rejecting any of them, you can learn to pass beyond the frontier of feelings. Passing beyond the frontier of feelings, you can enter into a meditative oneness with God that utterly transcends what feelings can contain. At the same time you can begin to discover how God gives herself wholly and completely in and as the river of your feelings. You can grow in a meditative awareness of all that feelings convey about the pathos and tenderness of what it means to be human.

The Body

Last, I was mistaken in assuming that when entering the monastery I could leave my body outside the gates. I knew, of course, that I would still have my body in the monastery, but I did not think my body would be relevant. I recall being surprised and disappointed by the blunt realities of my body. My head was shaven. I was wearing monk's robes. I was bowing and chanting and doing all the ethereal, monkish things monks do. And yet my knees bothered me from kneeling for long periods on the hardwood floors. If I didn't take a shower after working in the pig barn, I would smell bad. If, unknowingly, I meditated while sitting in a patch of poison ivy, I would regret it. (I actually did that once, and I actually did regret having done it!) From diarrhea to erections to coming down with nasty colds and the flu, my body was surely with me. I asked to be delivered from my body. It was as if I were asking God to let me live just a half inch off the floor. That was all I was asking. I wanted some small degree of being able to rise above the gravitational pull of the blunt realities of my own body. But I remained, of course, subject to gravity and to all the realities of my bodily being.

Then I discovered that I could learn to be present, open, and awake, neither clinging to nor rejecting my bodily being. If I was tired, I could learn to be meditatively aware of the intimate texture of my fatigue. When I was eating in silence in the refectory, I could learn to lift my mug to my lips and taste my coffee, feeling its warmth in my mouth. If I could not sleep in the large dormitory, I could lie awake on the straw mattress in my cubicle, listening to all the monks snoring away in the otherwise silent night. I came to appreciate the vegetarian diet, the paced rhythms of manual labor and prayer, and the set time for sleeping as ways that helped me to settle into and appreciate my bodily being.

I discovered meditation to be a way of honing the edge of this meditative awareness of my bodily being. I use to love taking long walks in the woods. I would sit on the ground, my back against a tree, and just listen to the sound the wind makes as it blows through the trees. Sometimes a deer would pass by, and I would be sitting so still it would, if the wind was right, walk right past me without realizing I was there. I would lean against the tree, feeling it against my back and listening to my breathing, and settle into my bodily sense of myself in silence. It was the same for me standing in the big abbey church and sitting in the monastic library. My body was always my grounding place in God's presence in the world.

This is the approach to meditation that I am encouraging you to try as well. Sitting still in meditation, learn to settle into the ungraspable immediacy of your bodily stillness. Sitting still and straight, settle into a deep meditative awareness of each life-sustaining breath. Learn to listen so deeply to your breathing that your very consciousness begins to take on the primordial, life-sustaining texture of your breathing. If you are tired as you meditate, learn to settle into a deep, reverential attentiveness to your bodily fatigue. If you are rested as you meditate, learn to listen and become one with the sense of bodily well-being that being rested brings. If there is a pain in your back or legs, or if your stomach is upset, or if the room is hot or cold—learn to listen deeply to the intimate texture of these and all aspects of your bodily being. Be meditatively attentive to, but do not get caught up in, the urges within you, both those that are fleeting and those that linger. Learn to be present, open, and awake to all that your bodily being reveals itself to be. Without clinging to all that is pleasant, without rejecting all that is unpleasant, let your bodily being be—in a restful, open awareness of all it so unthinkably is. Sitting in this way, you will learn, little by little, to neither abandon nor invade the graced mystery of your bodily being.

Scripture says, "The word became flesh and dwelt among us" (John 1:14). As we sit in meditation, we realize that these words are revelations, not just of the historical Christ but of ourselves as well. We sit in meditation pondering, breath by breath, the Word becoming flesh in the breath of us, in the very bodily being of who we simply are. We sit listening to God bodying himself forth in and as our bodily being. We listen to each breath, realizing, in some obscure manner, that we are listening to God breathing into us the gift of life. We realize, in ways we cannot explain, that each breath is carrying us all the way home into God, from whom each breath comes.

HEARING THE LORD'S VOICE

Saint Benedict says something relevant to this point in our journey that is at first somewhat perplexing. As he writes of the life-long journey of learning to listen to God, he says, echoing Scripture, "[I]f today you hear his voice harden not your heart." Now, why would we harden our heart in the moment of finally hearing the voice of the Lord we so deeply long to hear? It is because Jesus is the lord of love and emptiness. He emptied himself in love in everything he did and said. He kept on emptying himself in love no matter what, even to the point of emptying himself in love in his own death. His heart was pierced. Blood and water flowed out, so that there was no Jesus left in Jesus. And when there was nothing left of Jesus, then only love was left, which was the only thing that was really there all along. And the same is true of us. And yet in our ego self, we fear being emptied so completely that nothing will be left of us but love alone. And so, bereft of this redemptive liberation, we continue roaming about in our discontent.

Saint Benedict's words come from one who knows just how precarious things become the closer we get to what we are looking for. The ego self has lost so much already. The hard knot of the ego's illusions about itself has already been loosened to the point that the center barely holds together. And now in comes the Lord's voice inviting us to follow him in letting everything go *completely* as the only way to be free from the illusion of all that is less or other than love alone.

Truth is, the imagined center out of which we try to live our lives has already given way completely. All of our concerns about how things are going and how the journey will turn out are awash in the mystery that Christ came to reveal. The mystery is that nothing we can do can make God love us more.

Nothing we have done, or ever could do, can make God love us less. The measure of God's love for us is never in what we do or say. The sole measure of God's love for us is the measureless expanse of himself, perfectly poured out and given to us, in and as our standing when we stand, our sitting when we sit, our laughing when we laugh, our crying when we cry.

This is what Christ came to reveal: that nothing is missing anywhere. Our very life is itself the manifestation of the union with God we seek. But our ego self just doesn't get it! And so in the end we learn to extend the compassionate love of Christ to ourselves in our inability to realize how invincibly precious and one with God we are in all our wayward ways.

In summary, we have been exploring a rich and robust way to understand the monastic-meditative journey of self-transformation into God. We sit, giving ourselves to God, who from all eternity gives herself completely to us in and as our thinking self and all its thoughts, our remembering self and all its memories, our desiring self and all its desires, our feeling self and all its feelings, our breathing, bodily self and each life-sustaining breath we take, our unfaithful self and all its foolish and regrettable infidelities.

As we sit in meditation, all that we simply are is laid bare in a quiet, loving openness to God, who is eternally laid bare in and as all that we simply are. Of course, at some level we know of this unitive mystery, even before we begin meditating. After all, we have read the parable of the prodigal son and other words of Jesus inviting us to awaken to the oneness with God that is our life. We have known fleeting moments of spontaneous meditative awareness in which our oneness with God was intimately tasted and surrendered to. It is just that in meditation we come to realize this Good News as clearly and intimately as we know the palms of our own hands.

It is true that even as this knowledge grows within us, we continue to forget what we so clearly know. But no matter, for each time this occurs we renew our Christlike compassion for ourselves. In renewing our Christlike compassion for ourselves, we once again know ourselves to be invincibly precious and one with God in our forgetfulness of God's never-ending oneness with us. As we learn to stabilize ourselves in this Christlike compassion, we learn to see how precious and one with God others are in all their wayward ways. It is this communal dimension of our contemplative self-transformation that Saint Benedict had in mind in stressing the importance of community life as a spiritual practice. And it is in our compassionate interactions with others that our eyes are opened to a vital dimension of meditative living in the midst of the world.

In the following story I will share how I first came to experience Alcoholics Anonymous as a communal expression of the monastery without walls. As part of my doctoral training in clinical psychology, I worked at a thirty-day inpatient treatment center for alcohol and drug addiction at a large Veterans Administration hospital. The patients in this treatment center had devised an initiation rite. By the time I was there, this rite had become an ongoing tradition, part of the process a person had to go through to be admitted to the unit.

The initiation rite was held in a large room in the ward. The fifty or so members in the unit sat with their chairs facing inward around the four walls of the room. The middle of the room, around which the members sat, was empty of all furniture except for two chairs facing each other about four feet apart. The alcoholic seeking to be admitted to the unit was led into the room by one of the members, who instructed the newcomer to sit down in one of the two chairs. As the newcomer was led into the room, the alcoholics seated along the four walls of the room would all be looking downward, providing no eye contact, no smiles, and no indication to the newcomer of what to expect.

Once the newcomer sat down, the member of the unit presiding over the rite would sit down in the other chair across from him, look him straight in the eye, and ask, "What do you love the most?" The newcomer, who was, in most cases, fresh in off the streets, still shaky from the effects of alcohol abuse, would often blurt out something like "My wife." At which point the silence of the room would be abruptly shattered by all the men lining the four walls loudly yelling out in unison, "Bullshit!" Startled and unnerved, the newcomer would find himself sitting in the midst of the collective, surrounded by the serious-as-death silence of all the men around him still looking downward, giving him no point of human contact except their abrupt challenge to his self-destructive self-deception.

The interviewer would then, without delay, repeat the question: "What do you love the most?" The newcomer, this time with some trepidation, would often say something like "My children." At which point the group would once again yell, "Bullshit!" This would continue until the newcomer would, finally, say, "Alcohol." At this point everyone in the room would break into applause. The newcomer was instructed to stand. The members of the unit would line up, single file. In complete silence, each would approach the newcomer to hold him for a moment in a sincere embrace, welcoming him into their midst. Sometimes I would see tears coming to the newcomer's eyes, and tears would come to my eyes as well. I could sense that this was perhaps the first time this man had been touched, really touched, in a long, long time. This moment did not mark the end of the journey but the beginning of a long one.

Whenever I was present at one of these initiation rites, I felt

I was suddenly in the monastery without walls. All the essentials were present: The difficult passage through the gate. The senior member of the community to watch over the process. Seeking a freedom that one's own will is powerless to attain. Finding in this very powerlessness a taste of that amazing grace that sets us free each step of the way. Passing on to others the generosity of God that has been passed on to us.

This long journey is the one we are all on together as we learn to extend compassionate love to ourselves and others. Looking out through eyes transformed in meditative compassion, we see the world God has loved so deeply as to become completely hidden in it. We see others who, like us, go about suffering in the mistakes their egos make as to who they are and what they are about. Moved by compassion, we are impelled to do what we can to pass on to them what has been passed on to us in the silence of our meditation and in our daily life.

CHAPTER 6

The Self-Transforming Journey

What can be scary and wonderful about meditation is that it actually works! There is something about sitting, silent and still with all our heart, attentive to our breathing, that loosens the tight knot of our customary ego experience of ourselves. There is something about sitting silent and still, neither clinging to nor rejecting anything, that opens up an experience of oneness with God beyond what ego consciousness can grasp or contain.

As we begin to settle into a daily meditation practice, our old, familiar, ego-based ways of experiencing ourselves yield and give way to a wholly new, meditative experience. In the midst of this self-transforming journey, we ask with quiet, heart-felt urgency: How am I to understand what is happening to me? How am I to deal with this mysterious and sometimes oh-so-painful dying away of who I, up till now, have experienced myself to be? How am I to understand this new sense of spiritual fulfillment and oneness with God that is being born out of this dying process? And how can I learn to offer as little resistance as possible to this intimately realized oneness with God that is, little by little, becoming my very life?

Sharing how I personally understand these four questions provides a way of summarizing the approach to Christian meditation that I am taking in this book as a whole. We will then see what the anonymous fourteenth-century English author of the classic work *The Cloud of Unknowing* and the sixteenth-century Spanish mystic Saint John of the Cross have to say about these four fundamental questions. Turning to the writings of these two mystics will provide a way of moving forward in our ongoing efforts to familiarize ourselves with the richness of the mystical heritage of the Christian faith.

UNDERSTANDING WHAT IS HAPPENING TO US

Spiritual awakenings are wonderful and, in some ways, disruptive events. In the aftermath of a spiritual awakening we know that something has happened that has in some way transformed us. Such is our situation as seekers of a more meditative way of life. We know that at one time we felt no desire to seek God in meditation. Then something happened. An awakening of some sort laid bare the roots of our very being, setting our lives off in a wholly new, more interior direction that we now want to understand. This desire to understand is driven not by idle curiosity, but rather by a hope that we might continue on this more interior path with greater clarity and fewer misguided efforts and delays.

To fully understand the transformations that are occurring within us, we would have to have the mind of God, whose indwelling Spirit is secretly guiding us along this self-transforming path. But this does not mean we cannot come to some kind of basic grasp of the ultimately ungraspable nature of the transformations that are occurring within us. There is, in fact, a deep-seated need for us as human beings to get our bearings in our own life, to grow in authentic self-knowledge, so that we can live our lives in a mindful and effective manner.

One way to grow in this self-knowledge is to look back to the moments in which we were unexpectedly initiated into a meditative experience of oneness with God. Everything becomes highly personal at this point. Each of us is living out of our own unique edition of the one universal story of how we, as human beings, discover and respond to the divine origin and fulfillment of our lives.

As I think back to the origins of my own spiritual awakening, I see myself in my mind's eye back in Akron, Ohio, at the age of twelve, sitting in the back of Saint Bernard's Church, strangely bathed in a sweet, nurturing presence. As you look back to those moments in which you were first granted instances of spontaneous meditative experience of oneness with God, you will most likely be remembering details quite different from my own. But what all such moments share is that they dislodge us from our customary tendency to identify with our ego consciousness of ourselves. It is not that ego consciousness is annihilated in such moments; our capacity to think, remember, desire, feel, and have bodily sensations continues to exist. It is just that the eruption of meditative experience, as fleeting and subtle as it might be, transcends our thinking, our remembering, and all other parameters of ego consciousness.

As our moments of spontaneous meditative awareness pass, we return to ego consciousness, but we do so changed. For now we know *by experience* that, although we are surely ego, we are not simply ego. We know by experience how claustrophobic

and one-dimensional ego consciousness, estranged from meditative awareness, tends to be. We feel the sense of inadequacy
that will continue to pervade our life as long as ego consciousness continues to be our primary base of operations. We realize
that we must transcend ego consciousness as having the final say
in who we are and what our lives are about. We must venture
into deeper waters. We must learn to live in more daily abiding
meditative awareness of the depths we have so fleetingly
glimpsed in our moments of spontaneous meditative experience. In specifically Christian terms, we desire to experience directly for ourselves the presence of God that Christ came to
reveal and proclaim. We desire to see through Christ's eyes the
loving presence of God in all that we see. We desire to be transformed to the point that Christ's experience of oneness with
God becomes our habitual way of experiencing our day-by-day
lives.

When I was in the monastery, I was given permission to
spend time each day in an abandoned sheep barn. Eventually I
was allowed to build a small hermitage of sorts on the barn's
ground floor, which I furnished with a small table, a candle, a
kneeler, and a few books. A burlap sack served as a curtain for
the one small window. That sheep barn no longer exists. After I
left the monastery, a small wood-burning stove was put into the
small ground-floor room I used as a hermitage, which resulted
in the barn's catching fire and burning to the ground.

I spent most of my time in the loft of the barn, where I
would pray and read. I would sit on a bail of hay, looking out at
the meadow and surrounding woods. One of the books I read
there was *The Cloud of Unknowing*. In reading this book, I felt
as though its anonymous fourteenth-century author knew of my
struggles to understand the changes I was going through. I
would seek to find in its pages as much detailed information as

I could to dispel the confusion I felt about how to practice contemplative prayer. I read the anonymous author's words:

> If you ask me precisely how one is to go about doing the contemplative work of love, I am at a complete loss. All I can say is I pray that Almighty God in his great goodness and kindness will teach you himself. For in all honesty I must admit I do not know. And no wonder, for it is a divine activity and God will do it in whomever he chooses. . . . I believe, too, that Our Lord deliberately chooses to work in those who have been habitual sinners rather than in those who, by comparison, have never grieved him at all. Yes, he seems to do this very often. For I think he wants us to realize that he is all merciful and all mighty and that he is perfectly free to work as he pleases, where he pleases and when he pleases.[1]

To hear this great mystic admit he did not know gave me permission to admit I did not know. More significantly still, his humble admission helped me to begin to understand that I was being led by God along a path in which I had to be willing not to understand, on my own terms, what was happening to me. Nor could I know just where my self-metamorphosing path would end. For how could my finite mind understand the infinite ways of God into which I was being led?

The very fact that we are beginning to understand that we are experiencing things we cannot conceptually comprehend is itself the beginning of a new, more spiritually grounded form of understanding. The anonymous author, in fact, begins his book by attempting to help us understand that at the beginning stages of the meditative path we are in transition between two different ways of understanding. We are, in fact, between two different ways of being. He writes:

> There are some presently engaged in the active life who are being prepared by Grace to grasp the message of this book. I am thinking of those who feel the mysterious action of the Spirit in their inmost being stirring them to love. I do not say they continually experience that stirring as experienced contemplatives do, but now and again they taste something of contemplative love in the very core of their being.[2]

When the author of *The Cloud of Unknowing* uses the term *active life*, he is referring to a way of life in which our identity and sense of security tend to be bound up with all that we have attained and are capable of attaining through our own efforts. The author invites us to see ourselves going along, minding our own business, living the active life, when suddenly a blind stirring of love in the very core of our being blesses us with an awareness of God's loving presence that utterly transcends what our own efforts could ever account for or attain.

We can neither comprehend nor control this blind stirring of love that comes welling up, unannounced, into the midst of all we try so hard to comprehend and control. We can only open ourselves to this blind stirring of love. We can only make ourselves as vulnerable to this blind stirring of love as we can be, in the hope that in doing so we will awaken to a oneness with God in which such notions as comprehending, attaining, and controlling simply have no meaning.

At the initial stage of our journey we experience this blind stirring of love only "now and again." But the author suggests that there are "experienced contemplatives" who experience this stirring continually. And this fills us with a sense of hope that one day we, too, might, with God's grace, habitually experience this blind stirring. But the point is that we are to understand that God's love has already begun to dislodge us from our customary sense of ourselves. And the divine love that is dislodging us from ego-based ways of experiencing ourselves continues to lure us on into ever deeper, more habitual states of realized oneness with God.

For many of us the onset of our meditative path begins, as the author of The Cloud of Unknowing suggests, with a precipitating event that awakens us to a wholly new, more meditative way of experiencing God's presence. God comes with a wake-up call, announcing a love that transcends all that our ego can account for or attain. The awakening event initiates a journey in which God's indwelling Spirit leads us into the depths of the love that has awakened us.

But sometimes it does not work this way. Sometimes God moves in on us in a covert operation of love that we know nothing about. Then, at a certain point, God sets in motion in us a perplexing inability to pray and reflect on the things of God in the manner to which we are accustomed. We are not, in this scenario, awakened to some qualitatively richer way of realizing God's presence. Instead, the divine mystery, secretly at work in our hearts, dismantles our ability to derive satisfaction from our customary ways of praying and reflecting on the things of God. The whole experience can be quite disheartening. But then, as we learn to rest in this powerlessness, a new, more subtle and interior way of realizing God's presence slowly begins to emerge within us.

Saint John of the Cross is a great teacher to those who are sincerely trying to understand why their accustomed ways of praying and practicing discursive meditation using thoughts and images no longer console and reassure them as before. He compares the experience of this purifying and transformative process to that of passing through a *dark night*, in which God weans us away from our tendency to base our security and identity on anything less than God. I count myself among John of the Cross's grateful readers.

One of the things I found most helpful in Saint John of the Cross's writings is his presentation of the following three signs by which beginners are to discern they are being led into more interior, meditative forms of prayer.

The first of these three signs is, he says, "the realization that one cannot make discursive meditation or receive satisfaction from it as before."[3] We can look back to the days in which we derived a sense of spiritual satisfaction from reading the Scriptures, prayer, and discursive meditation, using thoughts and images of God. But now these forms of prayer and reflection leave us dry and unfulfilled. In presenting this first sign, Saint John of the Cross is careful to add that the inability to derive satisfaction from our customary ways of praying and reflecting on the things of God is not, in and of itself, a sign that we are being called to more contemplative forms of prayer. For, as he points out, our "inability to imagine and meditate" may be due to our "dissipation and lack of diligence."[4] Our prayer is a barometer measuring the way we live our life. Difficulties in prayer are often an indication that we need to check things out, to see what is going on in our life that is compromising or doing violence to the way we know God wants us to live.

The second sign is "the disinclination to fix the imagination or sense faculties on other particular objects, exterior or interior."[5] That is, with the onset of this second sign, our situation is not simply that we cannot derive satisfaction from reflecting on the things of God. For we notice that thinking about the things of this earth does not provide satisfaction either! Saint John of the Cross is careful to note that the experience of not deriving satisfaction from thinking about either the things of God or the realities of everyday life is not in itself a sign that we are being called to more interior, meditative ways of experiencing God's presence. For, he says, the inability to derive satisfaction from thinking about anything at all may be due to "melancholia . . . in the heart or brain capable of producing a certain stupefaction and suspension of the sense faculties."[6] We would say today that the reason we are not deriving any satisfaction from thinking about the things of God—or anything else, for that matter—is that we are depressed. One sign of depression is a difficulty in concentrating. Another sign of depression is the inability to experience satisfaction or pleasure in our daily experiences.

This does not mean we cannot be both depressed and in the dark night! It is just that it is important not to confuse the two. Depression is associated with feelings of worthlessness, a sense of hopelessness about the future, and other symptoms that diminish our ability to live and enjoy our life. The dark night is a painful and confusing loss of our customary ways of praying and experiencing God's presence in our life. We are left feeling barren yet free, in a strange new place we do not understand.

For Saint John of the Cross, "the third and surest sign is that a person likes to remain alone, in a loving awareness of God, without particular considerations, in interior peace, and quiet and repose, and without the acts and exercises . . . of the intellect, memory and the will. Such a one prefers to remain only in the general loving awareness and knowledge . . . without any particular knowledge or understanding."[7]

It is said of Saint of John of the Cross that he used to love to stay up alone at night, sitting in silence at an open window, looking out at the moonlit world. There is something vast and ungraspable that quietly grants itself in such silent, solitary attentiveness. The moments spent quietly surrendered to a general loving awareness are neither defined nor sustained by thoughts or feelings or anything the ego tends to use to sustain itself. In such moments, we are sustained by a general loving awareness that slowly grows and deepens the more we allow ourselves to settle into it.

In reflecting on this general loving awareness, Saint John of the Cross adds: "I am not affirming that the imagination will cease to come and go—even in deep recollection it usually wanders freely—but that the person does not want to fix it purposely on extraneous things."[8] As you sit, silent and still, in the general loving awareness of which Saint John of the Cross speaks, thoughts and images continue to pass through your mind. You notice the coolness or the warmth of the room, the ticking of a clock, a dark barking somewhere off in the distance. You are aware now of your own breathing, now of your hands resting in your lap. You feel no need to try to become unaware of any of these things. Nor are you inclined to focus on any of these things. There is no method. There is no goal. There is only a general loving awareness that slowly grows and deepens as you continue to rest wordlessly in it.

In this general loving awareness, all that is opaque becomes translucent, then utterly transparent. All that is tightly bound begins to loosen. The incomprehensible nature of simple things—the chair over there in the corner, the books stacked by the door—begins to manifest itself to our nonintrusive gaze. The perception of being somehow inside oneself looking out at a world external to and other than oneself begins to dissolve. Something of the divinity of what just is begins to appear in the silent sincerity of simply being present in the present moment just as it is.

We may, in reading such words, understand all too well what Saint John of the Cross is talking about. It is just that this understanding frightens us. It is entirely too much and too little for our ego to endure. And yet in hearing such words our heart breaks with longings to realize this blessed oneness with God. Great patience is needed as we quietly and persistently continue to yield to the general loving awareness in which alone we find our true rest. Little by little we grow in our understanding of what is happening to us. We come to understand that our customary tendency to identify with our ego consciousness is beginning to yield and give way to a more interior, meditative kind of experience. We come to realize that our thoughts, memories, desires, feelings, and bodily sensations are proving to be less and less adequate in their ability to sustain or account for the intimately realized oneness with God that is slowly growing within us. Little by little we come to realize that oneness with God is the true and endless nature of our thoughts, memories, desires, feelings, and bodily sensations. Little by little, we realize oneness with God to be our very life, the very reality of all that is real.

Imagine that you have fallen asleep in a small boat that is moored with two ropes between two piers. Imagine that one rope moors your little boat to your customary ways of experiencing and understanding your relationship to God. The other rope moors your little boat to your customary ways of experiencing and understanding your relationship to yourself, others, and all other earthly things. Imagine that as you are sleeping soundly in your little boat, God quietly unfastens the rope that moors you to your customary ways of experiencing his presence in your life and drops it into the water. God then quietly goes around to the rope connecting you to your customary ways of experiencing yourself in relationship to the things of this earth, unfastens it, and drops it into the water as well. Then God, trying not to laugh and wake you up, gives your boat a little nudge that sends it out into open water. When you awaken hours later, you sit up to discover you are out in the open sea, with no land in sight! And so it is that God, in the darkness of night, unmoors us from our customary ways of relating to things both divine and human. We are left in a strange and solitary silence, in which an utterly unforeseeable union with God begins to emerge.

Saint John of the Cross says, "To come to the knowledge you have not you must go by a way in which you know not."[9] Reading this statement in our ego consciousness, we cannot understand what he might mean. Reading this statement in the general loving awareness that is slowly becoming our home, we discern in his words an echo of the unspeakable mystery that we are, little by little, learning to understand. And yet it is this very understanding, born of our loving, silent surrender to God, that is bringing about a corresponding loss of our customary ways of experiencing ourselves. And so we ask: How am I to deal with this mysterious, subtle, and sometimes oh-so-painful dying away of who I, up until now, have experienced myself to be?

DEALING WITH THE DYING AWAY OF WHO WE USED TO BE

We can understand what is happening to us in meditation by understanding that our customary, ego-based ways of experiencing ourselves are yielding and giving way to more interior, meditative ways of being, ways that transcend all that ego can attain. We welcome this self-transforming process, realizing it to be the way we awaken to our eternal oneness with God. But this does not mean that this transformative process is not at times immensely difficult.

Reflecting on the process of metamorphosis as it occurs in nature provides a helpful vantage point from which to grow in this understanding. It is amazing how a caterpillar spins about itself a hiding place from which it later emerges and takes flight as a butterfly with delicate, iridescent wings. Our faith proclaims that this is what happened to Christ. He lived as a human being who freely entered into the hiding place of death, to emerge, deathless, filled with light and life, and utterly transformed. Our faith proclaims that in following Christ we experience the same thing. As Saint Paul expressed it in his second letter to the Corinthians: "Therefore if any man is in Christ, he is a new creature; the old things have passed away; behold, new things have come" (2 Cor. 5:17).

A caterpillar that emerged from its chrysalis only partially transformed—a caterpillar with wings—would be too heavy to fly. It is the same with us. As long as the transforming power of faith has yet to penetrate and transform the roots of consciousness itself, we are like a caterpillar with wings. As long as our ego consciousness remains intact as our habitual base of operations, we hear the call to fly to God but we remain earthbound. We have faith in God's providential care; and yet a headache, a spat with a neighbor, or a flat tire is, at times, enough to undermine our inner peace. We have faith in Christ, a faith telling us to "fear not"; and yet the uncertainties of what the future might hold still leave us anxious. We hear Christ calling us to love others as he has loved us; and yet we are afraid to listen too intently to the suffering of others. We avoid looking into their eyes as they speak, because we are fearful of the claim their suffering may make on us.

There may be moments of spontaneous meditative experience in which we fleetingly realize the metamorphosis from ego consciousness into full-blown meditative consciousness. A moment of yielding ourselves to the intoxicating smell of a single blood red rose, or a moment of silently gazing into the bottomless well of an infant's eyes, can instantaneously awaken us to the divinity of what just is. But as long as the meditative awareness awakened in such moments is not yet habitual, we remain a caterpillar with wings. We remain bound in ego consciousness in the long stretches between flashes of momentary liberation.

We sit in meditation so that the last traces of our tendency to identify with egocentric consciousness might finally dissolve as our habitual base of operations. We meditate that we might continue thinking, but no longer live by thought and all that thought can comprehend. We meditate that we might continue remembering, but no longer be limited to memory or all that can be remembered. We sit that we might continue willing, but no longer be limited to our own will or what our will is capable of attaining. We sit that we might continue feeling, but no longer be limited to our feelings or all that can be felt. We sit that we might continue being our bodily self as long as our life on this earth shall last, but no longer be limited to our bodily self and all the bodily self can be. We sit that we might live in God, and for God, and by God in all we do and say. We meditate that we might live in a habitual awareness of God living in us, for us, and by us in all that we simply are.

It is in actually committing ourselves to daily meditation that we come face-to-face with the realities of how deeply entrenched our tendencies to remain identified with ego consciousness are. Truth is, our own ego-based sense of ourselves that knows nothing beyond itself is afraid to open to unknown depths, transcending its circle of influence and control. We will go half way, in a willingness to become a caterpillar with wings. For such an undertaking not only leaves our ego intact but also expands it as an ego that has attained spiritual gifts or mystical states of oneness with God. But any notion of surrendering ourselves to something as radical as a complete metamorphosis *of consciousness itself* is too much to risk. The possibility of realizing a life that is at once God's and our own is beyond what we can comprehend.

Imagine a little girl who is crying because she does not want to go to her first day of kindergarten. Her parents know how important it is not to accommodate her fears by telling her she does not have to go to school. At the same time, they can understand why she is afraid at having to suddenly enter into a new world that is so much bigger than the one she has known up to this point. They feel something of her fears as well, in that they know their little child is being transformed in this decisive moment that requires that they let go of their little girl, who is not so little anymore. But something in them knows that the only real answer is to trust the unrelenting momentum of life, in which they and their little girl are being carried along. There is, between these parents and their little girl, a tender place of loving encounter. Even as they help her get ready to go out the door, they are listening and responding to her tearful concerns. Even as they are approaching the classroom, they are trying to reassure her and let her know that if she but gives it a chance, she will discover new friends and all sorts of surprises.

When we sit in meditation, we take the little child of our ego self off to school, where we must learn to die to our illusions about being dualistically other than God. We must also die to any grandiose delusions that we are God. In meditation we learn to wait with compassion and patience until we are ready to take our next faltering step into a yet deeper realization of oneness with God. This tender point of encounter is Christ, understood as God in our midst, listening, loving, and helping his children across the threshold into eternal oneness with God. This, then, is one way of understanding how to deal with the ongoing loss of our old and familiar ways of understanding ourselves. And this is how we can, with Christlike compassion, be present to the self-metamorphosing process in which, little by little, breath by breath, love dissolves the illusions and fears born of our estrangement from the infinite love that is our very life.

To see what light the author of *The Cloud of Unknowing* sheds on this matter of dealing with difficulties and the sense of loss experienced in meditation, we first have to present his guidelines for practicing meditation. Recall for a moment that, in sharing his guidelines for meditation, he is speaking to us as one who has experienced a blind stirring of love in the very core of his being. He invites us to recognize in this blind stirring of love a call from God to enter into the mysterious depths in which our spirit and God's spirit are one. Desiring to respond to God's call, we ask just what we are to do that might allow this realized oneness with God to occur. The author of *The Cloud of Unknowing* responds, saying:

This is what you are to do: lift up your heart to the Lord, with a gentle stirring of love desiring him for his own sake and not for his gifts. Center all your attention and desire on him and let this be the sole concern of your mind and heart. Do all in your power to forget everything else, keeping your thoughts and desires free from involvement with any of God's creatures or their affairs whether in general or in particular.[10]

Imagine that you are standing in the mountains in the middle of a pitch-dark night. Suddenly, you see a flash of light in the distance. Someone comes up, and you ask if they saw the flash of light. "No," they say, asking, "Where was it?" And you point off in the darkness toward the place the flash came from. That is, even though you do not know the exact location or the nature of the flash, you can still point in the direction from which it came. In a similar fashion, the author of *The Cloud of Unknowing* is saying, in the above passage, that you can quietly sit and interiorly face that deep place within yourself in which the blind stirring of love occurred. Interiorly facing the hidden depths of your awakened heart, you can lift your heart up to the divine love that has awakened it. You can sit in the simple intention of giving back to God the love he has given to you. Thus, something we observed about Saint John of the Cross is true of the author of *The Cloud of Unknowing* as well. For each of these two Christian mystics, meditation is not so much a method as it is a way of being utterly sincere in a loving stance of sustained openness to God.

The anonymous author then goes on to say, in the above passage, that you are to sustain the stance of loving openness to God by refraining from dwelling on any thoughts about God that might come into your mind. Throughout the book he refers to this stance of naked love, free of any intentional thinking about God, as dwelling in a "cloud of unknowing." The author of *The Cloud of Unknowing* is, at this point, following the teachings of another great Christian mystic, Dionysius the Aeropagite, whose work entitled *The Mystical Theology* influenced not only our anonymous author but also Saint John of the Cross, as well as numerous other Christian mystics and theologians.

The basic point of this lineage of Christian spirituality is that we are to be grateful for all that we can know of God through ideas of him revealed to us in Scripture. That is, we are to be grateful for knowing that God is good, that God is love, that God is our creator, and so forth. But this knowledge of God through our thoughts about him should not blind us to the absolute transcendence of God, utterly beyond all our thoughts about him. With such considerations in mind, the author of *The Cloud of Unknowing* urges us to respond to God's invitation to oneness with himself by remaining as best we can in the "cloud of unknowing," free of our customary reliance on our thoughts about God. For, as he tells us, "if in this life you hope to feel and see God as he is himself it must be within this darkness and this cloud."[11]

To round out the picture, the anonymous author suggests that as we sit with the cloud of unknowing above us, we are to sit with a corresponding "cloud of forgetting" beneath us. The *cloud of forgetting* is the term the anonymous author uses for a corresponding stance of holding in abeyance our tendency to dwell on our memories or to think about the things of this earth. Thus, suspended in a naked intent of love, between the cloud of unknowing above us and the cloud of forgetting beneath us, we are to slowly wean our self off our customary reliance on thoughts about God, ourselves, and all earthly things. We are to just sit, letting our love, stripped and naked of all thought, ascend to God, naked as he is in himself, utterly beyond all that thought can comprehend concerning him. We are to simply sit, allowing love alone to be our guide, our presence, and our path.

Having presented, at least briefly, some of the anonymous author's guidelines for meditation, we can go on to note how highly sensitive he is to how hard it can be to leave behind our customary reliance on thinking. In urging us to be faithful to the meditation practice he proposes, he is encouraging us to

diligently persevere [in this contemplative work of love] until you feel joy in it. For in the beginning it is usual to feel nothing but a kind of darkness about your mind, or as it were a cloud of unknowing. You will seem to know nothing and to feel nothing except a naked intent toward God in the depths of your being. Try as you might, this darkness and this cloud will remain between you and your God. You will feel frustrated, for your mind will be unable to grasp him and your heart will not relish the delight of his love. But learn to be at home in the darkness. Return to it as often as you can.[12]

The author of *The Cloud of Unknowing* does not say that because he knows how hard it is for you to free yourself from your customary dependence on thinking, he wants to give you some thoughts you can take with you into meditation, to console you as you wait for God. For this would be like offering an alcoholic a drink to help him through the rough spots of learning to be free from his destructive dependency on alcohol. Later on, we will be seeing how the anonymous author does suggest using a simple phrase or word, such as *God* or *mercy*, that we are to repeat each time we drift off into this or that thought. But even here he encourages us not to consider the word to be something to think about. To the contrary, we are to use the repetition of the word as a way of regrounding ourselves in a naked intent of love, void of any dependency on thoughts or images.

In the following passage the anonymous author puts words to what it is actually like to sit in meditation as we face the challenging task of leaving behind our customary reliance on our thoughts and memories of all things divine and human. He writes:

Your senses and faculties will be frustrated for lack of something to dwell on and they will chide you for doing nothing. But never mind. Go on with this nothing, moved only by your love for God. Never give up but steadfastly persevere in this nothingness, consciously longing to possess God through love, whom no one can possess through knowledge. For myself I prefer to be lost in this nowhere, wrestling with this blind nothingness, than to be like some great lord traveling everywhere and enjoying the world as if he owned it.

Forget that kind of everywhere and the world's all. It pales in richness beside this blessed nothingness and nowhere. Do not worry if your faculties fail to grasp it. Actually, this is the way it should be; for this nothingness is so lofty they cannot reach it. It cannot be explained, only experienced.

Yet to those who have newly encountered it, it will feel very dark and inscrutable indeed. But truly they are blinded by the splendor of its spiritual light rather than by any ordinary kind of darkness. Who do you suppose derides it as emptiness? Our superficial self, of course. Certainly not our true self; no, our true, inner self appreciates it as fullness beyond measure. For in this darkness we experience an intuitive understanding of everything material and spiritual without giving special attention to anything in particular.[13]

You have within you a practical, conceptual mind that allows you to focus on tasks, to figure things out. As you begin to meditate, this practical mind is out of its element. For in meditation there is nothing to figure out, nothing to achieve, nothing to acquire. As you sit in meditation, this practical mind will, understandably, feel frustrated. The author of *The Cloud of Unknowing* is telling you that nothing can be nor needs to be done to avoid this frustration that arises from committing your-self to a process that leaves your practical, conceptual mind unemployed, with nothing to hold on to or achieve. Hang in there, he says. Let the inevitable frustration occur. As it does so, notice how the deeper, more interior dimensions of your being one with God are beginning to come to the fore. Notice how as your ego self flounders, your deep self, one with God, drinks undisturbed from the deep pool of loving presence that medita-tion embodies. Let love lead the way, for thought cannot grasp God, who, in being love, is attained by love alone. In time the conversion process—in which you learn to identify less and less with your superficial self and more and more with your deep self, one with God—will mature and come to fulfillment. Be patient. Trust that God's generosity is at work, bringing you to a realized oneness with God infinitely beyond anything you might have imagined possible.

Saint John of the Cross also demonstrates great care and insight in attempting to help us tend to our heart as we under-go the loss of our accustomed ego-based ways of experiencing God's presence. In the following passage he first expresses the dilemma of being unable to experience God's presence within us. Then he goes on to provide insight into how to understand this dilemma and how it might be resolved. He writes:

> There is but one difficulty: Even though he does abide within you, he is hidden. Nevertheless, it is vital for you to know his hiding place so you may search for him there with assurance. . . .
>
> You inquire, "since he whom my soul loves is within me, why don't I find him or experience him?" The rea-son is that he remains concealed, and you do not also conceal yourself in order to find and experience him.

If you want to find a hidden treasure you must enter into the hiding place secretly, and once you have discovered it, you will also be hidden just as the treasure is hidden.[14]

Sometimes we tend to think that we can lure God out of hiding. There is, is fact, some truth to this. Prayer, meditation, a Christlike love for others—all can evoke a renewed and deepened sense of God's presence in our lives. But Saint John is addressing our situation following the onset of the dark night, in which our prayers and other acts of faith no longer work for us. We dance in front of the cave in which God hides; we call for God to come out and play and embrace us and let us know once again something of his loving presence in our lives. But God does not come out into our customary conscious awareness of ourselves. We know that God is within us, in some hidden manner we can neither feel nor comprehend. We are perplexed as to why our sincere efforts in prayer and meditation are not able to lure God out into our ego awareness, where we can "have" an experience of God's ever present nearness.

In the above passage, Saint John of the Cross invites you not to be discouraged, but rather to calm yourself and look very closely at what is happening. As you do so, you begin to discover that even the interior of your own heart is, for God, not nearly intimate enough a place for God to be as intimate with you as he desires. It is true that God no longer is showing up out here, where you can experience his presence in the manner in which you were able to in the past. But look closely and you will see that the empty space left by God's apparent absence has exposed a previously unrecognized passageway into the utter concealment of God. Look closer still and you will see that the general loving awareness in which you are learning to rest is this very passageway, through which you are being mysteriously led into a oneness with God, hidden from every mortal eye, including your own.

The transformative process in which we are led by God into the depths of God is so subtle it may seem as if nothing at all is happening. You are, after all, just sitting in a general loving awareness in which thoughts come and go. Memories come and go, as does your awareness of your breathing or the sound of the clock chiming the hour. But underneath all these passing experiences, the general loving knowledge imperceptibly continues to deepen as it translates your heart into the very hiddenness of God. This whole process is so utterly transparent and free of anything that would draw attention to itself that it may go on for quite some time before you even recognize it is occurring. It is this process that Saint John of the Cross is trying to help us understand. He says:

> Actually, at the beginning of this state the loving knowledge is almost unnoticeable. There are two reasons for this: First, the loving knowledge initially is likely to be extremely subtle and delicate, almost imperceptible; second, a person who is habituated to the exercises of [discursive] meditation, which is wholly sensible, hardly perceives or feels this new insensible, purely spiritual experience. This is especially so when through failure to understand it, one does not permit oneself to rest in it but strives after the other, more sensory experience. Although the interior peace is more abundant, the individual allows no room to experience and enjoy it. But the more habituated persons become to this calm, the more their experience of this general loving knowledge will increase. This knowledge is more enjoyable than all other

things because without the soul's labor it affords peace, rest, savor, and delight.[15]

Two people, falling in love, spend a great deal of energy, drawing love up from its hidden depths to keep it flowing, as it were, uphill, to nurture their needs for gratification in love. But as their love matures, the currents of love shift and begin to flow back down into the depths, pulling them along with it—into depths of love they never knew existed. It is even more so with the infinite love of God. We may, for quite some time, labor to make the river flow uphill into our conscious awareness of being consoled, reassured, and blessed on our own terms. But as the influx of love reaches a certain point of fullness, it begins to flow back into the oceanic depths of God, carrying us along with it into a deep, hidden, divine oneness with God that no one but God knows anything about.

UNDERSTANDING THIS NEW EXPERIENCE OF SPIRITUAL FULFILLMENT

As our old, familiar, ego-based ways of being cease to be our primary base of operations, a previously unknown sense of spiritual fulfillment begins to emerge. We seek to understand this new sense of spiritual fulfillment as best we can. One of the most helpful things for us to understand is that ego consciousness cannot comprehend that which is realized only in transcending ego consciousness. We can think about what it might be like to transcend our customary reliance on thinking. We can desire to realize a oneness with God that transcends what our desires can attain. But as long as our sense of self remains limited to our thoughts, our desires, and other aspects of ego consciousness, oneness with the divine fullness that transcends ego remains beyond our reach. The sense of spiritual fulfillment that is emerging out of the dying away of our egocentric ways of being is, therefore, a call to continue passing beyond thought and desire and all ego-based ways of being.

When we read what the mystics share with us about their experience of God, we discover that they do not speak of anything they can explain or define. Rather, they speak of an overflowing fullness of God's presence, utterly beyond anything they could ever explain or define. They give witness to the fact that the overflowing divine fullness that totally revolutionized their life was not realized by thinking, willing, remembering, or any other aspect of ego consciousness. Listen as the eleventh-century mystic Saint Bernard of Clairvaux shares with us his experience of the divine fullness transcending all references in ego consciousness:

> It did not come through the eyes, since it has no color; nor by the ears, since it makes no noise; nor through the nostrils, since it does not mingle with air; . . . nor by the throat, neither, for it cannot be eaten nor drunk. Nor did I discover it by touch, since it is impalpable. I rose above myself and found the Word was higher still. Curious to explore, I went down into my depths, and found in the same way that it was lower still. I looked outside myself and saw that it was outside all that was outside me. I looked within and saw that it was more inward than I. And then I recognized as truth what I had read; that in it we have Life, Motion and Being.[16]

And now listen to the fifteenth-century mystic Saint Catherine of Genoa as she, with equal eloquence, gives witness to an experience of oneness with God that transcends any and all reference points in ego consciousness:

> I see without eyes and I hear without ears. I feel without feeling. And taste without tasting. I know neither form nor measure; for without seeing I yet behold an operation so divine that the words I first used, perfection, purity, and the like, seem to me now mere lies in the presence of truth. . . . Nor can I any longer say, "My God, my all." Everything is mine, for all that is God's seems to be wholly mine. I am mute and lost in God.[17]

Even though the fullness of the divine that echoes in these passages may be beyond anything you have yet to experience, was there not some kind of *yes* going on inside you as you read them? Did you not recognize and, to some degree, resonate with the depth and beauty these passages embody? We should pay close attention to this recognition and this resonance. In doing so, we are awakened to the reassuring fact that our own ego is already being transcended in our experience of recognizing and feeling drawn toward that which transcends ego.

Imagine a caterpillar crawling along a branch. It looks up and sees a butterfly floating by with iridescent wings. "Oh" the caterpillar says, "what's that? And what is this strange sense of recognition and resonance that is going on within me in seeing the beauty of this butterfly? It seems to be so beyond anything I could ever hope or even imagine myself to be!" When we recognize and are drawn to the divine fullness the mystics speak of, we are like this caterpillar. Our attraction toward the oneness with God the mystics speak of reveals that our very nature bears within it the self-metamorphosing process by which, the mystics tell us, they were awakened to their eternal oneness with God.

We may never experience, on this earth, the fullness of God's presence that Bernard of Clairvaux, Catherine of Genoa, and the other great mystics were privileged to experience. But no matter, for the spiritual path is such that what holds true at its loftiest heights holds true at its humblest beginnings. What the mystics have to share about their sublime states of oneness with God casts a clear and penetrating light on the ground beneath our own feet. By looking at our own experience in the light of the experience of the great mystics, we are better able to discern how the first stirrings of the fullness of God are already at work in our life. This is why in reading the words of the mystics we are encouraged and reassured in knowing that we are on the path of realizing the overflowing fullness of God that they experienced in their life.

It is in this vein that I will now share a moment in which I experienced something of the fullness of God's presence in my own life. I share this story for two reasons—the first being that so much of what I am sharing with you throughout this book first broke into my life in a decisive way through this experience. Second, it is my hope that in reading about my experience you will be aided in looking back to the moments in your own life in which you were fortunate enough to experience something of the overflowing fullness of God.

The experience occurred in 1962. I was nineteen years old and had been in the monastery for about a year. For several months prior to this experience I had been going through a period of spiritual aridity. The well went dry. The sense of God's presence that I had been experiencing on an almost daily basis suddenly and mysteriously vanished. I read what Saint John of the Cross had to say about the dark night of the soul. I would talk with Thomas Merton in spiritual direction about what was happening to me. It was at this time that I began going each day alone to the loft of the abandoned sheep barn, where Thomas Merton, as my novice master, had given me permission to spend some time each day in prayer and meditation.

One hot summer day I climbed up the ladder into the loft, as up into a cathedral of light and heat. The air was heavy with the primordial, sweet smell of hay, which was neatly stacked in bails up to the ceiling along the back wall. I was sitting where I usually sat, on some bails of hay, which I had arranged near the open loft door that looked out over a meadow and the surrounding woods. I was reading the psalms. I stood up and began walking slowly back and forth as I continued reading. Everything within me was dry and empty in the hot, solitary silence. There was no sense whatsoever that anything extraordinary was about to happen.

Suddenly, I realized that what I had, up to that moment, thought of as the air was actually God! I was walking back and forth in God, breathing God. I was vividly aware that the oceanic presence in which I was walking back and forth was sustaining my life, breath by breath. And this presence of God that I was breathing, and in which I was standing and walking about, knew me, through and through, with oceanic compassion. There was nowhere to hide, nor did I need any such place. There was nowhere I could run from God. For even if I were to try to flee, God would be sustaining me, breath by breath, in my flight from him, and would be waiting for me, sustaining my life, breath by breath, when I arrived at my planned place of escape. I realized in some baffling, matter-of-fact way that since God is the infinity of the mystery of air, I was living my life in God and was being held by God always.

There were no feelings. No images. There was nothing imaginary about it. The realization that the air is God was as concretely real and immediate as the smell of the hay, the silence, the small book of psalms that I continued to hold in my hands. I was simply amazed. After a while I sat back down on the bails of hay near the door and looked out through God at the meadow and woods.

An occasional red wasp came buzzing in through the open loft door, to hover in the heat for a moment before ascending to the beams overhead to work on its mud nest. The pair of barn swallows that had built a nest along the inside wall beams darted and glided over the meadow. The tin roof made its slight pinging, crinkling noises as it expanded in the hot sun. A cicada whined, unseen, somewhere off in the trees. And I kept sitting there, breathing God, until I heard the bell ring for vespers. I walked back to the monastery breathing God. I chanted vespers breathing God. I ate supper breathing God. I fell asleep that night breathing God. It seemed to me as if this was what heaven must be like.

I woke up the next morning breathing God, and, in fact, I walked around in this state for several days. On Sundays we were allowed to take walks in the woods outside the monastic enclosure. I was walking along the dirt road that led up to a small lake in the woods where I would sit and read Saint John of the Cross. I was walking along, on this particular Sunday, breathing God, with my volume of John of the Cross under my arm. Just at the point at which the road curved and led from the open field up into the woods, I paused at a small tree that was hanging out over the road.

Standing there, breathing God, I reached up and touched one of the leaves hanging from one of the branches. As I did so, I looked up. There was one cloud in the sky. I said, out loud, "It's One!" The ground I was standing on, the leaf I was touching, the cloud in the sky, God that I was breathing, my own very self—were utterly, completely, ungraspably one! I walked a short distance up onto the edges of a large field. I sat there in the tall grass. A strong wind was blowing. I sat there all afternoon, not moving until I heard the bell ring in the distance from the monastery bell tower, letting me know that it was time to head back and go to vespers.

I do not remember the moment at which I lost the direct awareness of breathing God. As some point, perhaps later that very day, it dissipated. The air seemed to be, once again, just the air. Except that I knew my experience of the air as being just the air was but my unawareness of what I now knew the air to be. Then even this inner clarity faded. I realized that I had a long road ahead of me in learning to live in a habitual awareness of the fullness I had fleetingly realized.

For a long time I thought I would spend the rest of my life growing into what was granted to me in the sheep barn and in that moment when I reached out to touch that leaf that hung from the tree along the roadside. In some ways, I still think that way. On some days I am concerned that at my present rate of spiritual growth, senility may set in before this fullness is realized. But deep down I know that all such notions are but my persistent inability to live in the awareness of what I know to be true—namely, that God in all things and all things in God *is* the very reality of all that is real. The cutting edge of my present moment's inability to experience God's presence is itself the presence of God giving herself wholly and completely, in and as the intimate texture of my inability to experience God's presence.

Jesus called the divine fullness *the Kingdom of God*. He saw this divine fullness in all that he saw. He invites us to see this divine fullness in all that we see as well. Sitting in meditation, we accept this invitation to see in all that we see the divine fullness that Christ saw in all that he saw. We may be inclined to recognize this fullness more easily in a grand cathedral than in a bird we happen to notice momentarily sitting on one of the cathedral's spires. We may more readily experience this fullness in a verse of Scripture than we do in the graffiti scrawled on a fence.

Surely, from the vantage point of ego-based relative consciousness of relative reality, there is some truth to this incremental enrichment, in which the divine fullness is experienced as being more present in some things than in others. This is especially evident with respect to the mystery of evil that bears the mark of God's apparent absence. But as the mystery of the cross bears witness, even evil is, in some ultimate, ungraspable sense, assumed into the fullness that wholly pervades all that is, just as it is. From this point of view, we do not meditate to attain anything that is not wholly given, in and as the way the present moment immediately is. Rather, we meditate that we might realize that the present moment, in its deepest actuality, *is* the perfect manifestation of the mystery we seek. We meditate that we might realize that when we say the word *God* we are alluding to the infinity of the mystery the present moment manifests. And the present moment, just as it is, manifests the mystery we call God.

I encourage you to pause and look deeply into those moments in which your own heart was quickened by the graced awareness of God's surprising nearness. I encourage you to look for the ways in which you, in those moments, fleetingly tasted the fullness of God's presence. And I encourage you to look for the ways in which each passing moment in your life is woven with the threads of glory streaming out from those moments of realized oneness with God. Do not say that no such moments exist for you. For you would not be drawn to read this book if that were so. If you calibrate your awareness to a fine enough scale, you will recognize that utterly ordinary moment of holding a newborn infant, or of looking up into a black sky thick with stars. You will see how in these simple, unassuming moments you were granted a fleeting taste of the divinity of your life. The path ahead entails your willingness not to play the cynic, not to doubt the fullness of the divine presence that you, in your most childlike hour, recognized to be the ever present mystery of your life. The path ahead entails your willingness to open yourself to this ever present mystery, and to remain as open and responsive to it as you can be.

And I, of course, encourage you to continue meditating. For meditation is a way of opening yourself to this direct experience of the undifferentiated fullness of the divine mystery giving itself, whole and complete, in and as each thing that is, just as it is. Imagine that you are sitting in meditation. You have become silent—more silent, in fact, than you have ever been. Each breath, each sound, each thought, each aspect of the moment has become amazingly transparent and open. The last traces of your resistance to God are dissolving. Suddenly you realize, in some deep manner you cannot comprehend, that God is fully present in each thing that is, just as it is. You hear a car going by. What is that sound of the car going by, what is it *really?* You feel a chill in the room. What is that sensation of being chilled? What is it *really?* As you end your meditation and go over to close the window, what is that sound the window makes when you close it? What is it *really?* As you close the window, the question about the true nature of the sound it makes as you close it sends you back into the silent simplicity of meditation. Sitting silent and still in meditation, you silently say with your whole being, "Lord that I might see that my very seeing and all that I see *is* the ungraspable immediacy of your boundless presence."

To begin reflecting on what Saint John of the Cross has to say about the experience of the fullness of God's presence, we can first note the traditional distinction he makes between *substantial union* with God and what he calls *the union of likeness*. By our substantial union with God he is referring to the union in which we are preserved in being by God as our creator. He refers to the union of likeness as "the soul's union with and transformation in God that does not exist, except when there is a likeness of love."[18]

Everything John of the Cross has to say about union with God is understood by him as the art form of learning to be a great lover. For him, love is the way to God, who, in Christ, reveals himself to be the great lover *par excellence*. By following the guidance of the spirit of love within us, we are intimately instructed in how to be great lovers as well. One sign of all great lovers is that they experience the need to free themselves from all that hinders love. Consider, for example, John of the Cross's observation that "it makes little difference whether a bird is tied by a thin thread or by a cord. Even if it be tied by a thread, the bird will be held bound just as surely as if it were tied by a cord . . . as long as it does not break the thread."[19]

In the beginning of our journey we were held by heavy cords of sinful attitudes and behaviors that caused suffering to others and ourselves. As the spiritual journey progresses, the cords unravel to the point of being but slender threads of the illusion that anything less than an infinite union with infinite love will fulfill our hearts. God, in knowing that we do not have the power to break these threads on our own, places us in a dark night. In this purifying night, we learn to rest in a general loving awareness in which the threads of compromised love are finally broken.

The writings of John of the Cross are a good corrective for any notion that meditation can be adequately understood in terms of various methods or theological explanations. You go to meditate. As you sit there, silent and still, the essence of the moment is the mysterious manner in which your heart begins to taste something of a loving desire for God. Equally mysterious is the manner in which you are led, unseen, in a general loving awareness, into the depths of God by a love that melts away the last traces of all that is not God from your heart.

Saint John of the Cross searches for words and images that might effectively convey something of this mysterious process, in which our whole life is transformed in the hidden depths of a love we can neither grasp nor comprehend. At one point Saint John of the Cross depicts Christ as a divine lover who engages us in a game of love. As we go about our day, Christ, like a small, elusive deer, follows us about, peering around corners, waiting until we least expect him to make his move. He dashes out and wounds us with a desire to be one with God, then dashes off, leaving us to fend for ourselves with our love wound of unconsummated longings for God. Then, just when we least expect it, he dashes out and wounds us again. Saint John of the Cross says that the one who is wounding us with love knows where the sorest place in the love wound is. Christ goes right for this very sore place, making it still more deep and sore. Finally we cry out, "Why, since you wounded this heart, don't you heal it? And why, since you stole it from me, do you leave it so, and fail to carry off what you have stolen?"[20]

As we continue on this way, Saint John of the Cross says we come to realize that there is no real choice but to place ourselves in the hands of the one who is wounding us. We come to see that there is no real way forward except to surrender in the night to the love that wounds us with unconsummated longings. As we learn to allow ourselves to be undone by love's relentless ways, a new, previously unknown fullness in love begins to emerge. The night that we at first so dreaded, and in which we struggled to find our way, is now seen as God's tough-love program that takes no prisoners and leaves no trace of anything less than love. Grateful and amazed, we silently cry out, echoing Saint John of the Cross:

> O guiding night!
> O night lovelier than the dawn!
> O night that has united
> The Lover with his beloved.
> Transforming the beloved in her Lover.[21]

John of the Cross says that it is the nature of love not to rest until there is equality in love. Lovers, true to the ways of love, perpetually seek to help each other. The one who is up lifts up the one who is down. It is in taking turns, helping each other in this way, that they find their way into an ever more expansive equality in love. John of the Cross says that God, who is infinite love, keeps lifting us up in love, and will continue to do so until we are equal to him in love. God will have no Sabbath rest until our equality with him in love is realized.

It is in the context of this intimate experience of love dissolving away all that is not love that we come to the fullness of God's presence in our lives. John of the Cross writes:

A soul makes room for God by wiping away all the smudges and smears of [attachment to] creatures. By uniting its will perfectly to God's; for to love is to labor to divest and deprive oneself for God of all that is not God. When this is done the soul will be illumined by and transformed in God. And God will so communicate his supernatural being to the soul that it will appear to be

God himself and will possess what God himself possesses. . . . the soul appears to be God more than a soul.
Indeed it is God by participation. Yet, truly its being
[even though transformed] is naturally as distinct from
God as it was before.[22]

In this union the soul remains the finite creature created by
God, who is the infinite source of its being. And yet in the order
of grace and love, the soul can no longer distinguish itself from
God. In fact, God's love is so great and all-consuming that the
soul itself seems to be more God than a soul.

We will now turn back to *The Cloud of Unknowing* to see
what its anonymous author has to say about the spiritual fulfillment that is realized in the self-transforming journey of meditation and prayer. The anonymous author begins his book in a
manner that helps us to understand spiritual fulfillment by
situating it within the context of the stages of spiritual development that lead up to it. He lays out this developmental understanding in the opening chapter, in which he observes that
Christian life "seems to progress through four ascending stages
of growth, which I have called the common, the special, the
singular and perfect."[23]

The author invites us to look back to see how we have
passed through each of these stages of development in our own
spiritual journey. Beginning with the common way of life, he
writes, "You know yourself that at one time you were caught up
in the common manner of the Christian life in a mundane
existence along with your friends."[24] You are here being invited
to look back to the days when you perhaps attended church
simply because it served certain psychological needs and provided moral norms, void of any substantial sense of personal
religious experience and commitment.

You are then invited to look back to the ways in which a genuine spiritual conversion led you beyond the common way of living the Christian life into a manner of living that the author calls the "special manner of living" the Christian life. He writes:

> But I think that the eternal love of God . . . could not bear to let you go on living so common a life far from him. And so with exquisite kindness [he] awakened desire within you and binding it fast with the leash of love's longing, drew you closer to himself into what I have called the more special manner of living. He called you to be his friend and, in the company of his friends, you learned to live the interior life more perfectly than was possible in the common way.[25]

The anonymous author is inviting you to look back to the days when you lived in the glow of a genuine religious conversion, in which your awareness of God's love for you and your love for God transformed your life in a manner that truly was "special." In this conversion we sought the companionship and support of fellow Christians whose lives were also touched and transformed by God.

He then addresses the transition from the special way of life to the singular by asking, "Is there more?" That is, is there a yet fuller experience of oneness with God than is found in genuine religious fervor and commitment? "Yes," he says,

> for from the beginning I think God's love for you was so great that his heart could not rest satisfied with this. What did he do? Do you not see how gently and kindly he has drawn you on to the third way of life, the Singu-

lar? Yes you live now at the deep solitary core of your being, learning to direct your loving desire toward the highest and final manner of living which I have called the perfect.[26]

The perfect stage of life, he says, differs from the first three in that "the first three [stages of Christian life] may, indeed, be begun and completed in this mortal life, but the fourth, though begun here, shall go on without ending into the joy of eternity." By the *perfect* way of life, the author of *The Cloud of Unknowing* means the way of life lived by the blessed in paradise. Deeper still, he means the life the blessed in paradise live by virtue of their perfect awareness of living God's life, given to them by God as their own everlasting life.

The perfect way of life begins here on this earth, meaning that even on this earth we are living in and by God's sustaining love calling us to perfect union with itself. It is just that there are varying degrees to which we are aware of and responsive to this perfect life on this earth. The perfect way of life wholly permeates common life manner of Christian life, in which men and women live their ordinary daily lives, void of any substantial sense of personal religious experience and commitment. After all, each man and each woman, regardless of his or her degree of spiritual awakening, is living his or her life in God, who calls him or her to union with himself. But the common manner of living the light of divine perfection is filtered through thick layers of possessiveness of heart and unawakened ways of living one's life. In progressing to the special manner of living, one's heart becomes significantly more open to the perfect love of God that sustains us and calls us to itself. But in the special manner of life, one's primary sense of self remains essentially ego based. One's true life is illumined by and rendered translucent to the divine light. But one still tends to go about experiencing oneself as "having" faith, which is still experienced as belonging to the individual ego self one has always known one's self to be.

We enter into the singular life as we begin to experience and respond to a blind stirring of love in the very core of our being. The singular way deepens as we come to realize that something is happening to us, as we realize that we live now at the deep solitary core of our being, learning to direct our loving desire to the highest and final manner of living, which our anonymous author calls the perfect.

As we learn to yield to the blind stirring of love in the core of our being, we are awakened to a startling revelation. We begin to discover that we do not have to wait until we are dead to experience the fullness of God's own life that we are called to experience for all eternity. The catch is that if we, while still on this earth, are to experience this oneness with God that is the joy of the blessed in paradise, we must die to our tendency to identify with anything less than God. This is why we meditate: that we might, breath by breath, learn to live the singular way of life by learning to die to the illusions born of identifying with anything less than God. As this lifelong dying process unfolds, the perfect way of life lived by the blessed in heaven begins to shine through the intimate details of our daily living. The deathless life born of dying to all that is less than God begins to appear in the midst of ordinary living.

In the following passage the anonymous author directly pairs up the realization of the perfect life with the spiritual work of meditation, in which we sit in a single-minded intention to love and be loved by God, stripped of all thoughts and images. He suggests that each time our loving desire begins to be scattered by distracting thoughts, we can renew and gather our loving intention for God alone by silently repeating a single word. He writes:

> If you want to gather all your desire into one simple word that the mind can easily retain, choose a short word rather than a long one. A one syllable word such as "God" or "love" is best. But choose one that is meaningful to you. Then fix it in your mind so that it will remain there come what may. . . . Should some thought go on annoying you answer with this one little word alone.[27]

You go to your place of meditation. You bow and sit in meditative silence. You are not fooling around with methods. You are not stalling. The time for halfhearted measures is over. Your sitting embodies your whole being, now poured out in a single naked intention to love God, whose infinite love is the origin, ground, and fulfillment of your very being. Each time your mind drifts to this or that thought, you silently whisper, "God," or "love," or whatever your word might be. Then, with your naked intention to love God renewed, you rest wordlessly in that intention until the next distracting thought pulls you away into thinking. The realization that you have once again strayed from resting in the naked intent of love brings to your lips the silently whispered word "God" or "love," which once again grounds you in the naked intent of love for God.

The anonymous author then asks:

> Why do you suppose that this little prayer of one syllable is powerful enough to pierce the heavens? It is because it is the prayer of a man's whole being. A man who prays like this prays with all the height and depth and length and breadth of his spirit. His prayer is high, for he prays

in full power of his spirit; it is deep for he has gathered all his understanding into this one little word; it is long for if this feeling could endure he would go on crying out forever as he does now; it is wide because with universal concern he desires for everyone what he desires for himself.[28]

The anonymous author tells us that the transformative power of the word we use in meditation lies in the fact that the word embodies nothing less than the heights, depths, length, and breadth of our whole being, now absorbed in a single, naked desire to be one with God. Then he goes on to say:

It is with this prayer that a person comes to understand with all the saints the length and breadth and height and depth of the eternal, gracious and almighty God as Saint Paul says, not completely of course, but partially and in that obscure manner characteristic of contemplative knowledge. Length speaks of God's eternity. Breadth of his love, height of his power, depth of his wisdom. Little wonder then that when grace so transforms a person to this image and likeness of God, his creator, his prayer is so quickly heard by God.[29]

With artful subtlety the anonymous author first speaks of sitting in meditation, given over to a single desire for God that reveals the length of our spiritual being. By length he means that our desire for God has become so strong and singular that we would, if we could, go on crying out forever with this one word alone. Then, without breaking his stride, he says this length of our spirit "speaks of"—that is, opens out upon—the endless length of God's eternity. And so it is with each dimension of our spiritual nature laid bare in a single burning desire that flows into and merges with God's own nature. So it is that meditation lays bare our true nature, and in doing so lays bare God's nature given to us as our own nature.

We find in *The Cloud of Unknowing* a developmental unfolding of degrees of directly realizing even on earth the perfect life of God given to us as our own true life. The love path laid out by God begins in the common way of life, in which we are surprised by grace and led into the special way of life as one who seeks to follow Christ in all things. And the special way of life ripens into the singular way of life, so called because God alone is sought and surrendered to with such love that God and the soul are experienced as subsisting in a love that never ends. It is this singular way of life that is most transparent and open to the perfect way of life lived by the blessed in paradise. So it is that as we are transformed in this singular way of life, we no longer sense that death will bring about any essential change in the loving oneness that we now experience to be our very life.

This notion that death does not bring about any essential change is no doubt not entirely new to you. After all, our faith assures us that death is the passageway through which we discover the deathless nature of our life in God. Then, too, we are from time to time privileged to glimpse something of this nothingness of death: Imagine that as you are driving alone in your car you pass a cemetery. Suddenly someone you still love very much who has died comes vividly to mind. Right then and there, you and that person visit one another. As you are driving along the road, you experience that mysterious encounter that occurs when we who call ourselves the living realize once again that we are one with those we call the dead. As you continue driving along, it dawns on you that the road you are traveling on is taking you way beyond the corner grocery store. Soon enough you, too, will be what those still left behind will call dead. Only now in this moment of spiritual awakening, the awareness of your own approaching death is not disturbing. Rather, it comes as a source of reassurance, one with the reassurance that comes with seeing the sun that is just now setting, marking the ending of an another day in a life that never ends.

As we continue meditating, the singular life renders our heart more and more habitually transparent to the perfect, deathless life of God. Some years ago I had the opportunity to visit a nun named Jane Marie Richardson, who was at the time living as a hermit in the woods of Kentucky. We were sitting together in her hermitage, having a cup of tea and talking about her experience of living in solitude. She asked me what I thought about the value of keeping a journal. She said she was asking because, in the silence of her hermitage, she wondered what difference it made whether she noted and remembered her passing perceptions and observations. She was not saying it did not matter; rather, in the silence and solitude in which she lived, she wondered in what sense it did matter. Not knowing just what to say, I paused, waiting for words to come that might possibly allow the two of us to go deeper into the question she was asking.

As we sat together in a sustained moment of silence, she said, as if simply sharing what was coming into her mind at the moment, "The other day as I was sitting here in the hermitage, I suddenly realized that when I die nothing will happen. It became clear to me that it makes no real difference whether I am alive or dead." From the vantage point of ego consciousness, it is difficult to sort out just what such a statement might mean. For, after all, from the vantage point of ego consciousness, death is the cataclysmic event that makes *all* the difference, changing everything completely. And yet when she said what she did, neither one of us seemed surprised. It was as if we recognized together something of the deathless nature of a life in which all that is subject to death has simply ceased to be relevant or even real.

One way to understand this mystery better is to reflect on how it is realized in marital love: A woman's husband dies. From the vantage point of ego consciousness, his death absolutely altered his life, and dramatically altered hers as well. In the days, weeks, and months following his death, the gaping hole his absence leaves in her life is as big as a mountain. He is gone. His death has made a huge and painful difference. And yet she knows in her heart that his death has made no difference at all with respect to the depths of love itself, in which she and her husband were, and *still are*, so unexplainably one.

When our lives have been transformed in love, death makes no difference in the ungraspable sense in which we no longer identify with anything except the deathless mystery of love. Our faith tells us that God is the love that never dies, and that we are whom God is eternally loving into being. In meditation we are immersed in this love and transformed in it, to the point of realizing our oneness with the fullness of divine love that never dies. The French neo-Socratic thinker Gabriel Marcel observed that we know we have loved someone when we know we have seen in them that which is too beautiful to die. God sees in us that which is too beautiful to die. Which is to say, God sees in us the totality of herself, poured into us, in creating us as persons in God's image and likeness. As we meditate we learn to see who God sees us to be: all-glorious, and filled with the deathless love that is at once God's reality and our own.

CONTINUING TO BE FAITHFUL TO THIS PATH

The fourth and final question concerning the self-transforming path of meditation concerns how we are to continue being faithful to this path. The remaining chapters of this book will be devoted to an in-depth exploration of meditation practice as our grounding place in our ongoing fidelity to our self-transforming journey into God. Before we begin this in-depth exploration of meditation, we will first reflect on the ways in which the rich and seminal theme of entering the mind of Christ conveys the essence of the Christian tradition of meditation and the fulfillment in God to which it leads.

CHAPTER 7

Entering the Mind of Christ

S aint Paul writes in his Letter to the Philippians, "In your minds you must be the same as Christ Jesus"(Phil. 2:5). We become the same as Christ Jesus in our minds through a lifelong process of conversion in which Christ's mind and our mind become one mind, one way of seeing and being in the world. The faithful practice of meditation is a way of learning to follow the spirit's prompting in being led along this self-transforming path into the mind of Christ. Let us then explore the ways in which we enter Christ's mind in meditation. Such an inquiry will take us into the innermost recesses of Christian faith. These inner recesses consist of neither beliefs nor institutional structures, but rather a self-transforming journey into the vibrant center of reality itself. As our inquiry unfolds, a portrait of Christ will emerge in which we can recognize our own true face as one destined by God to be one with God forever.

NONDUAL ONENESS WITH GOD

The first aspect of the mind of Christ we will explore here is that of nondual oneness with God. By this I mean a state of mind in which we realize we are so one with God that God is no longer experienced as being other than ourselves. We will reflect on this aspect of the mind of Christ, first as it was manifested by Christ in the Gospels and then as it is manifested in us in meditation.

At the Last Supper, one of the disciples, Philip, boldly requests of Jesus, "Show us the Father and it will be enough" (John 14:8). He is saying, in effect: let us see God and we will not grumble. One would hope that in seeing God there would be little left to complain about. For in seeing God nothing would be missing. Everything would be complete. Our ultimate fulfillment as persons created in the image and likeness of God would be realized.

Our faith tells us that after death we shall see God "as He is" (1 John 3:2). We will know God, even as God eternally knows us. But here is Philip, representing the seeker in each of us, having supper with Jesus, asking to see God during supper. There is a present-moment immediacy to Philip's request. Let us see God now, he says, during the intimacy of this meal, and we will not need dessert. We will not need anything. For the God-given desire for God that burns in our hearts will be fulfilled.

The boldness of Philip's request is surpassed by the boldness of Jesus, who responds to Philip by saying, "He who has seen Me has seen the Father" (John 14:9) Jesus tells Philip that without even realizing it, his request to see God is already being granted. For Jesus realizes that in seeing him Philip *is* seeing God. Philip's request is couched in dualistic terms, in which he is asking to see the divine mystery as something not yet seen. Jesus responds in nondualistic terms, characteristic of one who realizes that the vision of the divine that Philip is asking for is already occurring.

When we meditate, we pass beyond the dualistic understanding of Philip so as to enter into the nondual consciousness of Christ. As we sit, silent and still, we become as open and receptive as we can be to the life-changing realization that the oneness with God we seek is already occurring, in and as our simply being who we simply are.

I do not have the power to explain how this happens. What I can do is invite you to reflect on what actually happens as meditative awareness begins to awaken within you. If the moment of awakening occurs as you are reading the Scriptures, you might leave the Scriptures open to the passage that prompted your heart to rest silently in God's presence. But as your silent, meditative resting in God's presence deepens, the passage becomes, as it were, a fissure in the rocks, granting access into the depths of realized oneness with God that is at once Christ's life and your own.

There is nothing fancy about it. You are simply resting in a state of attentive openness to God. Look and see how in this moment you are thinking nothing. It is not that no thoughts are arising in your mind. But, as Saint John of the Cross put it, you are not inclined to intentionally focus on any of the thoughts that may be passing through your mind. As you settle into this meditative openness, the thinking self that experiences itself to be other than God falls into the background, as a nonthinking, meditative self, one with God, begins to emerge. What is true of thoughts also holds true with memories, desires, and bodily sensations. Meditative awareness simultaneously beholds and transcends all aspects of the ego self in its perceived otherness from God.

Notice, too, that as meditative awareness deepens, you are less and less inclined to claim some higher ground from which to sit in judgment on anything. As you sit in meditative awareness, you might notice ego-based stirrings prompting you to lay claim to whatever heightened spiritual awareness you may be experiencing. But insofar as you are grounded in meditative awareness, you do not claim for yourself anything you may be experiencing. In opening your hands to show someone what you have acquired in meditative awareness, your hands are empty. In searching for the credentials that meditative awareness has bestowed on you, you find yourself to be without credentials. You are left poor, empty, and with nothing to stand on. You are left in that vulnerable openness to God that is free of relying on or identifying with anything less than God.

As you pass in meditative silence beyond the frontiers of thought, memory, and all ego-based modes of being, the curtain of perceived otherness from God is lifted. The oneness with God that is your very reality and the reality of all that is real is realized. Now look very closely at those moments in which you have rested, even to some degree, in this childlike openness to God. Is it not so that the more simple and heartfelt such moments become, the truer it is that you cannot find a place at which you leave off and God begins? Nor can you find the place where God leaves off and you begin. Nor are you even inclined to try. For such efforts would seem odd and out of place in these moments in which you are drawn simply to rest, like an unlearned child, like a lover in the beloved's arms, in this never-ending oneness with God.

If a fellow seeker were to approach you, as Philip did Jesus, in this moment and ask to see God, you would not be so foolish to think or suggest that you *are* God. For, if anything, your experience of oneness with God has made you keenly aware of your absolute nothingness without God. It is just that in fidelity to the oneness with God to which you have been awakened, you would not be so foolish to think or suggest that God is in any way dualistically other than the sheer miracle of your presence in the present moment. For in the oneness to which you have been granted access, all the ego's perceptions of being dualistically other than God have been transcended in an intimate realization of a simple oneness with God, in which no otherness whatsoever can be found.

It is in this intimate and mysterious manner that you know the request of your fellow seeker coming to you asking to see God, is already being granted in seeing in you one who has been graced by that simplicity in which everything but oneness with God has fallen away. You realize that this meditatively realized oneness with God that you have been privileged to experience is your true nature and the true nature of everyone, including the one who is now before you, asking to see God. You see, too, that their tendency and yours not to see this oneness with God is the source of all sorrow. You recognize this sorrow to be the sorrow Christ came to deliver us from, by inviting us to enter into his mind of nondual oneness with God. In this Christ consciousness, sorrow has no foundations, and only the endless bliss of God remains.

TRINITARIAN MYSTICISM

When Jesus disclosed to Philip his nondual oneness with the Father, he went on to say, "And I will ask the Father, and he will give you another Helper, that he may be with you forever: that is the Spirit of truth whom the world cannot receive, because it does not behold Him or know Him, but you know Him, because He abides with you and will be in you" (John 14: 16–17). The early Christians' prayerful reflections on these and similar teachings of Jesus led to an understanding of God as a loving Father whose living Word had become flesh in our midst, and whose indwelling Spirit inspires and guides us in our daily life. This uniquely Christian way of understanding God merged with Greek thought to form the Christian belief that God is infinitely simple and one, while at the same time being a trinity of Father, Son, and Holy Spirit.

The Christian understanding of God as trinity was already developing in the Christian community by the time the fifth-century bishop Saint Augustine wrote his classic work on the Trinity. But it was the genius of Augustine's religious imagination that forged one of the most compelling and elegant visions of God as Trinity.

There is a story about Saint Augustine writing about the Trinity. As the story goes, Augustine had become bogged down in his efforts to put into words just how God could be perfectly one God yet three divine persons. In fact, his dilemma was deeper than this. He realized he could not conceptually comprehend the *actual mystery* of God as one God in three divine persons. Augustine was walking alone one day along the beach, absorbed in the incomprehensible nature of his subject matter. He stopped and watched a child playing at the water's edge. The child was first going down to the water, bending down to fill a spoon with water. The child would then walk back onto the beach, being very careful not to spill any of the water, and would pour the water into a small hole in the sand. Augustine watched as the child carefully repeated this maneuver many times. Finally, Augustine approached the child and inquired what she was doing. The child said she was trying to put the ocean into that little hole in the sand. Augustine laughed and told her she would never be able to do it. The child laughed and said, "Neither will you get the mystery of the Trinity into your mind." At which point the child vanished into thin air!

In that precise moment Augustine found himself where the mystics found themselves in their prayerful reflections on the Trinity. The paradoxical nature of one God in three divine persons creates an impasse beyond which the conceptual mind cannot go. As the mind stays with this impasse, the meltdown of conceptual thinking liberates a meditative awareness of oneness with God. Suddenly, we find ourselves immersed in the divine mystery we cannot conceptually comprehend! It is not that Augustine's theological formulations are not lucid and profound thoughts that can be studied and appreciated in their own right. Rather, that no matter how lucid, the mind cannot grasp the mystery of the Trinity any more than that little girl could have managed to get the ocean into that hole on the beach.

The Christian mystics naturally gravitated toward the Trinity in their efforts to express the inexpressible mystery of God they were privileged to experience. They saw the Trinity not as a dry, abstract doctrine, but as the Christian love poetry of the divine mystery, in the face of which all words prove to be poor translations of what remains ultimately ineffable and hidden in silence. To cite but two of countless examples of the Christian mystics using Trinitarian language, note first the following passage, in the writings of the thirteenth-century German mystic Mechtilde of Magdeburg:

Lord, heavenly Father, you are my heart.
Lord Jesus Christ, you are my body.
Lord Holy Spirit, you are my breath.
Lord, Holy Trinity, you are my only refuge
    and my eternal rest.[1]

And listen to the thirteenth-century Flemish mystic Jan van Ruusbroec's use of Trinitarian language in expressing the non-dual oneness with God realized in contemplation:

> All enlightened spirits are raised above themselves into a modeless state of blissful enjoyment which overflows whatever fullness any creature has ever received or ever could receive. There all exalted spirits are, in their super-essential being, one enjoyment and one beatitude with God, without difference. This is what Christ desired when he prayed to his heavenly Father that all his beloved might be made perfectly one, even as he is one with the Father in blissful enjoyment through the Holy Spirit. . . . I consider this the most loving prayer which Christ ever prayed for our salvation.[2]

A Trinitarian understanding of the mind of Christ brings us into a realization of God's own divine life. To see how this is so, we must pay careful attention to the fact the persons of the Trinity are in no way whatsoever three separate individuals, each with its relationship to God and the other two persons of the Trinity. Any notion of even the slightest degree of separation or otherness among the persons of the Trinity violates the infinite simplicity of God's oneness. Being a person is then something infinitely richer than being an individual. Being a person means being, not someone *with* a relationship *to* God, but rather being a divine relation that wholly manifests and is God.

This is where the conceptual mind begins to experience its meltdown. We can grasp easily enough what it is to be an individual with a relationship to God. Indeed, this is how we experience ourselves. But to grasp what it means to say that the persons of the Trinity are not individuals with a relationship to

God, but are rather divine relations, each distinct, yet wholly and completely God is poetic language we have to silently sit with as a way of opening our mind and heart to the Christian tradition's understanding of the mystery of God.

Let us then see what meditating together on the persons of the Trinity reveals to us about the endless richness of all that entering mind of Christ implies and alludes to. Our Trinitarian meditation begins with the *divine nature*, as referring to the utter mystery of God as transcending all that can be known or expressed in any way whatsoever. To begin here is to begin on our knees, filled with awe in the presence of the infinite, ugraspable mystery of Reality Itself. To begin with the divine nature is to begin where liturgy becomes worship and where meditation becomes an awe-filled and endless silence. To begin here is to begin where monasteries firmly place their cornerstone. It is to begin where all reality has its endlessness and mysterious origins, and where all reality, including ourselves, finds its equally mysterious and endless end.

The hidden mystery of the divine nature is eternally expressing itself or manifesting itself as divine relations of knowledge and love, that Jesus reveals to us as Father, Son, and Holy Spirit. God the Father is God as origin. From the Father flows the Son. Sometimes it is said that God the Father is God as knowing and God the Son is God as known. That is, that God the Father eternally knows himself, and the Son is who the Father eternally knows himself to be, as the Wisdom of the Father. The tradition also refers to God the Father, eternally speaking himself or expressing himself, in which case the Son is called the Father's Logos, his living Word. Sometimes it is said that the Father, eternally expressing himself in his Word, eternally contemplates himself in the Word. And so the eternal origin of contemplation lies hidden in God's own eternal life. The tradition says the infinite knowledge of the Father and the Son, as one, generates an infinite love that is the Holy Spirit. Sometimes it is said the Holy Spirit is the fullness of the oneness of the Father and Son. This paradoxical language of one God in three distinct persons is the Christian love poetry of the divine.

One startling consequence of this Christian love poetry of the divine mystery is that if we were to try to find the person of Christ the Word as someone who *has* a relationship *with* the Father, we would search in vain. For there is no divine person of the Word who is in any way whatsoever less or other than all the Father is. There is no Christ the Word who *has* a relationship *with* the Father. There is only that relationship of perfect oneness that is God's living Word.

In this same manner, there is no God the Father who is in any way whatsoever more than or other than all the Son is. For the Father expresses and gives himself wholly and completely as his Word. In expressing and giving himself as the Word, the Father holds nothing of himself in reserve that is not wholly given and expressed as all the person of the Word is.

And what is true of the Father and the Son is true of the Holy Spirit. The Holy Spirit is not someone *with* a relationship to the Father and the Son. Rather, the Holy Spirit *is* the perfect love that arises from the perfect knowledge of the Father and the Son. There is, then, no Holy Spirit who is in any way whatsoever other than all the Father and the Son eternally are.

The Gospel according to John begins this way:

In the beginning was the Word;
The Word was with God
And the Word was God.
He was with God in the beginning,
Through him all things came to be,

Not one thing has its being but through him.
All that came to be had life in him
And . . . the Word was made flesh.
He lived among us,
And we saw his glory,
The glory that is his as the only Son of the Father.
(John 1:1–14)

This passage, read in the light of the believing community's understanding of the Trinity, provides an expanded and enriched way of understanding Christ's words to Philip: "He who sees me sees the Father." Jesus can be understood as telling Philip something truly extraordinary. He is saying, "In seeing me you are seeing the Father's self-expression made flesh before your very eyes." In yielding to the mystery that was revealed to him in this moment, Philip entered the mind of Christ. Philip realized himself to be enveloped in the nondual oneness with God that must have constituted the aura of mystery and grace of that moment. When we sit in meditation we sit with Philip. We enter the mind of Christ in entering into that oneness with God that is at once Christ's life and our own. Immersed in this oneness, we know that anyone who would look for us as someone dualistically other than God would search in vain.

BEING A CREATED PERSON

We can go on to explore entering the mind of Christ as alluding to a deeper understanding and experience of ourselves as persons, created by the Father through Christ the Word. When God created you, God did not have to think up who you might be. God the Father, eternally contemplating you in Christ the Word, eternally knows who you eternally are and are called to be from before the origins of the universe. As Saint Paul says, "Your life is hidden with Christ in God" (Col. 3:3).

Who God the Father eternally contemplates you to be in Christ the Word is who you are before you were ever born. This is the unborn you that never began, for there was never a point prior to which God did not eternally know you in Christ the Word through whom all things are made. The infinite simplicity of God admits no division. In this poetic meditation on your true self before you were born is a meditation on you in God as God, in no way other or less than all that God is.

In creating you as a person, God the Father wills into being who he eternally knows you to be in Christ the Word. God utters his fiat of creation, his "let it be" that brings you into being, giving you a nature. There are angels, who are created persons with an angelic nature, and human beings, who are created persons with a human nature. In your human nature you are a finite creature of God endowed with the capacity to know and to love. Why? So that you might, through your human nature, come to know God by learning to love God and to give yourself back to God, who is the origin, ground, and fulfillment of your life as a person created by God the Father through Christ the Word.

Moments of spontaneous meditative experience can be understood as flash points of awareness as the person we are breaks forth into human consciousness. Suddenly, we realize a oneness with God that we intuitively recognize to be at once God's identity and our own. In moments of meditative awakening we obscurely sense that who we are and who God is is, in some inscrutable manner, one mystery. Sustained in this awareness, we realize that if we were to try to find ourselves as someone other than God, we would search in vain. If we were to search for God as other than ourselves, our search would be equally futile. For we realize that God is given to us, wholly and completely, in a oneness that is at once all that God is and all that we really are. We are not God. But we are not other than God, either. We as persons are who God eternally knows us to be in his infinite knowing of his infinite actuality. And in this paradoxical truth lies the essence of what it means to be a human being destined for eternal oneness with God.

Our moments of spontaneous meditative experience can be understood in this context as moments of fleetingly awakening to our unborn self "hidden with Christ in God" (Gal. 3:3). To sit in meditation is to sit, silent and still, open to the unborn mystery of Christ, the Word given to us by God as our own true self. Entering the mind of Christ, in this context, means to awaken to this oneness with God that is at once all that God is and all that we really are. Meditation practice is a way of opening ourselves to this graced realization of this oneness with God that is the very person that we are. To meditate is an act of our human nature. By this I mean, in part at least, that meditation is an act of our human will. In meditation we freely choose to be the person we eternally are and are called to be. To meditate is to enter the mind of Christ in freely choosing to realize our oneness with the Christ the Word's oneness with the Father.

We are now at the axis around which all the mystics revolve in quiet unison as each seeks, in his or her own way, to express the paradoxical mystery of our being finite creatures of God who, as persons, are called to awaken to our eternal oneness with God.

In the passage cited earlier we saw that when Ruusbroec reflects on Christ's prayer for his disciples that they might be one "even as we are one," he puts the emphasis on Christ's little phrase "even as." For to be one with God, even *as* the Son is one with the Father, is to be infinitely, perfectly one with the

Father. It is in realizing this oneness, Ruusbroec says, that "all enlightened spirits are there raised above themselves into a modeless state of blissful enjoyment, which overflows whatever fullness any creature has ever received or ever could receive." In saying this, Ruusbroec is affirming a state of oneness with God that is *above and beyond* anything we as creatures can experience. Ruusbroec affirms that we are and remain finite creatures, infinitely less than God, and yet we enter one enjoyment and one beatitude with God *without difference*.

Meister Eckhart is the boldest of the mystics in speaking of this uncreated ground of all created persons that we are awakened to in meditative experience. Eckhart speaks of the Father as eternally giving birth to all that he is as Christ the Word. And in one continuous act of birthing, God the Father is eternally giving birth to that in us that is as fully God as the Son. Eckhart writes:

> The Father gives birth to His Son in the soul in the very same way as he gives birth to him in eternity, and no differently. He must do it whether he likes it or not. The Father begets His Son unceasingly, and furthermore, I say he begets me as His son and as the same son. I say even more; not only does he beget me as his son, but he begets me as himself and Himself as me, and me as his being, and His nature. . . . All that God works is one; therefore He begets me as his son without any difference.[3]

Eckhart is not calling into question the Christian belief in ourselves as finite creatures of an infinite God. Rather, he is using the Trinitarian language of his Christian faith to put words to an experience of nondual oneness with God. Lovers say to each other, "We are one." They know that their words are true at a level that transcends, yet leaves intact, the level at which they remain distinctly two people who are quite clearly other than each other. So too with Eckhart, who, while respecting our status as finite creatures of God, turns to Trinitarian language to express an understanding of the generosity of God. Eckhart says that God is so generous to us that he pours himself out and gives himself to us as wholly and completely as he pours himself and gives himself to the Son. As Eckhart expresses it, "Everything scripture says of the Christ is entirely true of every good and holy man."

Thomas Merton speaks in this same manner:

The Father is a Holy Spirit, but he is named Father. The Son is a Holy Spirit, but he is named Son. The Holy Spirit has a name known only to the Father and the Son. But can it be that when He takes us to himself, and unites us to the Father through the Son, He takes upon himself, in us, our own secret name? Is it possible that we come to know, for ourselves, the name of the Holy Spirit when we receive from Him the revelation of our own identity in Him? I can ask these questions but I cannot answer them.[4]

We could go on and on with this chorus of mystic voices. But enough has been said to make the point: We are not God. And yet we are not other than God, either. To enter the mind of Christ is to enter into this paradox of nondual oneness with God in which we remain finite creatures of God called to awaken to our eternal oneness with God.

BEING HUMAN

Scripture says that "the Word became flesh." Christ, the divine person in whom our personhood and our human nature subsist, took on our human nature. Entering the mind of Christ means to enter into God's own oneness with himself in the persons of the Trinity. And entering the mind of Christ means to enter into God's oneness with us as flesh-and-blood human beings.

Jesus was a human being. He woke up in the morning and got out of bed. He went to the bathroom, washed up, had something to eat, and got ready for his day. He stood up and sat down. He inhaled and exhaled. His beating heart sent his blood coursing through his veins. He saw and heard and smelled and tasted and felt what went on around him. If, while walking down a road with his disciples, one of his sandals became unfastened, everyone had to stop while he bent down in the road to fasten it. On hot days he was hot, and on cold nights he felt cold. As each day ended he got sleepy. He would say goodnight, get into bed, and go to sleep. He dreamed dreams. And the next morning he woke up one more time to all the things he and we do as human beings.

You get the feeling when reading the Gospels that when Jesus looked you in the eye it was vividly clear that you were in the presence of a very present, flesh-and-blood human being. To hang out with him, spend time with him, left no doubt that here was a clear-minded human being filled with love and a deep faith in the radical nearness and mystery of God in the day-by-day realities of being human.

You get the impression that Jesus was fully human from the ground up. He did not live out of his head. It was not mere ideas that he espoused, but deeply realized, deeply lived truths of what it means to be a fully alive human being. Saint Irenaeus said, "The glory of God is the human person fully alive." We see the glory of God in the fully alive human person of Jesus. And in this way we, in seeing Jesus, see the glory of the flesh-and-blood human being we simply are and are called to be.

When we meditate, we enter the mind of Christ from the ground up. We do not bypass our breathing. Rather, we sit and listen and settle into the mystery of breathing. We listen to our breathing, which has its hidden, uncreated origins in the Father's eternal contemplation of breathing in Christ the Word. When we sit still, we do not bypass the concrete immediacy of our bodily being. Rather, in sitting still we settle into the mystery of our bodily being that God the Father eternally contemplates in Christ the Word. When we meditate, we do not bypass our feelings. Rather, we settle into the mystery of all our feelings, as having their hidden, uncreated origins in the Father's eternal contemplation of our feelings in Christ the Word. When we sit in meditation, we neither continue thinking nor abandon thought. Rather, we sit, quiet and still, in deepening meditative awareness of the uncreated origins of the Father's eternal contemplation of thought in Christ the Word. Sitting in this way, we do not fly off into some eternal realm. Rather, we enter into the mind of Christ, which knows and is the divine generosity of the concrete immediacy of ourselves just as we are.

There are not two minds of Christ, one human and the other divine. Rather, the mind of Christ is the realized oneness of the divine and all that we are as human beings. Who we are in Christ is in no way reducible to our everyday, ordinary self. Nor is who we are in Christ in any way dualistically other than our ordinary self.

Sometimes we might get the impression that we are meditating to open ourselves to some kind of extraordinary experience beyond what we are accustomed to in our day-by-day life. And there is some truth to this. From the vantage point of relative consciousness of relative reality, there are incremental degrees of spiritual awakening to oneness with God beyond ordinary experience. But as the spiritual journey continues to deepen, it comes full circle back to where we started. We get up in the morning and touch our feet to the floor. And we know that this ordinary experience of this utterly ordinary event is the mystery of oneness with God manifesting itself in and as this very ordinariness. This is why we sit in meditation: so that we might settle into this ordinary mind; so that in becoming, at last, just ourselves, we might realize our eternal oneness with God. This ordinary mind, one with God, comes as an inarticulate certainty in the pit of the stomach. It comes as the kind of clarity characteristic of turning to see something beautiful and sensing immediately that it is beautiful. To enter the mind of Christ is to enter into the ordinary human awareness that God eternally contemplates in Christ the Word. To enter the mind of Christ is to enter into the ordinary human mind that God loves into being as your very ordinary awareness.

OTHERS

In speaking of himself as coming in glory at the end of time, Christ says that he will say to us, "I was hungry and you gave me to eat. I was thirsty and you gave me to drink; I was a stranger and you invited me in. . . ." We will ask when we did these things for him. And he will answer, "Truly I say to you that when you did it to one of these brothers of mine, even the least of them, you did it to me" (Matt. 25:35–37). Jesus taught that he was so one with others that what we do to others, we do to him. He taught that, just as he was one with everyone, so, too, we are one with everyone and are to give witness to this oneness by our love for everyone.

It is of course easier for us to sense our oneness with those we love. And it is easier to love those who love us and who are like us by virtue of such things as religion and ethnic background. Entering the mind of Christ certainly includes appreciating and honoring these and other ways in which we human beings recognize and express our loving awareness of our oneness with others. But just as clearly, entering the mind of Christ carries us beyond these ego-based modes of social awareness.

To enter the mind of Christ is to realize our oneness with the faces we see on television in the evening news. It is to realize we are one with that homeless person we saw going through the trash receptacle. The woman at the local market, the man who comes to check our gas meter, and all who have hurt us, abandoned us, and have otherwise wronged us, along with all the women and men we have never met—we are to realize that we are equally, fully one with every blessed one of them. We are to give witness to this awareness by our love for our fellow human beings. And we are to put this love into action by the ways in which we treat others, and by what we are willing to do for them as expressions of our love for them.

What comes through in the Gospels is that Jesus was someone to reckon with. There was a no-nonsense, straight-from-the-shoulder truthfulness about the way he related to others. He was not always necessarily nice. Jesus never said, "Blessed are the nice." But Jesus was always loving to the core, and in being so he gave witness to our lifelong journey of learning to be loving to the core as well. The act of entering the mind of Christ in our relationships with others is not pretending that real hurts and wrongdoings do not need to be acknowledged and dealt with. Entering the mind of Christ is not a premature, proclaimed love that merely clamps a lid on unacknowledged anger and hurt. It is not writing everyone a blank check of boundless love that pretends we are something we are not. It is rather learning day by day to be transformed in all that love is asking of us in learning to be a truly awake, Christlike human being. A lifetime of loving and being loved by those we love can go a long way toward softening the heart and bringing us into the richness and wisdom of what all life is about. On an ever grander and far more enriching scale, a lifetime of recognizing and yielding to a Christlike love for all men and women as our brothers and sisters and as children of God enlarges the heart to divine proportions.

When we meditate, we enter the mind of Christ by entering into meditative states of awareness of all that we hold in common as human beings. We sit, silent and still, and learn the intimate texture of thoughts, feelings, memories, and bodily sensations that all of us as human beings experience. In doing so we drop down into levels of oneness with others that transcends the differences between us. I am not you. But if I have intimately tasted my own aloneness, my own experience of thoughts arising and passing through my mind, my own breathing—then I already have in my intimate awareness of myself an intimate awareness of you.

This knowledge is not that of the words written on the pages of my mind; rather, it is a knowledge of the human experience of the mind itself. The experience is not simply my personal feelings about this or that. It is rather the intimate understanding of the texture of my own heart as feelings play across its surface, flow through it, and alter its state from one moment to the next. Grounded in this self-knowledge, I am grounded in awareness of oneness with you at a level that precedes and transcends the differences between us. I know you with an empathic, heartfelt knowledge of what it means to be a human being.

It takes time, but little by little we enter the social dimensions of the mind of Christ in awakening to how perfectly one we are with everyone living and dead. As this awareness slowly seeps in, we are able to grow, day by day, into a more patient, gracious recognition and acceptance of and gratitude for others. Little by little the graciousness of Christ's empathic mind of oneness with others is translated into a thousand little shifts in the way we think about people, our attitudes toward them, and the way in which we actually treat them day by day.

There is a strong bond between the mystical traditions of the church and serving the poor and those in need. Many of the great mystics demonstrated an extraordinary sensitivity to the suffering of others. Whether we are being inspired by a story about Saint Francis kissing a leper or by seeing how, in our own day, Mother Teresa of Calcutta spent her life serving the poorest of the poor, we are being inspired by the mind of Christ that flows from deep prayerful oneness with God. Inspired in this way, we are moved to act, to see what Christ might be calling us to do to help those around us.

SIN

There is a story in John's Gospel about a woman who was about to be stoned to death for being caught in adultery. Jesus tells the crowd, "Let the one who is without sin cast the first stone." As it turned out, not a single stone was thrown. Instead, each of the woman's accusers lets the stone drop to the ground as they walk away, one by one. When Jesus and the woman are together, with no one else around, Jesus asks, "Woman, where are they? Did no one condemn you?" She answers, "No one, Lord."

Jesus says to her, "Neither do I condemn you, go your way; from now on sin no more" (John 8:3–11).

This story embodies three aspects of the mind of Christ with respect to sin. The first is that Christ knew the stuff the heart is made of. He knew that anyone who is quick to punish sin in another is not without sin. To enter the mind of Christ is to know that even if all humanity would have been present at this scene, there still would not have been a single stone thrown that day. If we understand sin to mean our communal propensity to be unloving toward others and ourselves, then sin is woven into our hearts as human beings. To enter the mind of Christ is to recognize, enter into, and learn to understand this deep truth about ourselves.

As helpful and clarifying as it might be to be reminded of our common propensity to hurt ourselves and others, the story goes on to show that the mind of Christ embodies the moral imperative to "go and sin no more." To enter the mind of Christ is to become aware of our wayward heart as one motivated to repent of the sins of the past and to be committed to doing our best to sin no more in the future.

Meditation provides a vantage point from which we can observe at close range both of these aspects of the mind of Christ with respect to sin. The very simplicity of the intention to sit silent and still, neither clinging to nor rejecting anything, sets up a situation in which we discover inherent weaknesses in our inability to be simply present in the present moment. As we sit in meditation, we can watch our wayward heart in action as we wander off into this or that distraction. And the things the mind wanders off into are, at times, embarrassing. Meditation is a way of entering the mind of Christ by entering into a direct awareness of the wayward nature of our own heart.

Meditation also provides a way of entering the mind of

Christ by responding to his call to go and sin no more. In meditation we respond to this call at the most rudimentary level. For in meditation we respond to the call to repent of our indifference to our own estrangement from our deepest self, one with God. Each time we recognize that we have once again drifted off into this or that distraction, we simply renew our entrance into the mind of Christ by renewing our efforts to be present, open, and awake in the present moment in which we find ourselves. In this virginal awareness, a life free from sin is already under way. For I doubt very much if we would do all the things we do to abandon and hurt ourselves and others if we lived in perpetual intimate awareness of our preciousness as persons subsisting in the love that is our very life.

But the real crescendo of the story of the woman caught in adultery lies in Jesus's words "Neither do I condemn you." Scripture says that Christ was like us in all ways except sin (Heb. 4:15). Sin, we might say, negates the complete likeness between the way we are human and the way Christ was human. We are subject to sin and Christ was not. Big difference in the midst of so much likeness! But the essential thrust of who Jesus is as the Christ lies precisely in Jesus's response to this difference. For Jesus proclaims the difference to be irrelevant.

Sin negates the complete likeness between ourselves and Christ, but then Christ negates the negation by identifying with us as precious in all our wayward ways. What is more, Christ is always heading right toward the most sinful and shame-based place within us. He does not gravitate there to condemn us. Nor does he go there simply to invite us to shape up and change our ways. Rather, Christ goes there to break our heart wide open by revealing to us the mystery of the cross. In the mystery of the cross, Christ most radically reveals that we are totally loved in the very midst of all our sinful ways. This is

God's favorite thing: lying in wait for us to finally see and accept that which is most broken and lost within ourselves, so that we might see how invincibly loved and whole we are in this midst of our very brokenness.

Meditation opens up the clearing in which this blessed event of redemption happens time and time again. We sit silent and still, focusing on our efforts to be as present as we can be. Sometimes it goes fairly well. Sometimes it is a shipwreck. Sometimes we are consoled more deeply than we ever thought possible. Sometimes we are bereft of even the slightest hint that God loves us at all or even knows or cares about our sense of being so exiled from any sense of God's presence.

We go on with all these ups and downs that meditating day by day is made of. Then, perhaps in the midst of great sleepiness, perhaps in the midst of a tender touch of God's presence, perhaps in the midst of apparent indifference, everything drops out from beneath us, like the floor in a burning building. The roof caves in. There is nowhere to stand, save in the realization of being so absolutely loved and one with love as to render all that is not love irrelevant and essentially unreal. What seemed to matter just a moment before now seems simply not to matter. For we realize our heart is melting and is being washed away in the depths of a love in which nothing but love can be found. Tears might come. We might smile or burst out laughing. Or we might simply sit, breathing in a breath we know to be nothing but the love that is at once all that God is and all that we really are. We sit in the wordless wonder of realizing that God can no longer find the place where we stop and God begins. Nor can God find the place where God stops and we begin. Nor is God inclined to try to do so. For his child has come home.

The author Flannery O'Connor shares with us a vision of all humanity at the end of the world. All the lost, the broken, the forgotten, all the hardened sinners and the world's biggest fools are laughing and turning somersaults as they jubilantly lead all humanity into paradise. They are being followed by the righteous, who are concerned whether or not they are singing on key. When we meditate, our ego self does its best to sing on key by being as present, open, and awake as we can be. But then we discover that our self-monitoring self and the self that it is monitoring are being led by the folly of our own broken heart, won over by the love that is leading it through the wide-open gates into God. This folly is that of the cross, on which all the suffering dies away, leaving nothing but Christ—which is to say ourselves, one with God forever.

This lovefest goes best when nothing at all extraordinary happens. When you are simply sitting, simply being who you simply are. The clock chimes the hour, and everything, in all its utter ordinariness, is realized to be God, being poured out with infinite abandon in and as this blessed, never-ending ordinariness.

When Jesus sat around the fire at night with the disciples, talking about this and that, he no doubt at times simply listened to them talking among themselves. As he stirred the fire with a stick, he perhaps saw a single spark fleetingly fly upward into the night. Later, lying there, listening to their breathing as they slept, he heard in their breathing the love he knew himself to be. It is like that sometimes with us. In meditation, in daily life, we realize that we and everyone in the world, and everything in it, are manifesting the love our very life embodies. In this realization we enter the mind of Christ without going anywhere. We simply awaken to who we have always been from before the origins of the universe.

THE WORLD OF THINGS

The Gospel according to John says,

> *In the beginning was the Word;*
> *The Word was with God*
> *And the Word was God.*
> *He was with God in the beginning,*
> *Through him all things came to be,*
> *Not one thing has its being but through him.*
> *(John 1:1-14)*

From all eternity God the Father eternally contemplates, in Christ the Word, the eternal possibility of the world and all things in it. When God created water, God did not have to think up what water might be. God eternally knows what water eternally is, in Christ the Word, through whom all things are made.

This is why we can meditate on water. This is why we can sit at the water's edge, knowing that we can never exhaust the divinity that is manifested there. This is why we can meditate on a tree or a single flower, or walk in a forest or sit in the mountains, or look at the stars at night, and know that, in some mysterious way, we are looking into the face of God.

Saint Francis of Assisi talked to the sun, addressing it with affection and respect as Brother Sun. He spoke to the moon, speaking to it with loving respect, calling it Sister Moon. On one occasion he gave a sermon to the birds. It is said the birds in attendance listened attentively. On another occasion Francis had a heart-to-heart talk with a wolf that was troubling a local village. As a result, the wolf no longer bothered the residents of that town. It is said of Saint Columban that he died outdoors resting peacefully. When he died, a horse came over and put its head in Columban's lap and wept! There are a lot of stories like these about the saints. At one level these accounts may seem quaint, even naïve. But at another they speak in mythic language about a great and simple truth: to enter the mind of Christ is to awaken to the incomprehensible stature of simple things as eternally subsisting in the mind of Christ, the second person of the Trinity, in whom all things are made.

Carl Jung, in an essay on aging, asks how we can claim that the years have taught us anything if we have not learned to sit and listen to the secret that whispers in the brooks. The secret is the sound God eternally knows running brooks to make in Christ the Word. And so it is with fire, and stones and trees, and the way moss grows on fallen logs, and the smell that fields have after a rain. To enter the mind of Christ is to realize that the things of the earth are the things of God, in whom all things have their being.

Meister Eckhart had a clear and profound sense of reality having its reality in God. He wrote:

> God gives to all things equally; as they flow from God they are all equal. Indeed, angels and men and creatures are equal in their primitive emanation, by which they flow from God. Someone who would get hold of things in their primitive emanation would get hold of them as they are equal. If they are equal in time they are still more so in eternity, in God. If we take a fly, in God, it is more noble than the highest angel is in itself. This is how all things are equal in God and are God himself.[5]

It is in a state of meditative openness that we get hold of things in their primitive emanation as they flow directly from

God. In this openness we contemplate each thing as it is eternally contemplated by the Father in Christ the Word. We sit in meditation, silent and still, so that we might enter into that state of meditative openness in which we might begin to hear, in something as commonplace as the sound of a fly buzzing in the window, something as grand as the eternal presence of God. To enter the mind of Christ in this context is to see the glory of God in all things. This seeing results in a new sense of respect for the things around us, as a way of showing our respect and gratitude to God, in whom the reality of all things eternally subsists.

CHAPTER 8

Present, Open,
and Awake

There is no single way to meditate. There are, however, certain acts and attitudes inherently endowed with the capacity to awaken sustained states of meditative awareness that form the infrastructure of each specific way to meditate. These fundamental acts and attitudes constitute the guidelines for meditation that were presented and briefly elaborated upon earlier. Here, once again, are the suggested guidelines:

With respect to the body: Sit still. Sit straight. Place your hands in a comfortable or meaningful position in your lap. Close your eyes or lower them toward the ground. Breath slowly and naturally. With respect to your mind, be present, open, and awake, neither clinging to nor rejecting anything. And with respect to attitude, maintain nonjudgmental compassion toward yourself as you discover yourself clinging to and rejecting everything, and nonjudgmental compassion toward others in their powerlessness that is one with yours.

Here we will be exploring each of these guidelines in much more detail. We will also explore some basic guidelines for walking meditation. More precisely, we will be exploring the mystical dimensions of the *actual experience* of oneness with God that flows through the hidden recesses of each of these guidelines. Keep in mind that these guidelines are but suggestions for you to explore as part of your ongoing process of finding the ways to meditate that are most natural and effective for you. What matters is not which method of meditation you use, but the self-transforming process by which meditation leads you into more interior, meditative states of openness to God. The emphasis in what follows is not so much on how to meditate as on the transformative events that occur within us as we sit in meditative openness to God. The emphasis is on responding to these interior events that open us all the more to an experience of God's eternal oneness with us, which is our very reality and the reality of all that is real.

The first suggested guideline we will be exploring here pertains most directly to the mind—which is to say, to our awareness of thoughts, memories, intentions, feelings, and bodily sensations. The guideline with respect to the mind is to remain present, open, and awake, neither clinging to nor rejecting anything. Go to your place of meditation. Perhaps you might stand for a moment, renewing your awareness that you are in God's presence. You might say a brief and simple prayer expressing your gratitude to God for having been led to the path of meditation and asking for the wisdom, courage, and strength to be faithful to it.

Then, sitting still and straight, with your eyes closed or lowered toward the ground, let go of all that is preoccupying you at the moment. Choose to be present in the immediacy of the present moment by simply relaxing into being right where you are, just as you are. Settle into the intimate, felt sense of your bodily stillness. Settle into being aware of your breathing and whatever degree of fatigue or wakefulness you may be feeling in your body at the moment. Be aware of whatever sadness, inner peace, or other emotion may be present. Be aware of the light and the temperature in the room where you are sitting. In short, simply be present, just as you are, in the moment, just as it is. Cling to nothing. Reject nothing. Rest in this moment, in which there is nowhere to go, nothing to achieve, nothing to prove, nothing to tend to except being simply present. Relax. Give yourself a break. Simply sit in a "Here I am, Lord" stance of relaxed attentiveness and openness to God. Stay with that immediate experience of yourself in the present moment. Know and trust that God is already perfectly present in your simply being alive and real in the present moment just as it is.

It may seem strange at first to give ourselves over to this simple practice of unthinking wakefulness. But from a contemplative point of view, what is really strange is that the ungraspable immediacy of the present moment has become the land we know not. Strange and scary, too, that we would go through our whole life and not know something as foundational as simply being who we simply are, one with all that the present moment simply is. So much of the contemplative path has this strange mixture of perplexity and self-evident clarity. At the level of ego consciousness, we sit in meditation a bit perplexed and bewildered. Deeper down, we sit knowing and trusting that we are finding our way home to God in learning to rest in a slowly emerging awareness of the divinity of what just is.

This practice of being simply present, open, and awake in the present moment may take some getting used to. You may not be accustomed to being simply aware of all that appears as soon as you allow all preoccupations and concerns to fall away.

But with God's grace and patient, persistent effort, you will learn to stabilize yourself in simply being present. Rest in a simple faith that your simple presence in the present moment is a bottomless well of presence. Have faith that as you sit, silent and still, in meditation, you are being transformed as you descend ever deeper into the abyss of presence that we call God.

You will discover very quickly how elusive this immediate experience of simply being present tends to be. Within the first few moments of sitting in meditation you may discover yourself slipping away from present-moment attentiveness into your customary round of thoughts, memories, and concerns. This is ego consciousness reinstating its accustomed position as our primary way of being in the present moment. The strategy of self-transformation at work in meditation is not to fight with the ego's efforts to reinstate its domain. The strategy is rather that of sitting in a circle of simple presence that continues expanding outward to include any and all aspects of ego that may arise within it. The following example will illustrate this point.

When lovers share an intimate meal together, many things pass through their minds. They are, quite naturally, open to all that they see and hear and feel in their surroundings. They are aware of all kinds of thoughts, images, and memories flowing through their minds. They do not try, in some kind of forced or contrived fashion, to narrow down their awareness in an attempt to keep out anything they might happen to be aware of. And at the same time they instinctively watch over their hearts so that nothing breaks the flow of the growing meditative awareness of their oneness with each other. As they sit together in this way, they can sense those points at which they begin to drift away from their mutually realized sense of oneness. These initial tendencies to drift away are simply recognized and included as part of the experience of intimacy. Sometimes these little momentary driftings take care of themselves. Sometimes a conscious effort is needed to let go of whatever preoccupying concern may have arisen within them. Sometimes they do not catch the concern in time and the thread of their loving awareness breaks. Each time they realize a break has occurred, they simply renew and reinstate their loving sense of oneness with one another. They might share with each other what has distracted them, and in their doing so the distracting concern is drawn into the expanding circle of their mutually realized oneness. All that is included in the expanding circle of their love becomes an integral aspect of their love. In very much this same manner, our meditation embodies an expanding circle of loving presence that includes all that arises within it.

In the beginning stages of practice, the goal, if we can speak of goals, is to learn to be present, open, and awake to all that arises within you and around you. In order to do this you must do your best not to slip into ego-based ways of clinging to or rejecting all that is perpetually arising within and around you. For as soon as you become caught up and lost in the ceaseless contingencies of the moment, you lose your newly found groundedness in the present moment.

Be humbled and grateful in knowing that you are learning to awaken to your true nature in learning to be like God. Jesus tells us that God is like the sun, whose light shines on the good and bad, and like the rain, which falls on the righteous and unrighteous (Matt. 5:45). So, too, we are learning in meditation to allow the light of simply being present in the present moment to fall on all that enters our awareness in the present moment. Jesus said, "Judge not and you shall not be judged" (Matt. 7:1). Sitting in meditation, we put this teaching of Christ into practice in remaining present, open, and awake to ourselves just as we are,

without judging, without evaluating, without clinging to or rejecting the way we simply are.

I will, at this point, focus specifically on the thoughts that
enter our mind as we meditate. In doing so, I will return for a
moment to a basic teaching of *The Cloud of Unknowing*. The
anonymous author reminds us that in committing ourselves to
meditation we are to be grateful for all of God's blessings in our
life. But we are not content merely with God's blessings. For
those blessings have whetted our appetite, evoking within us a
desire to know God from whom those blessings flow. Likewise,
we are grateful for all that our faith reveals to us about God.
But we are not content with revealed ideas about God. We
desire to know God naked as he is himself, infinitely beyond all
ideas about God.

We are then to be aware of how priceless the gift of thinking
is. But we are also to be aware of how limited thought is com-
pared with the actual experience of that which transcends what
thoughts can grasp or words can adequately convey. This is
even so with earthly things. Someone out in the desert writing
the word *water* over and over in the sand is really onto a great
idea. But when we are really thirsty, all ideas of water prove to
be wholly inadequate, leaving us as thirsty as ever. In fact,
thinking of water makes us even thirstier. It is even more so
with God. Our own thirst for God might be awakened in reading the verse in the Psalms "As the deer longs for running
streams, so my soul thirsts for you, my God" (Ps. 42:1). We
might know that it is the Spirit of God within us that has awakened this thirst. But the verse and the insights surrounding it do
not quench this thirst but only cause it to grow stronger.

The more this thirst for God grows, the more apparent it
becomes that not even the most true and revealed thought
about God *is* God. The stronger the desire for God grows, the

more we realize that every idea of God, in being finite, is infinitely less than God, who is infinite.

Therefore, to the extent that we cling to any idea of God, clinging to that idea of God will be an obstacle to God. Thinking about God increases our thirst for God but does not quench that thirst. We come to realize that the only way to know God is to pass beyond the frontiers of thought by way of a loving awareness that realizes what the head cannot comprehend. And so we sit in meditation, gently and persistently freeing ourselves from our customary reliance on thinking and all that thinking can attain. We do not do this by banishing or annihilating thought, but rather by learning to establish ourselves in a non-thinking stance of being present, open, and awake to each thought that enters our mind as we meditate.

Ultimately we are not created by God to think about God. We are rather created by God for God, beyond all ideas of God. When we meditate we are not trying to think about God. Nor are we trying to banish all thoughts about God from our mind. We are rather attempting to realize our eternal oneness with the unthinkable immediacy of God in and as the immediacy of all that we simply are, one with all that the present moment simply is.

A distinction can be made between two different ways of experiencing the thoughts that enter our minds in meditation. There are those thoughts that are experienced as passing through the field of awareness, continuous with our overall experience of all that we are experiencing. As we sit in meditation, we are not trying to stop having thoughts that are experienced in this contextual manner. Nor are we trying to banish such thoughts once they have entered our awareness. As we meditate, we are not rejecting thought. Indeed, any attempt to do so is an intrusion of the ego into the moment as it simply is. For just as God creates the body to breathe, God creates the mind so that thoughts arise within it.

Just as the floor, the furnishings, and other details of the room in which we sit in meditation manifest the exteriority of the present moment, so, too, the thought that is just now passing through our mind manifests the interiority of the present moment. We sit in meditation not to reject, rearrange, or otherwise impose our will on the concrete immediacy of the exterior and interior aspects of the present moment. To the contrary, we meditate that we might learn to recognize and live in the simply given and unfathomable nature of all that lies within and all that lies without.

As we sit in meditation, we can see how each thought, if simply observed, without being clung to or rejected, simply arises, endures, and passes away. Just as the day or night in which you are meditating is arising, enduring, and passing away; just as your whole life is arising, enduring, and passing away; just as the whole universe is arising, enduring, and passing away—so, too, the thought you are *now* experiencing is arising, enduring, and passing away. The flow of thoughts we experience in meditation is not an adversary to be conquered. It is rather the presence of God manifesting herself, giving herself wholly and completely in and as the arising, enduring, and passing-away nature of thought and of all manifested reality.

What we must deal with, however, are those thoughts that are experienced as carrying us away from the concrete immediacy of the present moment. These are thoughts we experience as distractions. To meditate even for a few minutes is to experience the ubiquitous nature of distractions. We are sitting still and straight in meditation, intending to be as present, open, and awake in the present moment as we can be. Then, before we know it, a thought carries us away from present-moment attentiveness. Lost in thinking the thought that has carried us away, we are no longer safely at home in the virginal immediacy of the present moment in which we sit.

Actually, it is not that a certain kind of thought, with certain kidnapping qualities, carries us away. Rather, it is truer to say that as a thought comes unexpectedly down the path that leads through the open field of our awareness, we jump out of the bushes and mug it! If the thought is of some pleasant, profound, and beautiful thing, we try to hold on to it, so that it will not go away. If the thought is of some painful and disturbing thing, we jump out and mug it by trying to drive it away. Whether we cling to or reject the thought, we are drawn away from present-moment attentiveness into the ego-based domain of thinking our thoughts.

As soon as we have become aware of having once again drifted away from present-moment attentiveness into thinking our thoughts, we are to simply reinstate our intention of resting—present, open, and awake—in the immediacy of the present moment. As we renew our present-moment attentiveness, we can be reassured that we are renewing our awareness of the divine mystery that is manifesting itself in and as each thought that arises, endures, and passes away within us.

At first, and for quite some time, we tend to drift off into thinking without even realizing we have done so. As soon as we realize this has occurred, we simply renew our intention to remaining present, open, and awake in the present moment. As we mature in our practice, we are able to recognize the initial tendency to drift away from present-moment attentiveness into thinking as an event that is occurring within the open field of our awareness. Sometimes simply being aware of this first tendency to drift off into thinking is enough to restabilize ourselves in present-moment attentiveness. Sometimes a gentle corrective act is needed to renew and sustain uninterrupted present-moment attentiveness. Sometimes we do not catch the slippage into thinking in time to prevent the loss of present-moment attentiveness—in which case, we simply reinstate present-moment attentiveness by ceasing to think about whatever the thought may be that seduced us away from the present moment.

Of course, the process of sustaining and reinstating present-moment attentiveness can be, at times, extremely difficult. At other times, it is very easy, almost effortless. What matters is not the varying degree to which we are successful in sustaining a certain state of inner calm or clarity. Rather, what matters is our sincere intention to do our simple best. What matters even more is knowing and trusting that God is one with us, in the midst of our efforts, loving us, accepting us, drawing us invincibly to herself, regardless of what state of mind we are in. We, of course prefer times when we are able to sit in almost effortless sustained openness to God to times of great struggle. This is only normal. But it is helpful to remember that it is our trust in God's oneness with us just as we are, and not as we are trying to be, that most decisively opens up our growing realization of oneness with God in meditation. It is this trust in God, come what may, that paradoxically does more than anything else to stabilize us in a sustained state of being present, open, and awake in God's presence.

What has been said here of thoughts also pertains to all the *memories* that enter our awareness as we meditate. As we sit in meditation we are to remain present, open, and awake to each memory as it arises, endures, and passes within us. As we do so, we will sense the initial tendency to start remembering the memory that has come to mind. But to the extent that we slip into identifying with our memories, we become once again bogged down in overly identifying with our remembering self, which is growing older by the minute. As we allow our memories to carry us away into the shadow land of all that we used to be, we lose our rootedness in the virginal newness of the present moment. Each time we realize we have slipped out of present-moment attentiveness by getting caught up in our memories, we are to simply renew our present-moment attentiveness to these memories as they arise, endure, and pass away.

What holds true of the thoughts and memories that come to mind as we meditate holds true as well for desires that stir within us. By *desires* I mean the initial inclinations of our will to cling to what is pleasant and to reject what is unpleasant. As we sit in meditation we are to be simply aware that as a pleasant thought arises and endures in our mind, so, too, arises the natural inclination to linger with that thought, to hold on to it so that it does not go away. Likewise, as an unpleasant thought arises within us, we can observe the initial inclination to push it away as soon as possible. As we sit in meditation, we are to simply observe these initial tendencies to cling or reject, without identifying with them. As we learn to let go of our tendency to cling and reject we are awakened to God, one with us just as we are in the immediacy of the present moment, just as it is.

The situation in meditation, with respect to desire, is comparable to a man who loves a woman so much he can scarcely bear the fullness of the love that is growing within him. He secretely wills for them to be one in ways he dare not mention to her. But, oh, how he waits for that moment when she might say she, too, desires the oneness that he desires.

The point at which the woman does awaken to his love for her is not a moment in which she gains anything that was not already there. It is rather a moment in which she is awakened to a love that is already there. And the moment when she responds to this love is a moment when she gives to the one who loves her, a gift beyond anything that he might hope for or imagine.

So, too, between God and us. Jesus reveals that to us that God is brimming over with a single burning desire to be one with us. God is waiting for that look in our eye, that inclination in our heart, indicating that we desire this same oneness. God desires us to realize a oneness with himself that is already the infinite fullness of all that we really are and are called to be. The moment when we awaken to this love is the moment that gives back to God the love God gives to us. The circle of love completes itself in a union that has no name. God desires that we awaken to this divine desire that is our life. God desires that we, in our graced awakening, might yield ourselves over to this desire completely. For our heart, rendered supple and vulnerable to divine love, is the wide-open gate through which God comes riding in to take us by storm. He takes us with a bliss and a glory that are entirely his own—and, by virtue of his boundless generosity, entirely our own as well. The fullness of this glory and bliss lies fully present yet hidden in the sincerity with which we sit in meditation. It is in sitting in meditation with all our heart that this hidden bliss and glory is realized in ways too interior and intimate to describe.

I will be focusing in some detail on feelings and bodily sensations a bit later in these reflections, and so will mention here simply that the same guiding principles of being present, open, and awake pertain to feelings and bodily sensations as well. As we sit in meditation we are to be present, open, and awake to the feelings and bodily sensations that flow through us as we meditate. As we do so, we will experience firsthand how each time we slip into our customary tendency to reject or cling to our feelings and bodily sensations, we cease to be grounded in present-moment attentiveness. Each time we realize we have slipped away from present-moment attentiveness by drifting off into feelings and bodily sensations, we are to simply reinstate being present, open, and awake to the feelings and bodily sensations arising, enduring, and passing away within us. As we continue on in this way we are awakened to God bodying herself forth in and as our bodily being.

CHAPTER 9

Sit Still

The next suggested guideline for meditation is to sit still. Sitting still is practical in that it helps to still the restless stirrings of our mind. Each time we realize we have drifted off into this or that distracting thought or concern, we can simply renew our awareness of our bodily stillness as our anchoring place in present-moment attentiveness. Practiced in this way, sitting still becomes a way of being present, open, and awake, neither clinging to nor rejecting anything.

As you continue on in your practice you will discover the ways that are most natural and effective for you to foster and sustain more interior, meditative states of openness to God. Perhaps the meditative awareness of your bodily stillness will remain but one aspect of your basic stance of remaining present, open, and awake in the present moment. You might discover, however, that renewing your awareness of your bodily stillness is your most effective way of renewing and sustaining your meditative openness to God. What is more, you may find that resting in the mystery of your bodily stillness is the way that

God is leading you into an ever-deeper experience of oneness with herself. If this should prove to be the case, you will discover that quiet attentiveness to your bodily stillness is itself a self-transforming way to God. You could, in fact, spend your whole meditation time grounding your practice in meditative awareness of your bodily stillness. If you did so, you would discover that you would never use up your bodily stillness; you would never exhaust body stillness as a pathway into God. The same holds true of each of the guidelines presented here. For each has its basis in an aspect of our very being, endowed by God with the capacity to awaken us to God. Keep in mind the central point stressed by Saint John of the Cross: what matters most is to rest in a general loving awareness of God. Sustained awareness of your bodily stillness is relevant and helpful insofar as it helps to sustain and deepen this general loving awareness.

Whatever the focus of your groundedness in present-moment attentiveness might be, I encourage you not to be indifferent to your bodily stillness as you meditate. Do not pass right by your bodily stillness as if you are on your way to far greater, more spiritual realities. Learn, instead, to sit still with all your heart. Remain quietly attentive to your bodily stillness as long as you are interiorly drawn to do so. Be utterly sincere in your attentiveness to your bodily stillness as you allow your bodily stillness to embody your heartfelt sincerity. It is in this way that you will begin to discover directly, for yourself, that sitting still is a doorway through which you might pass into God.

By learning to sit still, we can learn to be still. In learning to be still, our present-moment attentiveness deepens, becoming an act of incarnate faith, giving witness to ourselves and to the whole world that ultimately there is nowhere to go. In our ignorance, we do not know that this is so. In our ignorance, we tend to confuse the relative order of ego consciousness—with all its places to go, goals to reach, and needs to be met—with the divine depths in which we sit. Subject to this confusion, we sit in meditation assuming that our difficulties in meditating profoundly, or living contemplatively, are due to our disturbingly slow progress along a disturbingly circuitous path to a disturbingly distant destination. We sit in meditation and say with a sigh, "I wonder if I will ever get there."

But as we continue to sit in meditation, we slowly begin to understand the nature of our confusion. We begin to see that our difficulties consist not of our slow progress in getting "there" but rather of the challenges we face in simply being *here*, fully present, open, and awake in the present moment. As we continue to sit in the body-grounded stillness of meditation, we begin to see as well just why it is so hard for us to be here. We see how we are still buying into the fear-based scenarios from our childhood or from society in general. These scenarios have us believing that it is not enough to *be* who we simply are. We have to keep surging forward by *doing* things that will establish our worth in our own eyes, in the eyes of others, and, we imagine, in the eyes of God as well.

What is perplexing about our fear-based self-doubts is that at some level we know better. We believe the Good News of our faith—that we are wholly loved and one with God, right here and now, in this present moment, just as we are. We know by faith that all our ups and downs are shot clean through with the grace that has sustained us up until now. We have lived long enough to see, time and time again, how our moments of apparent setback and loss are no less fraught with divinity than our moments of apparent victory and attainment. We know and trust that the steady stream of God's sustaining love will be flowing full force in the hour of our death. We know that when that moment comes we will round the bend, coming back full circle to discover God waiting for us with open arms, welcoming us back into the depths of divinity from which we came.

It is in having grown weary of failing to see the divinity of all we gain and lose that we now sit still. As we learn to rest quietly attentive to the mystery of our bodily stillness, our meditation practice begins to take on the quality of a deep and trusting acceptance of the endlessly holy nature of the present moment just as it is. Sitting, quiet and still, we slowly learn to simply observe and accept the constantly changing nature of our bodily being. We learn to observe and accept how being quietly energized gives way to fatigue, which in turn gives way to an unexpected, renewed quiet alertness. We learn to just sit, quietly aware of our insights and distractions, our advances and setbacks both real and imagined. Little by little we come to realize that the flux and flow of our distractions and sleepiness, intermingled with our insights and breakthroughs, *is* the flux and flow of God's sustaining, providential presence.

As we sit, silent and still, in meditation, questions come welling up from deep within: What if all my inner peace and sense of fulfillment depended on nothing more or less than what just is? How could there ever be more than what just is? How could there ever be less? How could God be anything but the infinity of what just is? How could the sheer miracle of my presence in this present moment just as it is be anything other than the overflowing generosity of God? As we sit still, the reassurance that these questions embody encircles us, granting the peace that surpasses understanding.

Sometimes—often, in fact—it is not like this at all. Sometimes our fatigue and distractions prevail. But no matter, for the more seasoned we become in this simple practice, the more we come to realize that, regardless of what we are experiencing at the moment, we can know and trust that nothing is missing in it. Our times of restless fatigue and our times of sublime rested alertness have an absolute and equal value. This awareness grants the peace that surpasses understanding. This peace is accompanied by a sense of quiet awe in realizing that our experience in the present moment, just as it is, *is* the fullness of God, one with us just as we are.

Another aspect of the transformative power of bodily stillness is that we learn from our body how to be. As we meditate, we realize how hard it is to say, at any given moment, where our mind will be. Our mind tends to be always lurching ahead into concerns for the future or lagging behind in preoccupations with the past. But our wise and mysterious body neither lurches ahead nor lags behind the present moment. This is why we always know right where to find our bodily being. It is always right here, in the present moment, bodying forth the love that is loving us into being. Even in death our bodily being will be right there in the moment of our death, not leaving the present moment but falling into its eternal depths, disappearing from view.

It takes time for the mind to settle down enough to begin to quietly merge with the unassuming simplicity of simply sitting still. This helps in understanding why it is often recommended that each session of meditation last for twenty to thirty minutes. Sometimes it takes that long for the mind to tire enough of its endless circling in thoughts and memories to finally land and settle in the silent mystery of our bodily being. Little by little, the unrest we tend to carry about within us starts falling away. Breath by breath, the quiet awareness of our bodily stillness begins to catch hold and take over as our meditative groundedness in the present moment.

Love opens the eyes of lovers, allowing them to see the divinity of the body. Love opens the eyes of the mother, who, in nursing her infant, viscerally senses the divinity of the mysterious weight and warmth of her infant's bodily being. And love opens our eyes in meditation, enabling us to see the divinity of our bodily being. This seeing of the divinity of our bodily being is like waking from a dream. It is like falling backward in slow motion into the luminous depths of our bodily being. As this falling occurs, our center of gravity is no longer sustained in our ego consciousness. Our center of gravity is sustained in God, the infinite origin, ground, and fulfillment of our bodily being.

A large pendulum clock hangs on the wall of our living room at home. When my wife and I are home during the day, the clock's quiet tick-tock tends to be drowned out by the momentum of the daily round of chores and concerns. But in the evening, as we are sitting together in the living room, quietly reading, we will sometimes comment on how pleasant and reassuring it is to hear the clock quietly ticking away. It is in this same manner that we sit still, quietly attentive to what we might call the full-statured stillness of the present moment. Sitting still with all our heart is a pathway leading to the realization of this full-statured stillness.

Even if we are meditating for the first time, we already know something about this full-statured stillness. Our moments of spontaneous contemplative experience fleetingly grant something of this full-statured stillness to us. In that moment of looking up to see the face of a friend, as if for the first time, or that moment of standing motionless at a breathtaking sunset or holding a sleeping infant, we fleetingly glimpse something of the full-statured stillness that eternally pervades the fleetingness of all things.

As these special moments of meditative awakening begin to dissipate, we linger wordlessly about the scene, still held in the aura of the awe that envelops us. When we finally do leave the still-darkening horizon, or the friend's presence or the sleeping child, we do not do so with the sense of having fully entered into the stillness we were privileged to obscurely experience. To the contrary, we move on with the conviction that we had hardly begun to do so. Deeper still we move on in the awareness that even if we were to sit forever with this setting sun, with the friend or the sleeping child, we would never exhaust the contemplatively sensed inexhaustibility to which the moment fleetingly granted access. Our heart is stilled in such moments in the paradoxical sense of being so deeply moved in realizing that all we could ever hope or long for is somehow present yet hidden in the moment we were privileged to experience.

When we sit in meditation, we sit with a heart pregnant with faith in the revelatory nature of our moments of spontaneous meditative experience, disclosing to us the true nature of this moment in which we now sit. We may be sitting in the midst of great sleepiness or in a dry-as-dust deprivation of any sense of God's presence. Even so, we know that our fleeting moments of spontaneous meditative experience have disclosed to us the divinity of this moment in which we now sit. It is with this sense of faith in the divinity of the present moment that we learn to rest with confidence in the present-moment miracle of our bodily being.

I can attest to the fact that even after we have been meditating for years, we may still be fairly estranged from the interior stillness of the life we are living. This should not surprise or discourage us. We are, after all, ordinary human beings who have been blessed with a desire to live a more contemplative way of life. But, thank God, we are learning to sit in meditation with a heart pregnant with faith in the revelatory nature of our moments of spontaneous contemplative experience. It is in this faith that we sit in meditation, knowing, in the marrow of our bones, that if we could only see *all* that this moment really is, we would see God loving us into being. It takes time, but little by little we begin to grow in our reverential awareness of the way our bodily being so faithfully bodies forth, with such open-faced ease, the infinite mystery we call God.

The question arises as to what to do when your nose itches or your knee or some other part of your body starts to hurt. This question is not all that relevant with respect to the itch or the hurt, which is just passing through. The question becomes relevant, however, in the presence of the great big itch or hurt that decides to move in and stay awhile. What is often best in the face of such persistent bodily discomfort is to simply scratch our nose or to move our foot to a more comfortable position. This is so simply because it is the most natural and most human thing to do.

It is our common humanity that Christ became and in which he manifested the divinity of our ordinary human experience. As you scratch your nose, do so with all your heart, knowing deep down the endlessly holy nature of scratching your nose. Or as you move your foot slightly to a more comfortable position, do so with all your heart, knowing deep down the divinity that moving your foot manifests perfectly in the world. The key to meditation is to continue expanding the circle of meditative awareness so wide that we are meditatively awakened to the infinite value of every aspect of our being. This infinite value is granted by God, who gives the infinity of herself, wholly and completely, in and as every aspect of our being.

At other times, however, we may, in obedience to a more interior wisdom, sense the transformative power to be realized in freely choosing not to move our foot or scratch our nose. It is precisely at this point that our bodily stillness becomes a way of freely choosing to enter the mysterious domain of the impotence of choice.

Each of us possesses the ability to choose to do our best to remove ourselves and others from the difficulties that befall us as human beings. We are, in fact, bound by the moral imperative not to remain passive in the presence of that which compromises or violates our own God-given preciousness or the preciousness of others. But if we are always leaping in and fixing the situation—immediately scratching what itches, immediately moving what hurts—our practice in bodily stillness never ripens. Our practice is never allowed to carry us all the way home, into the hallowed clearing where all our lives converge in our powerlessness to change all that we are powerless to change.

The stillness of our practice begins to ripen as we freely choose to enter the mysterious domain of the impotency of choice. As we do so, our bodily stillness begins to embody the suffering we experience in losing a relationship we are powerless to restore, leaving a home we are powerless to return to, becoming ill with an illness for which no cure can be found, growing older, realizing that our own death draws near. In short, sitting still becomes a way of freely entering any and all situations in which we suffer in our powerlessness to free others and ourselves from the suffering that befalls us. Sitting still in this manner becomes a way of being like God, who, in Christ, freely identifies with us in our powerlessness to free ourselves from suffering and death

I was once attending a weeklong silent Christian Zen retreat led by Rev. Hans Koenen, a Jesuit priest from the Netherlands. It was an intensive retreat during which we were meditating five, six, or seven hours a day. We were encouraged to pace ourselves, being careful not to push ourselves beyond our limit. At the same time we were encouraged, if we were inclined to do so, to stay up late or get up early to meditate even more. Our meals were taken in silence. We were encouraged to read very little, if at all. We were encouraged to walk slowly and mindfully from place to place.

The extended periods of meditation were difficult for me. I was experiencing a lot of both physical and emotional pain. Koenen presided at a liturgy each evening in the meditation hall, during which we all sat on our meditation cushions lining the four walls of the room.

Four or five days into the retreat, we were having the evening Eucharist. All during that day my physical and emotional pain had been particularly intense. My legs and back hurt. I felt depressed and lost in waves of troubling emotions and memories. As the day wore on, I settled into a quiet place in this suffering. By not resisting it, I entered more deeply into it and it, nonobtrusively, entered more deeply into me. As I was sitting in this pain during the liturgy, Koenen passed the chalice, saying as he did so, "Drink this cup, which contains the suffering of the whole world." We all sat in silence as each person drank from the chalice, then passed it on to the person sitting on the next cushion.

As I touched the chalice to my lips, tears came to my eyes. I realized in that instant that my suffering did not belong to me but was in some mysterious way the suffering of the whole world, manifesting itself in and as my experience of suffering. I realized my suffering did not belong to me alone but in some mysterious way belonged to God, who, in Christ, touched the chalice of human suffering to his lips and drained it in big, long, loving swallows that left it empty of any suffering that is not wholly in God.

The stillness of our practice brings us directly to the critical juncture at which we either despair or go deeper. To despair is the outcome of having placed all our hope in our frequent inability to make things turn out as we wish. To go deeper is to drink the cup of our common destiny, in which divinity flows unimpeded through our communal powerlessness.

It is in death that we see most clearly the communal powerlessness in which our destiny converges at some hidden place in the depths of God. Just recently I was giving a meditation retreat. Someone at the retreat came to me to tell me about the woman she had been living with for many years in an intimate and loving relationship. She told me that during the previous year her friend had died of cancer. The cancer had been a long, drawn-out ordeal. Toward the end many people were coming in and out of the house to visit, to bring food and offer whatever help they could.

Her friend suffered a great deal. In the end she went into a coma. One afternoon, the woman who was telling me this story said, she was sitting with her dying friend. There was no one else in the house. She was simply sitting, silent and still, with her silent and still, dying friend. Suddenly her friend opened her eyes, looked right at her, and smiled a celestial smile, then closed her eyes and died. The woman told me, her eyes filling with tears as she spoke, that she would never forget that smile. She said that in that moment it was clear to her that her friend had already passed over into God. She said that in that moment she knew what it felt like to be smiled at from an open window into heaven. Her friend's smile embodies the endlessly holy nature of our communal powerlessness, utterly transparent to the divinity that shines invincibly in it.

And so the meditative practice of stillness is a self-transforming practice in which we realize that we radically belong to God, who enigmatically sustains us in our powerlessness to sustain ourselves. To speak in this manner is not to claim that we are delivered from our desolation. Rather, it is to give witness to being delivered from the delusion that our moments of desolation have any ultimate power over us. It is to give witness to the possibility of being transformed in desolation, such that we come to discover directly, for ourselves, the divinity beyond gain and loss that invincibly shines through all gain and all loss.

At another Christian Zen retreat I attended, Thomas Hand, the Jesuit priest leading the retreat, had us enter into each session of meditation by repeating from the Psalms the words "Be still and know I am God" (Ps. 46:10). He would say the verse, and we would repeat it after him. He would then repeat the verse, taking one word off the end each time, with us repeating the shortened verse after him, "Be still and know I am God. . . . Be still and know I am. . . . Be still and know. . . . Be still and. . . . Be still. . . . Be." This scripture text, distilled down to the black hole of a naked "Be," was immediately echoed by the ringing of a bell, the resonance of which, in becoming silent, left us in the communal stillness of meditation.

I have since come to begin group meditation in this same manner. For here, it seems to me, is a contemplative liturgy of the word, disclosing a mysterious meeting place with God. Our bodily being embodies this mysterious meeting place with God.

As we sit still in meditation we are obeying God, who calls us to be still so that we might hear God saying the "Be" that ushers us, moment by moment, into being. As we hear this divine "Be" that our bodily being embodies, we enter into God. We come at last to that point of stillness that is the still point of the turning world.

And so if you meditate each day for thirty minutes, sit still with all your heart, every day, for thirty minutes. If you meditate every day for thirty minutes until death, sit still with all your heart every day for thirty minutes until death. For the stillness of our practice is a stillness unto death. The stillness of our practice is, in truth, the stillness of death itself. Our faith assures us that this stillness is a wide-open gate through which we pass into the hidden, life-giving depths of God.

CHAPTER 10

Sit Straight

The next suggested guideline for meditation is to sit straight. Sitting straight is practical in that it enhances present-moment attentiveness by warding off the sleepiness and daydreaming that can overtake us as we meditate. Sometimes, when I am leading silent retreats, I will look down the rows of people as we sit together meditating. First one head, then another begins to droop slightly forward, as now this, now that person begins to drift toward sleepiness. This is most likely to happen when the group is meditating in the middle of a hot afternoon. Occasionally, someone will actually begin snoring! Sometimes it is my own head that begins drooping as I become drowsy during the meditation.

Sitting straight is a preemptive strategy that helps to prevent sleepiness from occurring. Then, when we realize we have already begun to drift toward sleepiness, renewing our bodily posture becomes a corrective strategy that renews our sustained meditative awareness. But if we are not careful, the act of renewing our bodily posture can disrupt the delicate, meditative calm that is slowly deepening within us. And so, each time we begin to drift toward sleepiness, we renew the straightness of our posture, *being careful in doing so not to disturb our delicate, slowly deepening meditative awareness.*

When a parent is carrying a sleeping child off to bed, the parent lays the child down very carefully. The parent will slip his or her arm out from under the child, slowly and gently, so as not to awaken it. It is with this same loving concern that we renew the straightness of our posture in meditation, being careful, as we do so, not to disturb the ever so subtle relaxation of bodily stillness characteristic of deep meditation. As this process is repeated countless times, our bodily relaxation continues to deepen as we remain quietly grounded in meditative openness to God.

The relaxed stillness of meditation brings us to a fork in the road. Down one path lies the gentle slope leading into sleepiness. We know this gentle slope well. We travel it every night when we go bed. Down the other path lie ever deeper states of relaxed meditative wakefulness. As we sit in meditation, we approach this fork in the road time and time again. By faithfully renewing our posture in a manner that does not disturb the deepening meditative state of relaxed alertness, we navigate our way past this fork, taking the meditative path into the depths of God.

The present moment is a wide-open gate leading into the depths of God. God, the angels. and those whom we, who call ourselves the living, call the dead are all just on the other side of the gate, trying to get our attention, ready for us to come through and join them. In our egocentric estrangement from meditative awareness we do not see how wide open this gate always is. Nor can we see the celestial welcoming committee, cheering us on, inviting us into our divine inheritance. When we sit still and straight, this gate begins to come into view. By remaining wide awake and, at the same time, utterly relaxed, as if about to fall asleep, we begin to pass through this gate, which marks the point at which our egocentric unawareness dissolves into a deep, abiding awareness of oneness with God.

Breathing plays a part in this as well. You will notice how, as your meditative awareness deepens, your breathing becomes more and more subtle as your body becomes more and more still. Something similar happens spontaneously in the hypnogogic state, in which we can be in our bed halfway between waking and sleeping. The body is still and inert, almost as if it were made of clay, while the mind is awake, in a wondrous state of calm alertness. It is this utterly calm and lucid state that we enter into in meditation. We can say, as a way of echoing the Song of Songs, "I am asleep, but my heart is awake" (Sg. 5:2). Each time we renew the straightness of our posture as we meditate, we continue to become more and more relaxed, as if asleep, even as our heart becomes ever more awake to God.

As you very carefully observe the transformative process of sitting straight, you will see how it repeatedly passes through various phases, each with its own lessons in self-transformation. There is the phase of being so rested and alert that we are able, in almost effortless fashion, to remain poised and grounded in meditative wakefulness. While in this phase, we are quick to notice and correct the very first beginnings of each little instance of starting to slump forward or drifting toward sleepiness.

The image that comes to mind here is that of driving a car—say, out in the desert, along a straight road, at night, toward a far-off destination. As you drive along this road, you unconsciously make constant little corrections in your steering. In the very first instance of starting to veer off the road one way or the other you, without even having to think about it, keep the car heading straight with a minor corrective movement of the steering wheel. It is like this in meditation sometimes as well, except, of course, that the destination is one that lies not before us, but rather deep within and infinitely beyond us. But the central point remains the same: during those times when we are meditating, naturally rested and alert, we continue on by way of our constant little corrections of quiet vigilance.

The lesson here is that we come to oneness with God by learning to be faithful in little things. It is such a little thing to correct the straightness of our posture over and over. But in doing so, we manifest in the world a kind of integrity, a kind of fidelity that nobody sees. The gentleness with which we renew the straightness of our posture so as not to disturb the subtle deepening of meditative wakefulness is itself a manifestation of the gentleness of God. Seeing that this is so, even for an instant, is enough to make the heart sing in glimpsing how intimately God has woven her gentle ways into the sinews of our being.

Of course, we cannot always be rested and alert when we meditate. We will inevitably experience ourselves repeatedly passing through a phase in which we are so sleepy we can barely keep our eyes open. During such times, meditation is an arduous process in which a single thirty-minute session seems like an eternity.

What are we to do during such times? Sometimes, what is best is to engage in spiritual reading or more active forms of prayer in which it is easier to stay awake. At other times, the solution might be to simply return to the day's activities and try to meditate later, when we are more rested. Or we might try to practice walking meditation, which we will be exploring in a later chapter. What may be best is to simply go to bed and get some badly needed sleep.

Breaking off meditation in times of intense sleepiness and

fatigue is, however, not always the only or even the best option. If you have been meditating for very long, you know that some of the most momentous moments of spiritual awakening can occur out of nowhere in the midst of great struggle and sleepiness. In an instant, a fog bank of sleepiness and daydreaming can suddenly give way to great inner clarity. So the question remains: How are we to know when it is best to continue meditating, arduous though it might be, or to stop and try later, when we are more rested?

Part of the maturation process of meditation practice consists of learning to trust in an ongoing felt sense of just how to proceed at any given moment. When we meditated yesterday, faced with massive sleepiness, we stopped and read the newspaper. Meditating today, faced with massive sleepiness, we continue to meditate. Meditating at some time in the future, faced with massive sleepiness, we might remedy the situation by practicing meditation while standing, walking slowly back and forth, or kneeling on the floor.

Another spiritual lesson to be learned during times of great sleepiness is that the relationship between our desire to meditate and our sleepiness and other distracting influences is never adversarial. Our sleepiness is not an enemy to be overcome. Our wandering mind is not some alien force to be conquered or annihilated. To the contrary, our sleepiness and all aspects of our mind, at any given moment, are dimensions of our being. Our struggles in meditation are but ways of coming into ever greater degrees of awareness and acceptance of ourselves as a pathway toward realizing God's infinite awareness and acceptance of us.

When two people in a healthy relationship drift away from intimacy, each takes the responsibility to be honest and vulnerable in expressing to the other person this lack of fidelity to intimacy. There tends to arise, in such moments, conversations in which all kinds of hard-to-hear and hard-to-say things are heard and said. It can get messy. But if they stay the course through all the messy stuff, the couple learns to be intimate in sharing with each other their infidelities to intimacy.

In a similar manner, a lifetime commitment to meditation practice deepens in a willingness to struggle at times, in a non-adversarial manner, with sleepiness, daydreaming, and a host of other difficulties. Sometimes, because of these difficulties, we are not always faithful to practicing meditation. And when we do practice, our practice is sometimes halfhearted. But as we recognize and admit our vacillating ways, we can embrace our limitations as an integral part of the way we go deeper into an intimately realized oneness with God. Sitting straight in times of great sleepiness and fatigue is a nonadversarial act of integrity and commitment. Even as the sleepiness continues, our heart can, by way of this commitment, awaken to dimensions of ourselves as one with God that we have never known.

We have reflected on the times of almost effortless wakefulness, in which we learn to be faithful to little things. And we have reflected on times of intense sleepiness and distractions, in which we learn the art form of nonadversarial struggle that transforms and awakens the heart. We will now reflect on the times in which we experience, firsthand, the mercurial, paradoxical nature of our own heart.

Sitting still and straight, we make our descent into the depths of divinity that the present moment manifests. We do not make this descent by way of some scenic route that detours around all the unresolved chaos and emotional stirrings that dwell within. Rather, the descent takes us right through the middle of some of the worst neighborhoods inside our heart. If we are not careful, we can get mugged by our dark aggression toward our self. Or we can find ourselves abandoned by our self-abandoning ways. Then, just as surprisingly, we can find ourselves in open spaces and stately inner surroundings.

Feelings of fear or pain can suddenly come flooding in, overriding feelings of inner peace. At other times, feelings of profound loneliness can come welling up out of nowhere, only to give way to a consoling serenity we can neither account for nor understand. Our descent into the depths is impeded to the extent that we cling to or reject any of these experiences. Our descent continues on, ever deeper, as we simply sit—present, open, and awake to all that appears as it appears, to all that passes as it passes away. As we sit in meditation, we have a front-row seat for all the ups and downs of our own inimitable self. We experience firsthand how hard it is for us to be as divine and as human, as invincible and as fragile, as delightful and as cantankerous as we really are.

The great surprise is how God suddenly shows up in the midst of the constantly shifting feelings, thoughts, and memories that flow through us as we meditate. The more we come to experience our self to be a shantytown made of clouds, passing feelings, and secret wishes, the freer God is to move through us, blessing us with an awareness of his oneness with us just as we are. The more impoverished, paradoxical, and filled with surprises we realize ourselves to be, the freer God is to be God in us. By simply sitting still and straight, we remain quietly awake to all that lies within, where everything remains unforeseeable, open, and without fixed boundaries in any direction.

Just keep sitting still and straight. Do not waver in the midst of all your wavering. Do not lose heart in sincerely seeking to remain silent, still, and open in God's presence. Allow yourself to rest wordlessly in all that appears. Continue to renew the straightness of your bodily posture, being careful as you do so not to disturb the deepening bodily relaxation in which anything and everything continues to arise and fall away.

The nature of the transformations that sitting still and straight evoke brings us directly into the paradoxical realm of the limitless nature of all limits and the boundless nature of all boundaries. To begin seeing what this might mean, we have but to imagine ourselves holding a newborn infant. How limited the infant is! How small! How utterly vulnerable in being so powerless to get through a single day on its own! And yet we intuit the limitless nature of this infant's limits, the boundless nature of its boundaries, in intuiting that the infant is inherently worthy of a respect, even a reverence, that knows no bounds.

In its precise littleness, as if meticulously cut from God's cookie dough, in its mysterious weight in weighing hardly anything at all, in the imperial strength with which it grasps our extended little finger, it all but carries our heart away. In this moment we know, with an invincible certitude, that were we to die in the act of attempting to save the life of this infant, we would die in the truth.

Christ is God who becomes the limit. That is, Christ is God who becomes the vulnerability of humanity and, in doing so, reveals to us the limitless nature of our vulnerability, the boundless nature of all the boundaries that seem to hem us in on all sides. Our meditation practice brings us directly to this limitless nature of our limits, this boundless nature of our boundaries in which God and we are one.

This is a most extraordinary and paradoxical discovery. For if our very limitations are themselves limitless, what have we to fear? By what imaginings could anything limit us at all, now that we realize that our very limits, and the limits of others and all things, are limitless? If our very boundaries are boundless, what could ever confine us in any way? One of Dylan Thomas's poems ends with the line "And I sang in my chains like the sea."[1] The line suggests the oceanic freedom of God that arises within us, not by virtue of our having risen above our limits, but rather by our realizing directly the divinity of our limits, the boundless nature of our boundaries, one with God.

This is a good place to make two psychological observations. At the psychological level, meditation lowers our customary defenses that modulate the full range of emotions and memories that lie within. As we sit in meditation, things we have not thought of for years can suddenly come to mind. Sad feelings, angry feelings, sexual feelings, blissful feelings, soothing feelings, lonely feelings—all sorts of feelings can suddenly come flooding into our awareness.

We do not want to lose our ability to keep some of our painful affect and memories out of conscious awareness. We could not get through our day if we went around in the full conscious awareness of our own suffering and the suffering of those around us. The difficulty is that we can become so successful at hiding behind a cheery face that no one can find us. In fact, sometimes we are hiding so well we cannot find ourselves. In repressing our sad and painful feelings, we do not know what we really feel. In learning to be unaware of the painful things that we are carrying around inside us, we go around not knowing what we really know. It can be very lonely to wear masks that are so skillfully crafted that no one, including our self, even knows we are wearing a mask.

Sitting straight, in this context, embodies our willingness to allow the masks to fall off, laying bare previously unrecognized or unacknowledged aspects of ourselves. Most often, it is enough simply to allow the awareness, with its attendant feelings, to arise and pass through us. Sometimes, after the meditation session is over, we might do well to reflect on what we got in touch with in meditation. Perhaps we might journal it out, or talk it over with someone—perhaps a spiritual director, if we are fortunate enough and inclined to have one. Sometimes, too, such revelations can lead to the realization that things have simply gotten out of hand and we need to make some long-overdue changes. In more serious situations, the material that broke loose in meditation may require being worked through in psychotherapy.

It is in the context of the capacity of meditation to open up the boundaries of ego consciousness that a word of caution is in order. Those who have to work hard just to sustain their ego boundaries should use care in practicing meditation, which lowers psychological defenses and one's customary sense of ego boundaries. The same caution applies to those who are in therapy or on medication for major depression, anxiety, or some other psychological difficulty affecting one's ability to cope with painful emotions. This caution may apply as well to those who have experienced some loss or trauma they have not yet grieved and worked through.

It is not that people experiencing such difficulties should not meditate. Quite the contrary: with proper guidance and prudence meditation can be, for such people, a profound resource of healing. The key point is to always put safety first. The commitment needs to be that of not retraumatizing ourselves by venturing too far into that which we are as yet not ready to handle. Sometimes, the most spiritual thing we can do when the boundaryless aspects of meditation are too much for us is to back off, get our bearings as to what it is that is going on, and then gently reapproach the whole matter.

Our daily meditation should be a stabilizing force in our life, one that helps us to live our daily life in a happy, grounded, and effective manner. Any indication to the contrary is always a reason to pause and discern what corrective steps need to be taken to correct whatever it might be that needs correcting. If the situation seems to call for it, some psychotherapy might be helpful. The whole process of meditation has to do with our day-by-day willingness to be real with ourselves in the visceral intimacy of our bodies, our emotions, and our memories. In our willingness to see, accept, and befriend all that we are, we become more authentically open and real to ourselves and to others. We become more stabilized in a down-to-earth realization of God's oneness with us in life itself.

Finally, we can reflect on the experience of a body-grounded wakefulness that is so profound that no effort whatsoever is required to sustain it. In this instance, sitting straight refers to a sustained stance of looking right into the eyes of God. Some classical texts in the contemplative traditions speak of this state in terms of one's whole being becoming like the mirrorlike surface of a lake without the slightest breeze blowing across it. Entering this state of effortless, body-grounded serenity, we arrive at a resting place in which our self-transformation into God most clearly and decisively comes to pass.

As a way of arriving at some sense of this marvelous state, imagine that you are in a boat, crossing a vast expanse of water. There are many people on the boat. Music is playing. There is some kind of party going on. In a moment of carelessness, you fall overboard. Everyone on the boat is having so much fun they do not notice that you have fallen overboard. Treading water, yelling and waving, you watch the boat disappear off into the horizon. It becomes quickly apparent that you cannot tread water for very long, but you can float for a long time. So your survival strategy becomes that of floating until, you hope, those on board notice that you are missing and come back to rescue you.

Now, in order to float, you have to relax. For if you tense up, you sink. So there you are, all alone in the vast expanse of water, floating, relaxing, floating, relaxing. How would you be relaxing out there? Knowing your life depended on it, you would be relaxing *very seriously*. You'd be relaxing with all your heart. Each time fear arises, causing you to tense up, you would renew the letting go embodied in your life-saving relaxation. Tensing up, you relax; tensing up, you relax—a life-saving dance in the midst of the sea.

Then, a most extraordinary thing happens. Floating there, all alone, looking up into a boundless sky, you realize that you are being sustained in a vast presence that sustains you whether you live or die. At one level, it would be truly tragic to drown, to go under, to face the scary end. At another level too big to think about, there arises a bliss beyond feeling. There is granted a body-grounded realization that even in going under, you would remain sustained and safe. Floating there, beyond the dualism of life and death, in a timeless moment beyond time, anchored invincibly in the boundless sky, you realize that in drowning you would become what you eternally are. You would become one with the primitive sea of unmanifested presence that your very presence in the present moment is manifesting.

If, while floating in this wondrous awakening, you were to suddenly see the boat coming back to get you, you would no doubt experience a profound sense of relief and joy. In being pulled back on board, you might be overcome with emotion and begin to weep over the fact that your life was saved. But deeper down, within yourself, you would know that you were being pulled back on board as one transformed in a great awakening. Your thoughts cannot grasp it. There are no words for it. Even so, the truth remains: you were saved out there in the midst of the sea, where, in an unto-death dance of choosing to relax, choosing to let go, you found a life beyond the dualism of life and death.

It seems to me we can understand the essence of our practice in the light of this little story. Surely there have been moments in which we have fallen off the boat into the sea. At first these fallings were limited to our isolated moments of spontaneous contemplative awakening, in which we found ourselves momentarily awakened to the abysslike nature of the concrete immediacy of life itself.

The setting sun, the sleeping infant, the beloved's embrace— each moment of awakening ended in our being pulled back on board. Which is to say, it ended with our once again returning to our customary way of experiencing our customary self. But little by little, this pattern of falling and returning and falling and returning began to transform our character. We have begun to be transformed into someone whose daily living is becoming imbued with a quiet inner desire to live in a more daily abiding awareness of the divinity of the life we are living.

Sitting still and straight in meditation is our free choice to leap into the sea. Or perhaps, truer still, it is our free choice to ease ourselves over and over again into the fathomless sea of presence that the present moment manifests. It is our free choice to open ourselves to the realization that we are eternally sustained in this fathomless sea of presence that our very presence is manifesting.

CHAPTER 11

Slow, Deep, Natural Breathing

When you sit in meditation, your breathing naturally slows down. Quietly focusing your attention on your breathing is a way of slowing down and settling into a deep meditative awareness of oneness with God. Breathing out, be quietly aware of breathing out. Breathing in, be quietly aware of breathing in. Each time you realize you have drifted off into thoughts, memories, and other ego-based modes of being, simply return to your breathing as your anchoring place in present-moment attentiveness.

You might be inclined to renew your awareness of your breathing simply as a way of renewing and sustaining your meditative awareness of the present moment. You may, however, be interiorly drawn to follow the path of the breath as your primary way of opening yourself to a deep experience of oneness with God. If this proves to be the case, your practice will gravitate toward a quiet, wholehearted attentiveness to each breath. As you sit wholly attentive to this inhalation, wholly attentive to this exhalation, your awareness will slowly merge and become one with the simply given miracle of each breath. As you continue to entrust yourself to the sheer immediacy of each breath, you will be opening yourself to a deep experience of God, giving herself to you whole and complete in and as each life sustaining breath.

There are several ways of grounding yourself in awareness of your breathing that you can explore. You might imagine as you inhale that the air is going all the way down into your belly, your loins, your legs, down and through the soles of your feet. Then as you exhale, imagine you are exhaling from the soles of your feet up through your legs, your loins, your belly, your heart, and out through your mouth. Allow the air flowing downward and upward to create pathways of awareness and open acceptance of all that lies within.

There are two other approaches that you may find helpful in grounding yourself in awareness of your breathing. You can focus your attention on your abdomen as it moves in and out with each breath. Or you can focus your attention on the subtle sensation of the air at your nostrils as you breathe.

Your efforts in following the path of breath awareness might be enhanced by repeating a word or phrase with each breath. In a previous chapter, I mentioned using the phrase "I love you" as a meditative practice. Taking this as our example, as you inhale, listen to the incoming breath so intently that you can hear in it God's silent "I love you," in which God is flowing into you as the source and reality of your very being. As you exhale, breathe out your silent "I love you" back to God. As you inhale, be aware of the air as being God flowing into you, as the divine gift of your very being. As you exhale, allow your silent "I love you" to be your very being, flowing back into the depths of God. Simply sit, open to God breathing divine love into the depths of your being, as you breathe your whole being, as a gift of love, back into God. This one practice alone, engaged in with heartfelt sincerity and devotion, can awaken you to God's total and complete oneness with you as the giver, the sustainer, and the reality of the sheer miracle of your very being. As this realization of God's oneness with you grows, you will begin to realize how foolish it is to imagine that God is, in any way, distant from you. You discover how foolish it is to imagine that you could, in any way, hide from God, who is wholly one with all that is within your mind and heart, your very being.

If you do not find these strategies helpful, then simply sit, quietly attentive to your breathing. In its own quiet way, simply sitting still, quietly attentive to your breathing, opens up an awareness and acceptance of all that lies within. This entry into all that lies within occasions the encounter with God, who is one with all that lies within.

When we sit in meditation, we would do well to be attentive to our breathing, in much the same manner as a student sits with a world-renowned teacher of the spiritual path. The student listens intently to all the teacher has to say. Simply being in the teacher's presence conveys an inner knowledge of the path that cannot be put into words. In much the same way, sitting silent and still in meditation, we allow our breathing to mentor our newly awakened heart. As we sit in meditation, we listen intently to the lessons of self-transformation that our breathing embodies. In our willingness to learn these lessons, we are transformed and the union with God we seek is realized within us.

One lesson our breathing invites us to learn is that *the indwelling Spirit of God calls us inward, to join God in becoming one with all that lies within*. To say God is one with all that lies within means that God is one with our dreams, our hopes and fears, and all things remembered and long since forgotten.

God is one with our most intimate longings for things not yet realized, and with all the places within us that we do not know anything about. The reason we need to be called to be one with all that lies within is that we have become estranged from a meditative awareness of the interiority of ourselves. We have become strangers to the intimate recesses of our own heart. The Lord and master of heart is waiting within the depths of our heart. It is important that we enter into our own heart, so that God is not left waiting too much longer.

For a couple of years I was one of the Christian faculty members of the Buddhist-Christian conference in Boulder, Colorado. One of the Buddhist teachers there, a Zen master named Eido Roshi, said in one of his conferences that the devil is a tight diaphragm. He was referring to our tendency to go through life with a ligature tightly bound around our middle. Awareness of our breathing helps to loosen this ligature, granting access to all that lies within.

Truth is, we *are* known by God—so profoundly that we are only who God knows us to be. It is not God but we who have difficulty seeing and accepting all that lies within. We are the ones who are afraid to see and accept just how broken and whole, how fragile and invincible, how fleeting and eternal, how human and divine we really are. By sitting in meditation, allowing our breathing to create pathways of loving openness to all that lies within, we learn to rest, as God does, in openness to all that lies within.

Simply breathe in, wholly attentive to simply breathing in. Simply breathe out, wholly attentive to simply breathing out. Lean into each breath so far that your observing, note-taking ego loses it footing in the depth of a single breath. Rest in each breath until, little by little, the intimate texture of your consciousness becomes the free-flowing texture of your breathing.

Do not wait for anything more than this to appear. For how could there be more than God, given whole and complete, in and as the stark simplicity of each life-sustaining breath?

As breath awareness is a way of joining God in being one with all that lies within, *it simultaneously awakens you to join God in being one with what is outside yourself.* To say that God is one with all that is outside yourself means simply that God is one with all the trees and flowers and weeds that grow along the roadside. God is one with the great mountains of the world and with each tiny grain of sand. In short, God is one with the world and with each thing and person in it. How could this not be so, since God is the origin, infinite ground, and fulfillment of the whole world and all that it contains?

To see how awareness of your breathing can help you to join God in being one with all that lies without, consider this: If in ten seconds all the air were to be instantaneously removed from where you are now sitting, you would, of course, suddenly be unable to breathe. Such is your breath-by-breath radical dependency on the air that surrounds you. And the air that surrounds and sustains you also surrounds and sustains me, just as it surrounds and sustains all who live. The air, of course, is one with the plants, which are one with the sunlight, which allows the plants, by means of photosynthesis, to renew and sustain the oxygen in the air that you breathe. In short, in each inhalation, you take in the world of which you are a part, and without which you could not live. As you continue to meditate, this experiential oneness with the world around you grows and deepens. You learn to be more habitually aware of how one you are with everyone and everything around you.

Sit solidly, with all your heart. Sit as one who would rather be nowhere other than in this moment of being wholly absorbed in seeking God by being wholly absorbed in each breath as it is actually occurring. As you sit quietly, following each inhalation, you learn to be with God, who is one with all that lies within. As you sit quietly, following each exhalation out into all that is around and about you, you learn to be one with God, who is one with all that is external to yourself.

With each inhalation, all that is without flows inward. With each exhalation, all that is within flows outward. It is in our sustained meditative awareness to and oneness with this back-and-forth, in-and-out rhythm of our breathing that we come to a deep experiential awareness that all that lies without and all that lies within are one. As this realization deepens, it no longer seems as if we are looking out through the portals of our eyes at a world that is other than ourselves. To the contrary, we begin to realize that the line that separates us from all that is not us is much more porous than we imagined. We begin to awaken to the freely flowing interpenetration of the inner and outer worlds. As our consciousness merges with and becomes one with our breathing, we realize how our breathing weaves the seamless garment of the intuitively realized real world.

Another lesson learned in breath awareness is that of the neglected essential. I used to keep a small poster by my desk that someone had sent me. It said: "Things to do today: Inhale, exhale. Inhale, exhale. Inhale, exhale." Breathing does not tend to end up on today's to-do list, because breathing is not something we have to "do." That is, it is not something we have to remember to do, so it gets done. The breathing flows of its own accord, as the neglected essential without which all the "important" items on the to-do list could never get done.

What if our beating heart and our breathing required a continual repeated conscious choice? That is, what if, in order to take each breath, we had to consciously have the intention to breathe? What if, in order for our heart to continue beating, we had to continuously and consciously say to our heart, "Beat, beat, beat"? And what if you were absent-minded? Imagine the anxiety you would live in, realizing that your slightest diversion could result in death! Fortunately for all of us, such is not the case. Day by day by day, we are carried along by the neglected essential of life itself.

Imagine a man sitting in deep meditation, seeking perfect union with God. And imagine that, while sitting there, he has a massive heart attack and dies. We might say that his search for God met with sudden, unplanned success. Such is the thread that flows from God, the divine sovereign of the neglected essential of life itself. And yet we tend to get so caught up in all the nonessential things of everyday life that we rarely, if ever, pause to ground ourselves in the neglected essential of life itself. As we meditate, we are slowly healed of this hubris and folly of running roughshod over the simply given gift of life. We learn, little by little, to recognize God's radical nearness in the sheer immediacy of simply being alive in the present moment.

Finally, we can reflect on how breath awareness awakens us to God's presence in the pattern of letting go and receiving that permeates all of life. With each inhalation we receive air into ourselves. With each exhalation we let go of the air we have received. I realize you know this. Who doesn't? But a great deal of what is learned in meditation is arrived at in a willingness to become attentive to what we, in some unquestioned, matter-of-fact way, already know. When we meditate, we slow down so that we can begin to catch up with ourselves. We settle into unhurried, heartfelt attentiveness to all that is seemingly obvious. As we do so, something as simple as a simple breath becomes less and less obvious, and more and more fraught with the presence of God. The more we sit in meditation, the more we pause to ponder the simple things we tend to pass by in haste. And the more we slow down to ponder what simply is, the more we begin to understand that a great deal of our confusion arises from assuming that we understand things we do not understand at all. If we did understand the nature of our breathing and all the simple realities of our daily life, we would understand God. For God is giving herself, wholly and completely, in and as the incomprehensible stature of a single breath and of all things that are as they simply are.

When we meditate, we slow down to observe our breathing. As the silent attentiveness of meditation deepens, we enter into each inhalation. We discover, firsthand, the mystery of receiving that each inhalation embodies. We become very attentive to each exhalation. We enter into the mystery of letting go that each exhalation embodies. Sitting in this way, inhaling and exhaling, giving and receiving, we enter into the direct experience of the mutuality of giving and receiving.

Imagine trying to exhale one hundred times in a row without inhaling! This is not advised. Nor is it possible. For you can exhale only a breath you have inhaled. If you have not inhaled, there is no breath to exhale. All of life is like this. You and I and all our fellow human beings face the inevitability of our own approaching death. We are already on our way to losing our life on this earth. But had we never received the gift of life on this earth, we would not be facing the inevitability of losing it. For only that which is born dies. Only in having received life can we lose life. It is in having received the gift of life on this earth that the certainty of losing life on this earth arises.

The French painter Georges Rouault painted a nude woman in her final months of pregnancy. She's looking downward, as if lost in a moment of pensive silence. Her hand is on her stomach, swollen with life. The caption at the bottom of the painting reads: "Everyone must die, even the one who has not been born must die." Just as taking in a breath sets in motion the inevitable event of exhaling, so birth sets in motion the inevitability of death. This is the great truth that is so difficult for our ego self to come to terms with. Every birth sets death in motion. Every new beginning is the beginning of that which ends. Every gain is the emergence of that which will be lost.

But sit and watch your breathing, and you will see that the opposite is equally and fully true. You cannot sit for an hour and only exhale. For each exhalation opens up the empty space into which the next inhalation comes pouring in. It is understandable that we prefer birth to death. Who does not prefer the rising tide of one's powers to the inevitable decline of one's powers? Our ego self has a hard time with its own diminishment and death. After all, our ego self is not stupid. Each year, as we blow out the candles on a birthday cake that has one more candle on it than it had the year before, we can tell what is going on.

But look closely and see how often it proves to be true that a loss that was so difficult to endure at the time proved to be the staging area for receiving a previously unknown fullness of life. Look and see how true it tends to be that, had you not gone through the loss, your heart would not have been big enough to receive the unexpected gift that came flowing into the empty space that the loss left behind. Viewing all this on a bigger scale, it may seem unfair that, as we go through life, we do not start getting it together until we start falling apart. But look and see how, as life becomes tangibly more brief and fragile, there arises a previously unknown capacity to recognize and appreciate just how precious life is. In fact, as you look back over your shoulder to see just how you have become who you have thus far come to be, you will see many births giving rise to many deaths that in turn gave rise to many births.

As you sit, attentive to your breathing, you will eventually come to realize that even the present moment itself embodies the same dynamic mutuality of gain and loss that permeates your breathing. As you sit, silent and still, you can quietly observe that life is always occurring in the present moment. But the way things are in the present moment is never the same from one moment to the next. For the ever-present present moment, just as it is, *is* perpetually yielding to what we call the future, and in doing so *is* becoming what we call the past. If the way things are in the present moment would refuse to yield to the future, there would be no room for the perpetual newness of the present moment to appear.

Jesus said, "Unless the grain of wheat die and fall into the ground, it remains alone. But if it dies, it brings forth fruit a hundred-fold" (John 12:24). Jesus was talking, at once, about himself and about us. We tend to think of the birth, life, death, and resurrection of Jesus as events that happened one after another in sequential time. And, indeed, from the vantage point of our ego consciousness, such is the case both for us and for Jesus. Like us, he was born, lived, and died. And *then* he rose from the dead, to give witness to our yet-to-be-realized fulfillment.

But from the vantage point of meditative awareness, Jesus's life, death, and resurrection are occurring perpetually and simultaneously. For the life, death, and resurrection of Jesus are the revelation of the eternal fullness of the present moment. And the true nature of the present moment is the reality of the life, death, and resurrection of Jesus.

Little by little our awareness of this aspect of life begins to permeate our daily experience. We can begin to recognize those moments in which everything comes together, just as we had hoped, in the staging area of the inevitable loss of all that is currently being acquired. And, inversely, when we are in the midst of a painful downturn, we can know and trust that the painful loss is but the staging area for blessings as yet unknown. As time goes by, we learn to trust this rhythmic pattern in which our heart is being perpetually transformed and awakened to God's mysterious ways. Going deeper still, we come to realize that God is the infinity of this death-out-of-life, life-out-of-death rhythm of life itself.

In looking back over our shoulder we see just how we have become who we have become by way of this self-metamorphosing pattern of many births giving way to many deaths, giving way, in turn to many births. Peering into the unknown future, we can trust that this same pattern, at work in the heart of reality itself, will continue to prevail. We can look toward our own approaching death with confidence, knowing that it will be the final crescendo of this same pattern, in which we will exhale into God. As Saint Mechtilde heard God say to her, "Do not fear your death. For in that moment, I will breathe in my breath, and your soul will come to me like a needle to a magnet."[1]

CHAPTER 12

Eyes Closed or Lowered Toward the Ground

The next suggested guideline for meditation is to close your eyes or lower them toward the ground. Some people find it most natural to close their eyes while they meditate. Others find it most natural to leave the eyes open, lowered at a forty-five-degree angle toward the ground. Closing you eyes or lowering them to the ground is practical in that it helps to enhance present-moment attentiveness. To be always looking about contributes to a distracted state of mind, making it difficult to settle into more interior, meditative states of awareness. As your practice deepens, closing your eyes or lowering them toward the ground becomes an act of incarnate faith that embodies the desire to see God.

Both closing your eyes and lowering them toward the ground embody the visual dimension of the passage into more interior, meditative states of oneness with God. What matters is that your eyes embody a "Lord, that I might see" stance of openness to God.

Meditating with your eyes closed embodies certain truths of the meditative path. Sitting with your eyes closed embodies a darkness filled with an unseen light. As you sit, quietly gazing into this darkness, the unseen light can begin to appear. Sitting in meditation with your eyes closed embodies a spiritual wisdom in which you learn to see spiritual realities invisible to the eye. Freely choosing to close your eyes, then resting in this choice, embodies the desire to be a seer of things invisible to the eye. Closing your eyes as you meditate embodies the humble acknowledgment that you do not see God, who eternally sees you and, through his indwelling Spirit, is preparing your heart to see him face-to-face. To meditate with your eyes closed embodies entering the unknown depths, in which you have to feel your way along, learning to accept God's guidance. Meditating with your eyes closed dissolves the barrier that customarily exists between the waking and sleeping states. As this barrier dissolves, the mythic imagery of the unconscious is brought out of hiding into the light of day. Meditating with your eyes closed is like being in a pitch-dark room with someone you cannot see. Trust grows as you learn to stretch forth your hands to be led, step by step, in the darkness.

When I was in the monastery, I meditated with my eyes open. For a number of reasons I have continued to meditate with my eyes open, looking downward toward the ground. In fact, when I begin meditating, quietly becoming aware of what I see through my lowered eyes tends to be the way I most naturally enter into the meditative state. Sometimes my eyes will naturally close as I continue meditating, sometimes not. At any rate, I am most experienced in meditating with my eyes open and will therefore be focusing on this method here.

If you are among those who meditate with your eyes closed, you might want to explore some of the aspects of meditating with your eyes open that I will be reflecting on here. As a more general application, what I am about to share here may be more directly applicable to the transformative power of meditative gazing in the midst of nature, or at things in your own home or wherever you might be. Learning to see the inherent holiness of everyone and everything around us is a key component of contemplative living. On a broader scale, what is being shared here is germane to the traditional Christian understanding of life as a journey that culminates in a beatific vision of God. Meditation, in this regard, is a way of entering into meditative states consisting of interior ways of "seeing" God's presence in our daily lives.

Lowering your eyes toward the ground as you begin to meditate is practical, in that it helps to promote present-moment attentiveness. As you settle into your practice, lowering your eyes toward the ground becomes an act of incarnate faith, embodying your desire to see God in all that you see. It is in this stance of faith that the transformative event of gazing deeply into the divinity of the present moment comes to pass.

I say "comes to pass" because in lowering your eyes you are most likely, at first, to see simply your hands in your lap, the design in the carpet, or perhaps the cracks in the floorboards. You might notice the quality of light in which you see these things—the intensity of the midday sunlight, or perhaps the diffused light of a cloudy afternoon, or the faint light of a flickering candle as you sit meditating in the dark. As you settle into the silent, childlike attentiveness of your practice, there arises the contemplative experience of gazing into the endlessly holy nature of the cracks in the floorboard, the design in the carpet, your hands in your lap. You begin to see, through meditative eyes, that all that you see transparently manifests, in some overwhelmingly subtle manner, the unmanifested presence we call

God. Gazing into this depth of the divinity that the present moment manifests, you practice your practice. As you learn to sit in this way, day by day, this meditative way of seeing can slowly become your habitual way of seeing all that you see.

In order to understand and appreciate this visual dimension of meditation practice better, it might be helpful to recall that each guideline for meditation being suggested here is a way of freely choosing to assume the interior stance spontaneously assumed in moments of spontaneous meditative awareness. We can take the guideline to sit still as our example of how this is so. If, for example, you are out at night and look up at the stars, your quiet amazement might prompt you to stand motionless, so as to be as present to the moment as you can be. As you do so, you realize that you are being stilled in being so deeply moved by the awakening that is being granted and in which you sense something of the immense nearness of God. In continuity with the stillness that occurs in moments of spontaneous experience, you sit still in meditation as a way of inviting and evoking more interior states of openness to God.

Moments of spontaneous experience often have a visual dimension. But this visual dimension is subtle and not readily recognized until we pay close attention to it. So I will first point out this visual dimension and then go on to note how we invite meditative states of awareness by consciously choosing to incorporate this visual dimension into our practice.

As we carefully reflect on the visual dimension of moments of spontaneous experience, we discover that our vision in such moments has both focused and unfocused aspects that play about one another as the experience unfolds. To see how this is so, imagine that you are walking along the beach. You look about yourself, appreciating the beauty of the primordial meeting place of land and sea. As you look down, a shell at your feet suddenly stands forth with unprecedented clarity. Stopping, you stoop down, pick up the shell, and hold it in the palm of your hand. In that moment all else falls away as you become utterly absorbed in the shell's intricate beauty. Then you look up to see the countless shells stretched out before you. You see, once again, the whole scene of sky, shoreline, and birds. Then you focus in again on one thing, perhaps the wave that is, in this precise moment, washing up over your bare feet. Then your gaze once again opens up to the vast expanse of all that is about you. Then, looking down, you become once again momentarily absorbed in the shell in your hand—the one shell that it alone uniquely is, in this present-moment totality.

As your eyes move seamlessly from focusing on each specific thing to seeing the totality in which each thing plays its part, something quite extraordinary manifests itself. What is manifesting itself is the fact that the totality of reality that is the big picture of all that you see is, in some way, present in the reality of each shell, each bird, each thing that you see. And the reality of each thing is, in some way, present in the totality of all that you see. The totality in each thing, each thing in the totality nature of reality, is revealed in the way your eyes effortlessly move back and forth, focusing on each thing and then taking in the big picture of all that is seen. So it is that the now focused, now unfocused aspects of awareness work together, like a great bellows of the eyes, fanning the flames of enlightenment.

It is this visual dimension of our moments of spontaneous awareness that we freely choose to evoke in meditation by simply sitting, with our eyes lowered toward the ground. Sitting still and straight in meditation with your eyes lowered toward the ground is a way of entering into the interplay of the one-in-all, all-in-one nature of the contemplatively realized real world. Notice that, as with all aspects of meditation, the intentional aspect is sustained throughout, even as it is quickly transcended by the spontaneous occurrence of the meditative state that meditation is intended to evoke. With respect to the visual dimension of meditation, our intention is to open ourselves to seeing the way in which we see in moments of spontaneous meditative experience. To carry out this intention, we simply sit still and straight and gaze downward toward the ground. We then simply allow our eyes to be our eyes. We simply yield ourselves to the God-given nature of our eyes as they are left free to be themselves, free of the intrusion of the ego, with its intention that directs our vision toward this or that.

Imagine, then, that you are sitting still and straight in meditation. Through your lowered eyes you see the cracks in the floorboard or the design in the carpet. Your eyes naturally focus on a single aspect of the totality of all that you see. Perhaps your eyes land on a particular section of a single crack in the flooring that is a bit wider or narrower than the others. Or perhaps you see how the flooring shines in the sunlight, or how the carpet's edging is frayed in one particular place.

In fidelity to the practice, you are not clinging to this focused awareness. Rather, you let it pass of its own accord as your eyes take in the more global sense of the totality of all that you see. But in becoming aware once again of a more global awareness of all that is seen, you do not cling to this more global awareness. You do not choose this more global awareness over the beholding of the concrete immediacy of each detail of each thing that you gaze upon.

As you sit like this, giving yourself over to this gazing, there can come rising up out of the cracks in the floorboards, or the designs in the carpet, the concreteness of all that is seen—the intimate seeing of the all-in-one, one-in-all unitive nature of reality. This is the visual dimension of beginning to be present in the concrete immediacy of the present moment: beginning to see things that were there all along; caring enough to stop and notice. More than noticing, it means beginning to appreciate and enter into the endlessly mysterious nature of the concrete details of everything around you. It means beginning to see something of God in all that you see.

Jesus said, "The lamp of the body is the eye. If, therefore, your eye is clear, your whole body will be full of light" (Matt. 6:22). By learning to surrender our ego consciousness to this primordial wisdom of the eyes, our eyes become open windows through which the divine light comes flooding in, making us whole in realizing that we *are* in the presence of God.

There is spiritual wisdom to be found in the interplay of the focused and unfocused aspects of seeing the way reality really is. This wisdom is found in discovering how good it is to see clearly the concrete details of the world around us. By this I mean simply that it is good to be an astute observer of the details of all that we see. But to become fixated on the details without seeing the all-encompassing totality the details manifest is not to see the true interconnected nature of all the details that we see.

Likewise, to seek God, to seek enlightenment, to seek holiness, to seek mystical fulfillment, is good. For this is to seek our ultimate fulfillment in learning to see the big, ultimate picture of reality that our faith discloses to us. But to seek divine fulfillment as wholly other than and beyond the concrete immediacy of the present moment is to be blind to the immanence of God's transcendence. Which is to say, it is to be blind to the way our divine fulfillment is already at hand in and as the concrete immediacy of the situation at hand.

Our meditative gazing is the visual expression of a self-transforming journey in which we are set free of a twofold ignorance. Specifically, we are set free from the ego-based tendency to see things as separate from God, as we are set free from our simultaneous tendency to see God as being dualistically other than the concrete immediacy of things. In the contemplative gaze, the concrete immediacy of the present moment is realized to be the manifestation of the unmanifested mystery of God. And God is realized to be the infinity of the mystery of all that is seen.

We, of course, are not excluded from the contemplatively realized all-in-one, one-in-all nature of the real world. How could we be excluded, since we are the one in whom this all-in-one, one-in-all nature of reality is realized? Meditation is not a spectator sport in which we stand back and observe in objective fashion, with great admiration, a unity that is dualistically other than ourselves. The opposite is true: in meditation, we open ourselves to the transforming realization of our oneness with the mystery we seek, manifesting itself in and as our experience of this oneness. In specifically visual terms, we realize that we who are seeing, the act of seeing, that which we are seeing, and God are completely and unexplainably one.

As a way of attempting to explore the visual dimension of meditation further, we can reflect on the characteristics of gazing, as distinct from staring and gawking—three decidedly different modes of seeing. Staring has a harsh edge to it. We instinctively become somewhat guarded in the presence of the hostile stare. Gawking is the amazed and befuddled look of those who are momentarily captivated by the sight of something or someone that is outside the range of what they are accustomed to seeing. Gazing is a form of seeing that is much more refined than either staring or gawking. Gazing is the unobtrusive beholding that attains the innermost essence of that which is gazed upon. A mother wordlessly gazes at the face of her nursing infant. Lovers gaze at one another. And artists gaze upon that which moves and inspires them.

As an exercise in our religious imagination, if we were asked to choose whether staring, gawking, or gazing seemed to be most continuous with how the blessed see God in heaven, most of us would choose gazing. It seems counterintuitive to think of the blessed in paradise staring at God, with all the intrusive harshness that the word *staring* implies. Similarly, it seems counterintuitive to think that, in paradise, you can tell the new-comers—that is, those who have been in heaven for only a few centuries or so—because they are still gawking at God like open-mouthed tourists.

We speak in the Christian tradition of the beatification vision, in which we express our faith and our hope of seeing God for all eternity face-to-face. We do not know what this might mean. But is it possible that our loving gaze embodies a kind of foreshadowing of how we will, after we are dead, eternally gaze upon God? Is it possible that our loving gaze is in some manner the way God lovingly gazes at us? Meister Eckhart suggests something even bolder in saying, "The eye with which I see God is the eye with which God sees me."[1] We can then rephrase our questions in a yet bolder way and ask: Is it possible that God, God's loving vision of us, who we are, and our vision of God are all absolutely one? Is it possible that the loving gaze of our meditation practice is, even now—this single eye, with which God is seeing us—seeing God in the concrete immediacy of all that we see? I will tell you what I think. I think the answer is yes. It is possible. It is more than possible.

Finally, we can reflect together on the visual dimension of humility as a pathway to meditative oneness with God. To get at this, we can go back once again to our moments of spontaneous meditative experience. As a moment of spontaneous meditative experience is actually occurring we are awed and grateful in seeing something of God in the sunrise, the child at play, or whatever it might be that we are seeing. As the moment of spontaneous contemplative awakening passes, we are made painfully aware of how blind we tend to be to the divinity of the life that we are living.

Jesus said, "You have eyes to see and do not see" (Mark 8:18). We know by virtue of our moments of spontaneous meditative experience how true this is. We are endowed with the capacity to see the mystery that is always before our eyes. And yet we tend to go about not seeing the inherent holiness of everything around us. When you sit and lower your eyes in meditation, you might typically see nothing but the surface appearance of what is simply before your eyes. You might bemoan the fact that you are seeing what you know to be but the surface appearance of God's perfect and complete presence in the world. But you can also choose to gaze deeply into your inability to gaze deeply into the divinity of all that you see. Here is a spiritual path that is open to all of us. It is a self-transforming path marked out by a kind of humility of the eyes. In this humility we freely choose to see and accept how we tend not to see God's presence in all that we see.

Imagine a woman who looses her eyesight in a tragic accident. At first, she thrashes about in a tumult of mixed emotions. But then, by way of a painful and circuitous path, she calms herself and gazes with unseeing eyes into the darkness that has become her home. At the level of ego, the loss of her eyesight is truly tragic. But interiorly, at a level that determines the tonality of her presence in the world, she gazes into a great and always hard-to-come-by truth. She sees that loss leaves an empty space; a gaping hole in the should-be, always-thought-it-would-be world in which the ego tries so hard to live. It is into this empty space, opened up by the loss of her eyesight, that she now gazes. As she does so, she is transformed in seeing and accepting all that she sees.

There are those of us with twenty-twenty vision who, with respect to what matters most, do not see so well. There are also others who have lost their eyesight who, with respect to what matters most, have twenty-twenty vision. What often proves to be the case with the latter group is that they came to this interior vision by gazing deeply into their loss of sight, and all that the loss of sight has allowed them to see.

Something very similar to this happens to us as we learn to sit in meditation, gazing deeply into our inability to see the divinity that is always before our eyes. We gaze downward and see nothing but the plain old ordinariness of our hands resting in our lap. We gaze downward and see nothing but the ordinary floor. There is more than enough here to live on. For by such heartfelt gazing, we come to discover directly, for ourselves, the stuff of which the heart is made. In our willingness to see clearly how little we see, we are graced with a visual humility in which we know we are always standing at the edge of a vast expanse of things unseen.

It is as if each new moment of spontaneous contemplative experience, or each flash of awareness that comes in our meditation, comes like a lightning flash in the night that fleetingly discloses the divinity of the present moment. The darkness that quickly returns is the empty space, the gaping hole in the world of divinity in which we are trying to realize we are living. By learning to sit in meditation, gazing deeply into this blindness, our lowered eyes become the narrowed gate through which we pass into a deeper place.

As we sit, gazing into this depth, our eyes tell the story of our life up until now. We cannot tell this story in words. Our hearts break when we try. Words fail us in their linear limits, sequentially stretching out in many ideas what happens all at once, in the immediacy before thought begins. And so we sit, our story told, our identity revealed, in this wordless gazing into the depths of the moment in which we sit. As we are sitting thus, our meditation echoes the plea of the blind man in the Gospels: "Lord, that I might see."

Sitting thus, we gaze directly into the uncertain world in which the light of God perpetually shines.

We can bring these guidelines with respect to the body to a close, by reflecting briefly on the suggested guideline *to place your hands in a comfortable or meaningful position in your lap.* It may feel most natural for you to place your open hands palms downward or upward on each thigh. Or you may be inclined to rest one hand gently in the other, both palms upward.

You may be interiorly inclined to place your hands in a particular position simply because it is the position that feels most natural to you. Or you may be inclined to place your hands in a position that is personally meaningful to you. For example, you may find that sitting with your hands turned upward with the back of each hand resting on your thighs symbolizes an attitude of receptive openness to God. Or your upturned hands, one gently resting in the other, may symbolize an empty cup that you are waiting for God to fill. Or you may be inclined to hold your hands in still some other position that may have for you its own personal relevance. I have seen people on retreats sitting in meditation with the palms of their hands joined in prayer. I have seen people crossing their arms over their chest.

What matters, of course, is not the specific position in which you hold your hands but that the position of your hands forms an integral part of your wholehearted commitment to a work not made with human hands. The stillness of your hands in meditation expresses a Sabbath rest in which you cease all activity save that of actively sustaining a receptive openness to God.

CHAPTER 13

Walking Meditation

At this point we will pause in our reflections to explore some of the ways in which your practice of sitting in meditation might be enhanced by the practice of walking meditation. In fact, many of us practice walking meditation quite naturally, without ever really thinking about it. Look, for example, at how often taking a walk provides moments of meditative awareness in simply seeing, appreciating, and being out and about in God's world.

Having grown up in the Catholic tradition of the Christian faith, I found it meaningful to take part in liturgical processions and in the devotional practice of making the stations of the cross. When I was in the monastery, I would sometimes walk alone in the cloister, simply trying to be mindfully present to each step. And taking long walks in the woods became for me one of the ways in which I most naturally became more meditatively aware of God's presence.

I did not, however, begin to practice walking meditation as part of my regular meditation practice until I was first introduced to it in the mid-1980s as a Christian faculty member at a Buddhist-Christian conference in Boulder, Colorado, sponsored by the Naropa Institute.

The classes on Buddhist and Christian meditation practices were scheduled in a manner that allowed me, as a Christian faculty member, to participate in sessions led by Buddhist teachers. One of the classes I attended was led by a Zen master named Eido Roshi. He began the session by briefly presenting the fundamentals of sitting meditation practice. We then sat in silence for about twenty minutes of sitting meditation. He then introduced the fundamentals of walking meditation, after which we all stood and walked together in a long, slow, silent procession around the circumference of the room. Walking slowly, in silence, single file, around the room with Buddhists and fellow Christians was for me a powerful experience of the ecumenical potential of contemplative spirituality. For in walking together we were, I sensed, realizing our oneness with each other in ways that acknowledged and transcended the differences between us. And—what is more germane to our present reflections—I began to incorporate walking meditation into my own practice of meditation in the Christian tradition.

As with the directives given for sitting meditation, I present the directives for walking meditation with the assumption that you will be discerning the degree to which, and the manner in which, you might be interiorly drawn to incorporate walking meditation into your meditation practice.

Most people find that walking meditation is best performed barefoot or in their stocking feet. You may, however, prefer to leave your shoes on. Begin by standing straight and still, breathing slowly and naturally, with your eyes lowered toward the ground. Hold your arms and hands in any position that feels natural and comfortable. You might, for example, have your arms extended straight down at your sides, with hands facing in toward your thighs or with your open palms facing forward. It might be most natural for you to walk with your arms extended downward and your hands clasped behind you. Or you might naturally follow the Zen tradition of making a fist with one hand, then folding the other hand over it, and holding both hands in front of you at the level of your stomach or over your heart. Or you may find it most natural to join your hands together in front of you in a position of prayer.

Standing still and straight, with your eyes lowered toward the ground, breathing slowly and naturally, stand in the whole-hearted awareness of simply standing. Standing in this way, with deep devotion, is itself a deep practice, one empowered to awaken an intimate realization of the divinity of standing.

When it feels interiorly right to begin your first step, shift your weight to your right leg. Slowly and mindfully, lift your left foot off the ground, and slowly move it forward, lowering it to the ground about half a foot's length ahead of your right foot. Then, in one continuous, slow movement, shift your weight to your left leg. Neither pausing nor rushing, slowly begin lifting your right foot off the ground. Move it slowly forward and lower it about half a foot's length ahead of your left foot. Walk on like this, in one slow, continuous movement.

The essence of the practice is childlike mindfulness of each step. As you lift your foot, be wholeheartedly absorbed in lifting your foot. As you slowly swing your foot forward, be whole-heartedly absorbed in swinging your foot forward. As you lower your foot to the ground, be wholeheartedly absorbed in lower-ing your foot to the ground. As your foot makes contact with the ground, be quietly absorbed in your foot touching the ground.

If you find it helpful, you can use a word or phrase with each step. Each time your foot touches the ground, you might silently say, "Jesus," "God," "Life," or "Love." Or you can say a phrase with each step. At a Christian-Zen retreat I once attended, the leader, the Jesuit priest Hans Koenen, suggested using a phrase from Scripture: "Make straight the way of the Lord" (John 1:23). You could silently say, "I love you," as you lift your foot and begin swinging it forward, and then listen to God saying, "I love you," as you continue swinging your foot forward and touching it to the earth. If you are accustomed to using a word or phrase in your sitting meditation, you are likely to find the same word or phrase to be the most natural word or phrase to continue using in your walking meditation as well.

The word or phrase that feels most natural to you might be expressed as a question. For example, each time your foot touches the ground, you might silently ask, "What is this?" Or, as you lift your foot up off the ground, your question might be "What is this leaving behind?" As you move your foot forward and begin touching it to the ground your question might be "What is this moving on?" The conceptual mind is, of course, ready to jump in, suggesting the answer to such questions: "God," or "The mystery I seek," or "My lifelong path to God." But as we walk, the questions neither arise from nor are directed to our conceptual mind. Rather, the questions serve to awaken us to the concrete immediacy of our wholehearted absorption in each step as being nothing less or other than the all-encompassing mystery we seek, manifesting itself in and as this step . . . this step . . . this step.

If you find it helpful to do so, you can consciously incorporate your breathing into your walking meditation by inhaling deeply and slowly as you lift your foot and begin moving it forward, then exhaling as you continue to move it forward and lower it to the ground. If you are saying a word or phrase as part of your practice, you may find that it tends to blend naturally with the breath. Do not try to juggle all these various possibilities at once, but simply begin walking with childlike mindfulness of each step. You can explore the specific ways of practicing walking meditation at your own pace as you go along.

The walking should have a natural, flowing quality. Do not stop between each step. Do not lift your foot in exaggerated movements, as if yanking your foot out of a mud hole. Do not lift each leg high into the air in exaggerated movements, as if wearing snowshoes. Do not walk with an aura of impatience. Rather, walk slowly and naturally, in an even, flowing movement that embodies your childlike mindfulness of each step. Move as a huge old fish slowly moves through primordial waters. Move as a glacier moves across the land. Move as one who is awakening to the eternal stillness flowing out, unbroken and uninterrupted, in and as your foot lifting up, swinging forward, and touching the earth.

If you are practicing walking meditation alone at home, you might decide to walk slowly around the room. Walking in a circle embodies the circularity of life's journey, in which we move out from God and, without ever leaving God, follow the long slow curve of our life back to God.

The configuration of the room or your personal inclination may prompt you to walk back and forth in a straight line. If this proves to be the case, walk in a straight line until you come to a wall. When you get to the wall, stop, mindful of and attentive to the divinity manifested, just as we are every time we come to a point beyond which we cannot pass. Stand still with all your heart, allowing your standing to incarnate your faith in the divinity of standing. When it intuitively feels right, begin lifting your foot, turning it slowly about a quarter turn, and lowering it to the ground. Continue lifting and lowering each foot in a meditative awareness of turning about. When the turn is completed and you are facing back the way you came, stand motionless in mindful attentiveness of the divinity manifested in all the times we find ourselves heading back the way we came. When it intuitively feels right to do so, slowly lift your foot, beginning your walk back across the space through which you came. In other words, when walking back and forth, let the times of stopping and turning be integral aspects of an unbroken flow of meditative movement.

When walking very slowly in the manner described here, we are repeatedly balancing ourselves on one leg as we move the other leg forward. In doing so we sometimes wobble a little as we begin to lose our balance. This occasional wobbling plays its own part in walking meditation. As our sincere mindfulness of each step ripens, we will glimpse in each faltering step the art form of contemplative living as a process of learning to wobble well—that is, learning to waver with compassionate awareness of ourselves and of all people as ineffably elegant and precious in all our wavering ways.

Walking meditation naturally dovetails with sitting meditation. For most of us, most of the time, twenty to twenty-five minutes is a long enough period to spend in sitting meditation for us to settle into the meditative state, while at the same time being short enough to honor the arduous aspects of sitting motionless for long periods. Sometimes, however, it is just as a twenty- to twenty-five-minute session of sitting meditation is coming to an end that we begin to feel ourselves going deeper into a sustained state of body-grounded mindfulness of the divinity of the present moment. At such times, to stop meditating feels a bit like walking out of a play in the middle of the second act. It hardly seems right, and yet to go on much longer might not seem quite right either with respect to the importance of not pushing beyond our limits relative to the arduous aspects of sitting motionless for extended periods of time. Walking meditation provides a way of compassionately integrating the arduous aspects of sitting meditation with the felt need to give ourselves more time in which to allow the meditative state to deepen and expand. Sitting motionless for a full hour may be a bit too much for most of us. But sitting for twenty-five minutes, practicing walking meditation for ten minutes, and then sitting in meditation for another twenty-five minutes provides a balanced and compassionate way of practicing meditation for a full hour.

As each session of sitting meditation comes to an end, questions of contemplative living arise: As I learn to awaken to the divinity of sitting, can I, at the end of this session of meditation, learn to stand, awake to the divinity of standing? Can I learn to walk across the room, awake to the divinity of walking across a room? Can I open the door, awake to the divinity manifested every time I open a door? Can I pass someone in the hallway or out on the street, awake to the divinity manifested in our every encounter with another? Walking meditation is a living *yes* to these questions of contemplative living.

In practicing walking meditation we learn to navigate the transition from stillness to movement without breaking the thread of present-moment attentiveness. As we enter into the flowing movement of walking meditation, the unbroken thread of sustained contemplative wakefulness occasions an intimate realization of God, wholly poured out and given over to our foot lifting up, swinging forward, lowering, and touching the ground simply given the mystery of the earth.

Practicing walking meditation between two periods of sitting meditation can be done briskly, in a manner that has very much the same effect as splashing cold water on your face to renew and invigorate your awareness. Brisk walking can be done outdoors around the yard or garden, or indoors around the room or through areas of the house. Most people find that just one or two minutes of brisk walking, rather than ten minutes, is enough to renew and revitalize their awareness. What matters is that the brisk walking not dissipate but sustain in bodily movement the intimate wakefulness fostered in sitting still.

As we learn to move back and forth between sitting and walking meditation without breaking the thread of present-moment attentiveness, we begin to sense the possibility of sustaining contemplative awareness of the present moment in the midst of all our daily activities. Monastic life is a contemplative culture that invites a gradual metamorphosis of one's consciousness, such that the daily round of prayer and work are experienced as a single unitive movement of contemplative living. The dictum of Benedictine monasticism—*ora et labora*, "prayer and work"—calls upon the monk or nun to experience prayer and work not as two different activities, one opposed to the other, but as two modes of a single unitive experience of the inherent holiness of daily living. We who are seeking to live a more contemplative way of life in the midst of today's world must cultivate a contemplative culture in our homes and places of employment by creatively finding ways to make habitual a contemplative awareness of the inherent holiness of the life we are living.

The following exercise is intended to demonstrate how sitting meditation, walking meditation, and the performance of daily tasks might gradually flow together in a habitual state of present-moment attentiveness. The exercise consists of first choosing some household chore that needs to be done. I will use, as an example, washing a sink full of dirty dishes. Begin the exercise by first sitting in meditation for about twenty to thirty minutes. Then slowly stand, and walk in a slow, mindful manner to the sink. Stand at the sink, mindfully gazing for a moment at the dishes. Slowly and mindfully put soap in the sink. Fill the sink with hot water, attentive to the sound of the running water. With mindfulness, wash and rinse each item, mindfully placing each item in the drainer. When the dishes are finished, pull the plug; listen to and watch the water going down the drain. Rinse out the sink with mindfulness. Dry each item and put it in its proper place with natural and deliberate mindfulness. Wipe off the countertops with mindfulness. Then slowly walk back to your place of sitting meditation and sit for another twenty to twenty-five minutes. Then open a journal and begin writing spontaneously and sincerely about what it would be like to live in this way. That is, what it would be like to engage in your daily tasks—to open and close doors, take some boxes out of the garage, file papers, answer the phone—not as rude interruptions in a carefully sequestered contemplative life but, to the contrary, as living embodiments of the hands-on divinity of daily living.

The self-transforming potential of exercises such as the one suggested here can be heightened still further by setting aside retreat days devoted to the deepening of a habitual state of contemplative awareness of the present moment. Follow the promptings of your heart in what seems most natural and helpful relative to the pacing and number of hours to be spent in sitting and walking meditation. Prepare and eat simple meals with mindfulness. Keep all conversations with others to a minimum. If you journal or read anything at all, read and write in a mindful manner only that which awakens and deepens a sustained state of mindfulness of the divinity of the present moment. Let your prayers be sincere and childlike, with an emphasis on opening yourself to the intimate realization of

God manifested in and as the concrete immediacy of each passing moment. As you end your retreat day, ask for the grace of entering back into your daily routines more contemplatively awake and appreciative of the inherent holiness of your daily routines.

At first, and for quite some time, our efforts in being more contemplatively awake to the divinity of each passing moment require continual renewal. Catching ourselves in the act of rushing, we must consciously choose to slow down. Catching ourselves becoming overly reactive to stressful situations, we must choose to breathe into the situation a more genuinely present and compassionate way of engaging in the flow of what is happening. With time, however, this conscious effort transforms our daily awareness. With time we become ever more habitually awake to the inherent holiness of the one unending moment in which our lives unfold.

Participating in meditation retreats and attending regular sessions of a local meditation group provide the opportunity to practice walking meditation with others. In the meditation-intensive retreats that I lead, the participants take part in hour-long meditation sessions, seated in chairs or on prayer cushions or benches arranged facing inward around the four walls of the room. When the first twenty-five minutes of sitting meditation end, all stand in silence and walk slowly around the circumference of the room for ten minutes or for one rotation of the room, whichever comes first. Then all sit to complete the hour's meditation with another twenty-five minutes of sitting meditation.

Walking together in this way embodies fundamental lessons regarding the communal nature of life's journey. Walking slowly, single file, around the room, you are made aware that you cannot walk faster than the person in front of you. Likewise, walking slowly, single file, around the room, you are made aware that all the people behind you cannot walk faster than you. If you start walking slower and slower in becoming so absorbed in your private world of walking that you forget everyone walking with you, a problem begins to develop. Namely, all who are walking with you will begin to pile up behind you. By taking responsibility not to allow the distance between you and the person in front of you to increase, your absorption in each step opens up a sensitivity to the communal nature of your walking. Walking together embodies the realization that you cannot authentically live absorbed in your private inner world. The way you walk your daily walk impacts, for better or for worse, those whose lives are inexorably bound up with your own.

When the group's collective practice is deep and strong, walking together in silence can occasion a profound realization that the unforeseeable fulfillment we are moving into is always manifesting itself perfectly in and as the journey itself. I was once conducting a meditation retreat at which the participants were practicing sitting and walking meditation in the manner described here. Sitting next to me and walking directly behind me was Sister Julian, who had taught my mother in high school. Sister Julian, who was in her eighties at the time, had to use a walker. During the ten-minute periods of the group's slowly walking together around the room, the communal silence of the walking was rhythmically woven with her walker, which squeaked loudly each time she would move it forward and lean her weight on it to take her next step. I became aware of the sound of her squeaking walker. Then I became aware of my irritation. Then I became aware of being irritated with myself for being irritated. Then I became aware of being irritated with myself that I was still subject to getting irritated at myself for getting irritated. As I entered into the concrete immediacy of simply walking, this egocentric noise slowly fell away. I was left with a deepening, childlike awareness of belonging to a community moving together as one in a silence woven with the *squeak, squeak, squeak* of Sister Julian's walker.

Childlike fidelity unto death sounds just like this: *squeak, squeak, squeak!* The long walk into feeble limitations and beyond sounds just like this: *squeak, squeak, squeak!* The unbearable beauty of a person's unself-aware engagement in the primordial flow of life sounds just like this: *squeak, squeak, squeak!* The whole journey of life sounds just like this: *squeak, squeak, squeak.* Never, in the end, other than a human being coming to the end. Never, in the end, anything less than the deathless divinity, manifested in and as each step we take. This is deep walking. This is God manifested in and as this step . . . this step . . . this step.

Little by little this mindful, heartfelt walking becomes our way of following Christ in today's world. Little by little we learn to walk through life as Christ did—as an awake, compassionate human being. We will now turn to compassion as the attitude that is to permeate both our sitting and walking meditation so that, with time, compassion comes to permeate every aspect of our lives.

CHAPTER 14

Compassion

The guideline for meditation with respect to attitude is to maintain nonjudgmental compassion toward ourselves as we discover ourselves clinging to and rejecting everything, and to maintain nonjudgmental compassion toward others in their powerlessness—one with ours.

The unexpected strategy at work in meditation is that it invites us to engage in the simple task of simply being present, open, and awake in the present moment. Our efforts to do so become the context in which sleepiness, daydreaming, and all sorts of distractions make us keenly aware of how difficult simply being present can be. What is more, some of the thoughts, memories, and feelings that pull us this way and that can reveal just how petty and reactive we can sometimes be. Then, when we are graced with moments of spiritual awakening, we catch ourselves secretly giving ourselves a standing ovation for how mystical and spiritually refined we are becoming. We discover, too, how prone we are to being impatient and frustrated with ourselves in the midst of these difficulties. We see how we launch self-attacks about what slow progress we are making, how we are not very good at meditation, and so forth. Or we can be inclined to simply give up meditation altogether.

Our feelings of impatience and frustration with ourselves in meditation are certainly understandable, especially when they persist in spite of our best efforts to overcome them. But as we sit in meditation we can begin to recognize the subtle violence inherent in our impatience with ourselves. As our awareness and understanding of our limitations in meditation continue to deepen, we begin to gain greater insight into what is happening. We realize we are catching ourselves in the act of perpetuating violence toward our own wandering mind, our wayward will, or our sleepiness—in short, toward those very aspects of our self that need to be loved the most. We realize that to stop meditating simply because we feel we are not good at it amounts to abandoning the very aspects of our self that need patience and loving encouragement.

We see that the whole venture in meditation is going to be a rough ride unless we can learn not to invade and abandon ourselves in response to all the ways in which meditation exposes our limitations and shortcomings. It is precisely at this point that we begin to appreciate the liberating power of compassion.

Compassion is the love that recognizes and goes forth to identify with the preciousness of all that is lost and broken within ourselves and others. At first it seems as if compassionate love originates with our free decision to be as compassionate as we can be toward ourselves as we sit in meditation. As our practice deepens, we come to realize that in choosing to be compassionate, we are yielding to the compassionate nature of God flowing through us, in and as our compassion toward our self as precious in our frailty.

God is revealed in Christ as a compassionate love that recognizes and goes forth to identify with us as precious in our frailty. This is what Jesus reveals to us in the parable of the prodigal son (Luke 15:11–30). We all know the story of the son who goes off against his father's wishes and squanders his share of his father's money. When the money runs out, he realizes how foolish he has been and returns home. Because of what he has done, he feels he does not deserve to be allowed back into his father's graces. So he plans to ask if he might be a servant in his father's house. As he continues on home, ashamed and remorseful, he is not prepared for the moment in which he first looks up to see his father running toward him with open arms.

The father embraces the son as preciousness almost too precious to bear. The son is at once undone and restored to wholeness in a flurry of embraces received and given. The two of them stand together out on the open road, each laughing and crying at once. Each causes the other to lose his balance as each holds up the other. We can sense in their awkward dance of compassionate love the dance we all long to dance. For we all intuit a taste of heaven in the compassionate embrace that welcomes home one who has been lost.

The father in the story is not even interested in hearing the son's carefully prepared speech about his unworthiness. Even as his son is trying to get out his words of sorrow and regret, the father is already slipping a ring on his finger and telling him that preparations for a grand meal of celebration have already begun. In the actual moment of the encounter there is, for the father and son, nothing but their overflowing, compassionate encounter. The parable reveals God's version of reality. It reveals the way God *always* is toward us, regardless of how foolish and hurtful we may have been.

When we practice meditation we are like the repentant son

returning to his father's house. By the time we begin to meditate, we have probably come to realize how foolish we have
been in the past. We are sorry about the suffering our foolish
ways have caused ourselves and others. We are sincerely intent
on not being so foolish in the future. But like the repentant son
heading home to beg for his father's forgiveness, we are still
laboring under the illusion that our wayward ways make us
unworthy in the eyes of God.

We do not want to give up the illusion that our weaknesses
are obstacles to God's love for us. The perception that our
weaknesses are real in God's eyes is bound up with our egocentric perception of ourselves as outside God's sustaining love.
Entrenched in the ignorance of our imagined otherness from
God, we set out to meditate as a way of overcoming one obstacle after another so that we might succeed in reaching God. It
is in being subject to this ignorance that we become discouraged about our real and imagined slow progress in meditation
and in the spiritual life in general.

As the parable begins, the father saw that his son could not
be talked out of his foolish insistence on making himself miser-
able. And so the father, as an act of love, lets the son go off so he
can discover, in the process of exhausting his own resources,
the loving home he was so determined to leave. The same is
true of us. Seeing how we cannot be talked out of our ignorance, love sets up a kind of obstacle course that provides the
ego with spiritual goals it can attempt to achieve. "Here, try
this," love says. "See if you can sit present, open, and awake as a
way of being open to my presence in your life." The sincere ego
self, still dominated by the ignorance of imagining there is
something to achieve or attain, takes up the challenge. The ego
self struggles in its efforts until it exhausts completely all its own
means of overcoming its inability to realize the oneness with

God it desires. Then, just as all seems lost, we look up to see God running toward us with open arms. Suddenly we realize there is no place within us that is not encountered, embraced, and made whole in a love that does not even care to hear our litany of shortcomings and regrets.

Here is yet another way of putting it: Our egocentric self sets out with an egocentric understanding of the spiritual path. This egocentric understanding is that of having to jump over a bar that is set so high that only the most finely tuned spiritual athlete could ever hope to clear it. Our struggles with distractions, sleepiness, and indifference bring us to a point of near despair. We begin to fear that our doubts were true concerning our inability to master such a seemingly insurmountable challenge.

Then, just as we have become exhausted and spent in our futile efforts to rise above our own limitations, the saving event happens. Compassion steps out and places the bar flat on the ground! Approaching the bar, bewildered by the unthinkable simplicity of the task, we trip over it and fall headlong into God, waiting to reveal to us that we are precious in our frailty and strangely whole in the midst of our fragmentation.

Some of the mystics speak of what is called the *gift of tears*. Sometimes, tears may literally start streaming down our face. Most often, the tears are interior tears of realizing that we are so profoundly loved by God. We are loved without any foundations for being loved, except divine love itself. The tears stream all the more as we realize that everything in us that could be offered as a reason for our not being worthy to be loved results only in deepened and intensified experiences of love.

All this occurs in the ways in which you simply open yourself to God in meditation. As you keep sitting in your "Here I am, Lord" stance of openness to God, your precious, wayward heart is laid bare. As you continue breathing God's love into each new distraction and diversion, the imagined power and relevance of distractions and diversions dissolves in the silent love in which you now sit.

Of course, as it is actually experienced in meditation and in daily life, this process of establishing yourself in compassionate love takes place in the context of countless failures to be compassionate. But this proves to be no hindrance as long as we continue to be compassionate toward our self in our failure to be compassionate. As this process of yielding to compassion unfolds and deepens over a lifetime, we are amazed and filled with joy to discover that the more our meditation practice is established in compassion, the more surely we advance in the midst of our powerlessness to advance.

Imagine that you have a dream in which you are climbing a high mountain. You know that the valley below is the place where you grew up and in which you experienced painful things and made all sorts of mistakes. It is this valley of painful memories and self-doubt that you are now trying to transcend and leave behind by reaching the summit, on which you will be sublimely holy and one with God.

Suddenly, the summit comes into view. In that same instant the wind coming up from the valley below brings with it the sound of a child crying out in distress. Just as suddenly, you realize that there is no real choice but to renounce the hard-fought-for goal of the almost attained summit to go back down the mountain to find and help the hurting child. Turning back, you descend into the valley. Following the child's cries as your guide, you are amazed to discover that you have been led—just as you knew you would be—to the home you tried to leave behind in setting out to make your ascent into holiness.

Standing at the doorway of your own home, sensing the ungraspable and momentous nature of the moment, you gently open the door and look inside. Sitting there, in the corner on the floor, is your own wounded child-self, that part of you that holds the feelings of powerlessness and shame you tried so hard to leave behind. Respectfully approaching this hurting soul, you sit down next to the child on the floor. Perhaps, for a long time you say nothing. You simply sit there, grateful that you finally had the common sense to come back to the preciousness of your own wounded child-self.

Then a most amazing thing happens. Just as you are putting your arms around this child, you suddenly realize you are on the lofty summit of union with God! Suddenly you realize that in going forth to identify with the preciousness of your self in your brokenness, the lofty summit of oneness with God one with you as precious in your frailty is realized.

Here is yet another way of expressing the transformative power of compassion: As we yield to compassion, we are caught in the updraft of grace that carries us aloft. Then, in one single continuous movement of love, compassion draws us downward into the preciousness of all that is lost and broken within ourselves. The deeper the brokenness, the greater the momentum of the descent. The greater the momentum of the descent, the more deeply compassionate love descends into the innermost recesses of our doubts and fears. Suddenly encountering such love, our doubts and fears melt in the love that sets us free.

To be transformed in compassionate love does not mean that we do not have to continue struggling and working through our shortcomings and difficulties. It means being reassured and essentially at peace in the midst of our shortcomings and difficulties. For we have been graced to experience the Christ event, in which love identifies with the deep-down preciousness of ourselves in all our wayward ways. Established in this love, we are freed from the bondage of being invested in the outcome of our efforts to overcome and move past our shortcomings and difficulties. For, as we continue to do our best to deal with whatever needs to be dealt with, we know that right here, right now, just the way we are, we are one with the love that identifies itself with us no matter what.

Immersed in compassion, we look out through compassionate eyes to see the world in which we live. Here the dream in which we return to our wounded child-self takes on new, social dimensions. In this expanded version of the dream, you follow the child's cries to the home in which you grew up. You go inside to compassionately embrace the preciousness of the hurting child that still suffers within. Then a most amazing thing happens. Just as you are putting your arms around the child, it turns into your mother. It turns into your father, your brother and sister. It turns into that person at work who keeps giving you a hard time. It turns into every nameless face you have passed in the street. It turns into the world that "God so loved . . . as to send his only begotten Son" (John 3:16).

God loves and is one with the communal preciousness of all that is lost and broken in everyone who lives. So, too, you begin to realize that you are falling in love with each and every person in the world. As you go on in this love for others, you fail in it again and again. This is no obstacle so long as your failure to be compassionate toward others is realized as just the latest opportunity to renew your compassion toward yourself and others. What matters is that you have come to see a certain look of pain in the world's eyes. You know that look well, for that look has been in your own eyes as well. It is the look of sadness and confusion in not realizing how loved and lovable one is in the midst of difficulties and shortcomings. You begin to appreciate that every time you compassionately engage with another person, your reason for being on this world is honored and expressed.

For the world is the arena in which suffering continues to arise in the absence of love, and happiness continues to arise in the presence of love.

Meditation allows us to see the world through eyes of compassion. This compassionate vision of the world impels us to live in ways in which our words and behavior toward others embody compassion. Compassion forms the essential bond between seeking God in meditation and all forms of social justice. For the more we are transformed in compassion, the more we are impelled to act with compassion toward others.

Notes

CHAPTER 1.

DIVINE DESTINATION

1. T. S. Eliot, *Four Quartets* (San Diego, New York, and London: Harcourt Brace Jovanovich, 1971), 59.
2. David V. Erdman, ed., *The Complete Poetry and Prose of William Blake* (New York: Anchor Books, Random House, 1982), 39.

CHAPTER 2.

LEARNING TO MEDITATE

1. William Johnston, trans., *The Cloud of Unknowing* (New York: Image Doubleday, 1973), 54.
2. Jean-Pierre de Caussade, *Abandonment to Divine Providence* (New York: Image Doubleday, 1975).

CHAPTER 3.
MEDITATIVE EXPERIENCE

1. Romano Guardini, *The World and the Person* (Chicago: Henry Regnery Company, 1939), 31.

CHAPTER 4.
A LADDER TO HEAVEN

1. Guigo II, *"The Ladder of Monks"* and *"Twelve Meditations,"* trans. Edmund Colledge and James Walsh (New York: Image Doubleday, 1978).
2. Guigo, *Ladder of Monks*, 81–82.
3. Guigo, *Ladder of Monks*, 82.
4. Guigo, *Ladder of Monks*, 82.
5. Guigo, *Ladder of Monks*, 83.
6. Eliot., *Four Quartets*, 28.
7. Kieran Kavanaugh and Otilio Rodriguez, eds., *The Collected Works of Saint John of the Cross* (Washington, DC: Intitute of Carmelite Studies, 1991), 45.
8. Guigo, *Ladder of Monks*, 88.
9. Guigo, *Ladder of Monks*, 87.
10. Guigo, *Ladder of Monks*, 96.
11. Guigo, *Ladder of Monks*, 90.

CHAPTER 5.
A MONASTERY WITHOUT WALLS

1. Erdman, *William Blake*, 23.
2. D. Oswald Hunter Blair, *The Rule of Saint Benedict* (Fort Augustus, Scotland: Abbey Press, 1948), 39.
3. Blair, *The Rule of Saint Benedict* , 145.
4. Blair, *The Rule of Saint Benedict*, 3.

CHAPTER 6.

THE SELF-TRANSFORMING JOURNEY

1. Johnston, *Cloud of Unknowing*, 90.
2. Johnston, *Cloud of Unknowing*, 44.
3. Kavanaugh and Rodriguez, *Saint John of the Cross*, 189.
4. Kavanaugh and Rodriguez, *Saint John of the Cross*, 190.
5. Kavanaugh and Rodriguez, *Saint John of the Cross*, 189.
6. Kavanaugh and Rodriguez, *Saint John of the Cross*, 190.
7. Kavanaugh and Rodriguez, *Saint John of the Cross*, 189–190.
8. Kavanaugh and Rodriguez, *Saint John of the Cross*, 189.
9. Kavanaugh and Rodriguez, *Saint John of the Cross*, 150.
10. Johnston, *Cloud of Unknowing*, 48.
11. Johnston, *Cloud of Unknowing*, 49.
12. Johnston, *Cloud of Unknowing*, 48–49.
13. Johnston, *Cloud of Unknowing*, 136–37.
14. Kavanaugh and Rodriguez, *Saint John of the Cross*, 481.
15. Kavanaugh and Rodriguez, *Saint John of the Cross*, 191.
16. Lucien Hervé, *Architecture of Truth* (New York: Phaidon Press, 2001), 90.
17. Carol Lee Flinders, *Enduring Grace: Living Portraits of Seven Women Mystics* (San Francisco: HarperSanFrancisco, 1993), 130.
18. Kavanaugh and Rodriguez, *Saint John of the Cross*, 163.
19. Kavanaugh and Rodriguez, *Saint John of the Cross*, 143.
20. Kavanaugh and Rodriguez, *Saint John of the Cross*, 472.
21. Kavanaugh and Rodriguez, *Saint John of the Cross*, 359.
22. Kavanaugh and Rodriguez, *Saint John of the Cross*, 165.
23. Johnston, *Cloud of Unknowing*, 45.
24. Johnston, *Cloud of Unknowing*, 45–46.
25. Johnston, *Cloud of Unknowing*, 45–46.
26. Johnston, *Cloud of Unknowing*, 46.
27. Johnston, *Cloud of Unknowing*, 56.
28. Johnston, *Cloud of Unknowing*, 96.
29. Johnston, *Cloud of Unknowing*, 96–97.

CHAPTER 7.
ENTERING THE MIND OF CHRIST

1. Mechtild of Magdeburg, "The Flowing Light of the Godhead," trans. Frank Tobin. (Mahwah, NJ: Paulist Press, 1988), 186.
2. Jan van Ruusbroec, *"The Spiritual Espousals" and Other Works*, trans. James A. Wiseman (Mahwah, NJ: Paulist Press, 1985), 30.
3. M. Walsh, "Meister Eckhart: German Sermons and Treatises," vol. 2 (London: Watkins, 1979), 136.
4. Thomas Merton. *The Inner Experience* (San Francisco: HarperSan-Francisco, 2003), 37.
5. Reiner Schürmann. *Meister Eckhart: Mystic and Philosopher* (Bloomington: Indiana Univ. Press, 1978), 108.

CHAPTER 10.
SIT STRAIGHT

1. Dylan Thomas. *The Poems of Dylan Thomas* (New York: New Directions, 1989), 226.

CHAPTER 11.
SLOW, DEEP, NATURAL BREATHING

1. Sue Woodruff. *Meditations with Mechtild of Magdeburg* (Santa Fe, New Mexico: Bear and Company), 80.

CHAPTER 12.
EYES CLOSED OR LOWERED TOWARD THE GROUND

1. Thomas Merton. *Zen and Birds of Appetite* (New York: New Directions, 1968), 57.